# LUCIE
## AUBRAC

*Also by Siân Rees*

The Floating Brothel: The Extraordinary Story of the Lady Julian and
Its Cargo of Female Convicts Bound for Botany Bay

Sweet Water and Bitter: The Ships that Stopped the Slave Trade

The Ship Thieves: The True Tale of James Porter, Colonial Pirate

The Shadows of Elisa Lynch: How a Nineteenth-Century Irish
Courtesan Became the Most Powerful Woman in Paraguay

Moll: The Life and Times of Moll Flanders

# LUCIE AUBRAC

The French Resistance Heroine
Who Defied the Gestapo

**SIÂN REES**

Michael O'Mara Books Limited

First published in Great Britain in 2015 by
Michael O'Mara Books Limited
9 Lion Yard
Tremadoc Road
London SW4 7NQ

A CIP catalogue record for this book is available from the British Library.

Papers used by Michael O'Mara Books Limited are natural, recyclable products made from wood grown in sustainable forests. The manufacturing processes conform to the environmental regulations of the country of origin.

ISBN: 978-1-78243-387-3 in hardback print format
ISBN: 978-1-78243-390-3 in e-book format

1 2 3 4 5 6 7 8 9 10

www.mombooks.com

Cover design and typeset by Billy Waqar
Cover image courtesy of Getty Images
Designed by Kay Hayden

Printed and bound in Great Britain by CPI Group (UK) Ltd, Croydon, CR0 4YY

# CONTENTS

# INTRODUCTION

IN THE COLD dawn of 9 February 1944, Lieutenant Affleck of the RAF landed his heavy Hudson aircraft a few miles from London. Touchdown was fraught. Mud from the Jura mountains of eastern France had coated the wheels of the plane and frozen, although Affleck kept the fact from his four exhausted passengers. John Brough, a downed RAF pilot rescued by the French Resistance, alighted first. Next came twenty-nine-year-old Raymond Aubrac, wounded, grieving and carrying his sleeping two-year-old son in his arms. Finally, a woman's swollen, awkward figure appeared, wrapped in coats, scarves and blankets against the bitter wind, and the ground crew had their first, eagerly awaited glimpse of Lucie Aubrac, eight months pregnant, who had sprung her husband from Gestapo custody five months earlier and had been on the run ever since.

The following night Radio Londres, the BBC French-language broadcast, announced the Aubracs' safe arrival. 'A few weeks ago,' the speaker declared, Lucie Aubrac was 'the leader of a 12-member action group, who seized 14 patriots from the claws of the Gestapo.' Her story illuminated:

what the French resistance is, and how it has come to be so; the heroism of heroes and heroines who were not born heroes and heroines and who were made, like Lucie Aubrac, for a quiet and unremarkable life; why they fought and will continue to fight to their last nail, to their last tooth, for their country, like Lucie Aubrac, for the dignity of the centuries which it was her mission to teach, for their happiness, like Lucie Aubrac for her husband, for their future, like Lucie Aubrac for her children.[1]

'Aubrac' was the last, and the most enduring, of Lucie's many identities: the resistance name taken by her husband in 1942, retained to protect relatives in Nazi hands and eventually adopted as the family's legal name in 1950. Every French schoolchild knows it, and the legend of heroism attached to it. Over one hundred French schools, nurseries, hospitals and retirement homes are called after the Aubracs, both wife and husband were given state funerals and Lucie was recently mooted for 'pantheonization', the transfer of remains into the Panthéon in Paris, where France honours its best and boldest. The Aubracs upheld French honour at a bleak time in their country's history, but their courage under Vichy and during the Nazi Occupation was only one episode in their long lives. There is, however, shade as well as light in the Aubracs' story, for their trajectory from freedom fighters to revered senior citizens was not a smooth one.

Still young in 1945, both Lucie and Raymond Aubrac developed successful post-war careers, revisiting their wartime stories only when they retired in the 1970s. It was ultimately France's growing fascination with the 'Dark Years' that propelled Lucie back into the spotlight thirty years after the events which had first made her famous, when she found herself sought by documentary-makers, historians and schoolteachers anxious for their pupils to hear first-hand testimony of resistance. But as new evidence of wrongdoing also began to emerge, the comforting myths of mass resistance which had sustained post-war France began to fall apart, and even celebrated *résistants* such as the Aubracs came under hostile scrutiny.

The Gestapo officer who had tortured Raymond Aubrac in 1943 was Klaus Barbie, known as the 'Butcher of Lyon'. Extradited to France forty years later, he tortured the Aubracs all over again with accusations of treachery and betrayal. A sordid episode of resentment, jealousy, cowardice and opportunism saw the elderly community of former *résistants* turn on each other, and on the Aubracs. But the couple's legend survived, despite a beating at the hands of the press and people they had believed to be comrades in arms, and by the turn of the century they were again considered national heroes even if the polluted ripple of accusation and counter-accusation has never quite died. Their status as public figures restored, both found their opinions sought on contemporary as much as historical events: international politics and the growing discourse of human rights; the rise of religious fundamentalism and new types of totalitarian rule.

Lucie died in 2007, and Raymond was buried next to his adored wife five years later. Very few men or women with first-hand testimony of the Occupation now survive, but France's fascination with its own wartime self has continued even as that period retreats into history. Researchers have continued to uncover evidence of both heroism and treachery, and popular and academic focus has shifted with the generations: an emphasis on Resistance as the central element of the Occupation gave way to one on the deportation of Jews; investigations into deportation opened into wider research into collaboration, first political and then in all the grey areas inhabited by people living everyday lives in extraordinary circumstances; a narrative of united national resistance emerged to rival early claims by the Communist Party that *it* had led anti-Nazi opposition; that new narrative itself was then subsumed in an examination of the reaction of individuals; military history gave way to cultural history, cultural history to psychological examination, the role of men to that of women. But when it seemed that the Aubracs' biography must, surely, be written – the march from womb to tomb over, wartime and other archives excavated to exhaustion, the familiar details examined under each new lens – new light was suddenly shed on Lucie. The smoking gun threatened by Barbie in the 1980s was never fired: no convincing proof of collaboration or betrayal has ever been found. Rather, archival investigation after her death revealed a more enigmatic flaw, and one which fits the interests of our generation as much as tales of derring-do and treachery fit the preoccupations of hers: a flaw rooted not in actions, but in character – the individual, unrepeatable blend of circumstance, childhood, chance and neuropsychology which created the person who became 'Lucie Aubrac'. This book tells the story of that creation.

## CHAPTER 1

# LUCIE BERNARD

ALL HER LIFE, Lucie Aubrac was a storyteller, and her first and most enduring stories were spun around her childhood. At first, it was merely the place and people she was determined to leave behind. Later, she reimagined it as a springboard and a support, and finally, when she talked of it in her old age, it was a receding background against which a few recollections still flared like matches struck in the dark: the places and people which had marked her, and the signposts she had followed. Some of these remained constant in the narratives she created around herself. Ambition was one, and rebellion, and the fierce determination to seek and seize happiness. So were love, friendship and the compulsion to name and fight injustice. All of these coloured the way in which she lived, moulded and told her life.

It began on 29 June 1912, when Lucie Bernard was born in the small and undistinguished commune of Châtenay-sur-Seine, on the flat lands south-east of Paris. She was the first child of a young couple who had left peasant families in Burgundy, a fertile region of rolling hills, sunflower fields, vineyards and wide rivers, where generations of their ancestors had lived lives tied to the soil. Her parents, Louis and Louise Bernard, were the first to break away, moving to the capital where they ambitiously set themselves up in business just after their daughter was born. Baby Lucie's first months were lived in the scent of stewing beef and cheap wine, for the Bernards briefly ran a sold-by-the-glass bistro in the working-class arrondissement of Montparnasse on the left bank of the Seine. It did not last long. When Lucie was two her father contracted typhoid, the disease of the poor, and the family gave up their business and moved into lodgings.

A retrospective rosy light would shine on Montparnasse as the picturesquely poverty-stricken haunt of artists and intellectuals. In fact, it was an area of slums where working people lived in the meanest of conditions. Poverty, said the celebrated artist, writer and one-time resident Jean Cocteau, was a luxury in Montparnasse. Louise Bernard, feeding baby Lucie and supporting an ill husband, spent hard hours washing other people's linen throughout her second pregnancy. When little Jeanne was born in September 1913 the family left Paris altogether for the healthier employ of a countess in the department of Eure, to the north of the capital, where a recovering Louis worked as a gardener and Louise milked cows and sewed soldiers' uniforms when her work in the dairy was done. The improvement in their situation was brief. When Lucie was two and her little sister, Jeanne, not quite one, their father went away to war. They did not see him again for three years.

One and a half million French soldiers died in the First World War, and more than four million were wounded. Lucie was five when Louis Bernard came home in 1917, a traumatized and partly deaf stranger. By then they were back in Burgundy, where Lucie and Jeanne had spent the war years sometimes with their mother and sometimes with grandparents when their mother's series of employers preferred their dairymaid or washerwoman childless. The reunited Bernard family moved briefly to the employ of another of France's countless countesses, this time on an estate outside the coal-mining town of Montceau-les-Mines, still in Burgundy. Louis, recovering from the horrors of war as he had previously recovered from the horrors of typhoid, again took gardening work and Louise returned to the dairy. This, too, did not last long. After some altercation with an employer who treated her wounded gardener and his tireless wife with contempt, they abruptly left to rent a house in the little canal-side town of Blanzy, with the help of a parent and the war pension which was eventually paid. In Blanzy, life became a little easier. The couple rented a plot of land where Louis grew flowers and vegetables for Louise to sell at market, the two girls attended the local primary school, and the family found some security and permanence.

Lucie's infancy was thus characterized by movement and absence, hunger and hard work. But it was not unhappy: there were grandparents to step in, a mother who loved them, and a little sister she adored and for whom she would always feel responsible. And Lucie was blessed with curiosity and detachment from the earliest age she could recall. Her grandmother wanted her to kiss the statue of the Virgin. She refused: why should she kiss this piece of wood? When she caught a fugitive parrot and presented it to the countess whose cows her mother milked, that lady withheld the promised reward after the bird bit the little girl and she bled onto a precious carpet. How dare she! This was dishonesty. This was *unfairness*. Among the most vivid of these childhood markers was her first experience of racism. A large community of Polish workers lived in Montceau-les-Mines and one day Lucie saw 'a Polish woman, wife of a miner, carrying the body of her child who had drowned in the canal. Overwhelmed by sorrow, but upright and dignified. And a voice raised: "so heartless, those women!" A stupid, racist reaction which mistook this mother's dignity for coldness. That day, I understood what racism was.'[1]

Lucie would always remember the terrible deprivation of the

Montceau mining families, and the hard labour of the peasants in the villages where she went to visit her grandparents. The villages of the Mâconnais in Burgundy remain sunk in the stillness of *la France profonde*, a concept which still has a tenacious hold on French culture and politics, and which influenced Lucie's own view of her origins. All her life she swayed between France's traditional romanticizing of the peasant life (even writing out her parents' attempt to become Parisians to boost their credentials as tillers of the soil and tenders of the vine), and anger at the misery behind the rural idyll portrayed by writers and politicians who did not have to live it.

Lucie's own parents were not able to break their connection with the land completely. Before school, Lucie and Jeanne picked the flowers and vegetables which their mother would sell at market that day and all four of them did exhausting seasonal work in vineyards and orchards. Lucie recalled the 'terrible aches' in her growing body when she straightened after a day bent beneath a panier of grapes, 'and mama's anger; she said they [the landowners] were going to wear us out.'[2] She had better memories of her time away from the land: the security of the classroom where she discovered she was good at schoolwork, and her realization that her parents had great expectations of their daughters.

The key figure in Lucie's childhood and adolescence was her mother. Louise Bernard's status as de facto head of the house evolved during her husband's three-year absence during the war, when she had had to manage as best she could. Even when he came back, Louis was a reduced man. Looking at her damaged father, Lucie became a pacifist before she even knew the word. Louise never stopped working. If she was not milking cows she was planting and harvesting, running her market stall, picking grapes and gathering peaches, and then coming home to cook and clean and sew and launder, and at the same time ensure her two daughters did their homework 'on the oil-cloth, under the light, before she did the ironing, or served the dinner.'[3]

Louise Bernard grabbed at what she could get of the world beyond the kitchen and the field. She taught herself to read at the same time as her daughters, and then saved for newspapers and read them cover to cover. She was the first in their village to send off for the new-fangled 'catalogues' from the nearest *Bon Marché* store. Lucie was the only child in her school who had a dictionary. The teacher was sniffy: 'Hasn't your mother got better things to spend her money on than that?'[4] But Louise was determined that her daughters would continue the journey she had herself begun, and that they would not be forced down the ancient route of early marriage and too many children, worked to death between kitchen, childbed and farm. Her own mother had married at fifteen and had fourteen children; one of her sisters had married at the same age and died giving birth to her third child when she was still a teenager. Louise was lucky that she conceived no more children after Lucie and Jeanne. So was Lucie, for care of a string of younger siblings would have hobbled her before she had taken her first steps towards independence.

If Louise's early ambitions for herself had been thwarted, she was determined that her two bright little girls would go where she had not. She had decided that they would become either primary-school teachers (*institutrices* in French) or 'post office ladies', for these were two of the few ways in which working-class girls could move a step up the social ladder. In 1923, both Lucie and Jeanne were made 'Pupilles de la Nation', a status accorded the children of certain war veterans and one which brought a little extra money into the family. Even so, sending Lucie to the fee-paying *lycée* – the grammar school – in 1925 was far beyond the family's means. Instead, they scraped together the money for her to study for the entrance examination to a primary-school teacher training college. So determined were they to give Lucie the best possible start to her teaching career that in 1928 they arranged for her to study for the entrance examination not to the local training college near Montceau-les-Mines, a provincial second best, but to the Parisian establishment in the Boulevard des Batignolles. Sacrificing the hard-won independence of their little market garden, the Bernards crossed Burgundy to settle in Vitry-sur-Seine, among the drab outer suburbs of the capital, where Louis found another gardening job, and Louise went back to work in a factory.

For a year, seventeen-year-old Lucie prepared for her entrance examination. Her sister Jeanne left school and got work in the post office, and the whole family supported the star daughter. But in 1929, Lucie failed her examination for the college in the Boulevard des Batignolles and was rejected. The disappointment must have been severe but the Bernards persevered. Lucie prepared for the examination of 1930 – and again, failed. And again, they rallied, and supported her through a third attempt. At last she succeeded, and was offered a place to train in the 1931 intake! It was a moment of pride and celebration. Lucie's future as an *institutrice* seemed safe, and with it the entire family was lifted from insecurity and the parents had some expectation of easier times to come – at which point, Lucie changed her mind, and refused to take up her place.

Many years later, looking back to the wartime record which made her famous, Lucie would say that for her 'resistance was primarily *refusal*. Refusal has been a principle all my life.'[5] She never deviated from her principles or political beliefs, the most important of which was the guarantee of liberty, that most contested of words, to all people. Liberty, she said frequently, was directly linked to the same cherished principle of *refusal*, and *refusal* was linked to disobedience. Throughout her life she took it as a point of honour that if she felt like it she would break engagements – even failing to turn up to take lessons, later on, when she was teaching – justifying this as being her *own* right to liberty. In 1931, liberty was chasing her own dreams, and not her mother's dreams for her. Going against her parents' wishes might provoke a family drama, but that would pass. A whole lifetime of teaching infants and supporting her family, on the other hand, was simply too high a price to pay to please her parents. Nevertheless their retirement, as she realized many years later, perhaps more sympathetic to her parents' point of view than she had been as a nineteen-year-old, 'went up in smoke.'[6]

Lucie had decided that the constraints of becoming, and being, *mademoiselle la maitresse* were too great. She wanted more than her mother's vision for her: the years of studying and exam-taking had rendered what Louise saw as a bold advancement seem too timid a step to her daughter. Instead, Lucie had set her sights on graduating from the elite Sorbonne university with an *agrégation*, the degree which would qualify her to teach at a *lycée* and give her a status and salary far above those of an *institutrice*. It was a huge ambition.

* * *

In 1931, aged nineteen, Lucie Bernard embarked on the adventure of living alone in a great city. She had set herself a daunting task. To apply to university, she had first to pass the *baccalauréat* examination, which meant not only catching up with everything her wealthier peers had studied at their *lycées* but also teaching herself Latin from scratch. At the same time she had to earn her keep, for even if her family continued to house and feed her on and off for several years, she had tuition and examination fees to pay, and rent on a series of rooms in the Latin

Quarter which allowed her to live some of the time in the freedom she craved. She began applying for temporary jobs at primary schools, bending the details to present her situation in the most sympathetic light. Her failure to take up the training course offered in the Boulevard de Batignolles had been, she explained to prospective employers, due to her mother's bad health. And while both working and studying, she also launched herself into political activism and a social life which might on their own have absorbed the energies of a less driven woman.

Political engagement and romantic love would be the driving forces of Lucie's adult life, and she encountered politics first. Emerging from a childhood marked by hardship, she embarked on adulthood just as the Great Depression crashed over France. She would later say little about the effects of that bleak period on her own life. Perhaps it was pride, but perhaps it was her tendency towards the glass half full which lent her a distaste for recalling the unpleasant details of poverty: she never pitied herself, and she would certainly not let anyone else pity her. Nonetheless, the Depression affected her as it did all people dependent on the fruits of their own labour, and its impact was both material and moral. During the harsh winters of the early thirties, city life was marked by the obscene rub of utter poverty against uncaring wealth, and the inescapable presence of the dispossessed and the desperate.

Lucie's politicization was lived rather than learnt. If she had not already been aware of unfairness after a childhood in Montceau-les-Mines and rural Burgundy, she saw it now. 'The winter I spent on the streets,' wrote Morvan Lebesque, later a journalist but that year one of the thousands who slept rough in Paris:

> the winter of '32–33 ... it snowed and it froze; thousands of young men, forced out of their jobs by the crisis, struggled on to their

last penny, to the end of their tether then, in despair, abandoned the fight ... On street benches and at métro entrances, groups of exhausted and starving young men would be trying not to die. I don't know how many never came round ... In the rue Madame one day I saw a child drop a sweet which someone trod on, then the man behind bent down and picked it up, wiped it and ate it.[7]

Early in her Latin Quarter life, Lucie began a long and not always happy association with the only political party which called not for palliative measures, but for a change to the system which could allow such misery.

When she called at Communist Party headquarters at 120 Rue Lafayette, Lucie was directed to the *Jeunesses Communistes*, the Party's youth wing. The 'Communist Youth' was not as strict as the Party itself. Lucie's group of fifteen or so were mainly students, to whom the Party delegated a certain number of workers, and were less interested in the theory of Marxism than in action. Their militancy was eager but limited. They pasted posters to walls with flour and water glue, catcalled the right-wing parties during the street demonstrations which seemed more numerous each month, and linked arms along pavements to allow workers and the unemployed to carry out their own demonstrations unmolested. Lucie was an enthusiastic and committed member of the group, whose activities not only met her desire to address injustice, but also gave her friends.

On weekdays she would rise before dawn to hand out Communist tracts outside the Panhard motor-car factory as the workers went on shift. On Sundays she went to sell the Communist *Avant-Garde* newspaper outside churches, enjoying the provocation. One admiring Communist acquaintance called her 'a fighter, a dare-devil (*très casse-cou*)'.[8] Released from the prim expectations of a teacher training college and the dourer ones of peasant conservatism, away from the scrutiny of parents, her tomboy side emerged. Sometimes her enthusiasm for the traditionally masculine pursuit of fisticuffs surprised even her friends. 'She was a simple and combative fraternal comrade,' one wrote, 'always ready for a fight.' Another orator 'often kept her nearby when he gave speeches at factory doors ... she was a person of great possibility, sometimes strong-headed.'[9] Not everyone approved whole-heartedly, however. Rising Communist leader André Marty, a man with the dark skin and heavy moustaches of the South, had already been incarcerated for 'antimilitaristic actions', and would later be a leader of the International Brigades in Spain and a *résistant* against Nazism, yet 'reproved her publicly one day for behaving and dressing like a boy'.[10] He was a minority voice of small-c conservatism, however. The ebullient Lucie Bernard was popular among her comrades.

In Paris as in other European cities, politically motivated gangs from both Left and Right took to the streets in the thirties to fight their principles out with cobblestones and fists. The Boulevard Saint-Michel – boundary between the fifth arrondissement, where Lucie had been born, and the sixth, of which she was now a proud resident – was a battleground in the 1930s as it would be again in 1968, when unrest on the streets nearly brought France's capitalist economy to its knees. Lucie was in the thick of it, for 'militancy', she found, 'was an everyday part of life for students.'[11] Lucie and her group, however, were in the minority in the brawls and demos. As she knew from personal experience, further education was the preserve of a moneyed group, and the offspring of that group tended more frequently to the Right than they did to the Left. Like their British counterparts who rushed from Oxford and Cambridge to subvert the British General Strike in 1926, the students of the Sorbonne, the elite *grandes écoles* and all the other educational establishments clustered on the Left Bank took it upon themselves to beat down the threat of political Bolshevism and social liberalism, invoking the values of patriotism and order, and the spectres of decadence and decline.

Lucie's own communism was always situated within republicanism: she wanted the Communist Party to have a strong, perhaps the strongest, voice in the French parliament; she wanted social reform and a redistribution of resources, but she did not envisage a totalitarian state. The battle cry for the vast majority on the Left was not revolution, but the safeguarding of the Republic, the sacred political fruit of 1789 which enshrined liberty, equality and fraternity. The threat to democratic government in the thirties seemed to come not from the Left but from the resurgent Right which was sweeping through Europe: Benito Mussolini seized absolute power of Italy in 1925, Salazar created his autocratic 'Estado Novo' in Portugal in 1932, Hitler became Chancellor of Germany in 1933 and General Franco launched his coup in Spain in 1936. In Britain, Oswald Mosley created the British Union of Fascists in 1932, and after the shocked pacifism and fragile republican pluralism which followed the horrors of the First World War, left-wing parties and agendas in France also found themselves under ferocious attack. French far-right groups claimed that any and all parties on the left-wing spectrum, from moderate republicanism to outright Bolshevism, were sapping the strength of the country, aided by hostile groups such as Jews, Socialists, homosexuals and other 'degenerates'.

The student haunts of the Left Bank were fertile recruiting grounds for the right-wing groups which confronted Lucie Bernard and her comrades on the streets. *Action Française*, the most powerful, militated not against any particular government but against the republic itself, calling for the restitution of the monarchy which had been felled in 1789. The *Camelots du Roi* was its unruly youth wing, welcoming not only committed monarchists but anyone espousing Catholic, anti-Semitic and right-wing ideas, particularly if they came with the chance of a punch-up. Beside the *Camelots* marched the *Jeunesses Patriotes*, created in 1924 by a wealthy industrialist and inspired not by monarchy but by Mussolini's blackshirts, and the members of the secretive *La Cagoule*, 'the cowl', home to a very young François Mitterrand and still provoking conspiracy theories and political scandals today. The violence of these groups was not a mere turf war, nor a simple outlet for upper-class brutishness of the Bullingdon kind. On 6 February 1934, they were heavily represented in the army of thugs and rioters which attempted a physical attack on the French parliament in which sixteen people were killed and 2,000 injured. Although historians have tended to resist the theory that this was an attempted putsch on the model of Hitler's or Mussolini's, popular opinion at the time certainly regarded the 6 February riots as an attempted *coup d'état* against the republic.

By 1935, Lucie's robust and combative activity on the streets had convinced the leaders of the French Communist Party that she was someone who could be given responsibility. Senior officials had had an eye on her for some time, commissioning secret reports from members who knew her. Occasional worried rumours that she was leaning towards the Trotskyist heresy revealed more about the tail-chasing world of Communist Party headquarters than it did about Lucie, who was never very interested in political theory. Lectures and editorials had less impact on her than what she saw about her or heard discussed in the workers' restaurants she frequented. She was invited to headquarters and informed that she had been chosen to go to Moscow, one of the young people from working-class backgrounds whom Communist parties outside Russia were seeking to pick out and train as political staff. She was told to find an excuse to explain a long absence to friends and family. Lucie thought about it, but after her initial excitement, she decided Communist officialdom was not for her. Paris, her family (particularly her younger sister, Jeanne, now mother to a baby) and the politics of the street were more interesting to her than climbing up the greasy pole. More importantly, perhaps, she was moved by the old refusal to be limited by the demands of others. Lucie wanted to be in control of her own story: she might believe in some communist ideals, but she could not tolerate the idea of fighting for them from within the strictly policed ranks of the Party itself.

*Le refus* was accompanied in Lucie's private pantheon of political values by inclusivity, and the Communist Party was not the only, or even the greatest, element in her political education. For Lucie, political engagement and friendship were inextricably mixed. She was an insatiably sociable young woman: a talker, a proposer of parties and expeditions, someone who stayed up chatting until dawn. In her quest for social contact during her first months in Paris – the first she had ever spent not surrounded by close family – she had joined not only the Communists but an international youth group run by the Quakers in one of the cool, flat-fronted, white-shuttered houses on the Rue Guy de la Brosse, in the heart of the university district. A Quaker youth group might give the idea of decorous tea parties and table tennis but this one offered nothing of the kind. Rather, it was a support group and home from home for Communists, Socialists, displaced Jews and pacifists. 'The diversity of beliefs and opinions' fascinated her. 'I was curious about everything.'[12] For Lucie, there was nothing wrong or inconsistent in belonging to both the Quaker youth group and Communist Youth. Engagement, friendship, solidarity: these were all values to which she was passionately attached by personality as much as by politics. Eager to explore any experience that came her way, she would never accept that any single group had the right to her exclusive loyalty.

The Quakers did not only inculcate pacifism and tolerance of difference among the young people who came to the Rue Guy de la Brosse, but also organized social and sporting activities. Lucie met there the first representatives of her own country's middle classes, whom she regarded with an almost anthropological interest: 'I had never met bourgeois girls.'[13] These daughters of families similar to those who had employed her parents in the dairy and the garden were almost a race apart. Quaker connections opened new worlds to her as, despite the demands of studying for the *baccalauréat*, as well as earning her keep in primary schools, Lucie also began to discover the leisure pursuits of a class which was not tied to a plot of land or the shifts of a factory floor. She found that she loved risky sports, throwing herself down ski-slopes in winter, hiking in the mountains in summer, galloping as fast as she could, kayaking and swimming in the thunderous gorges of the Tarn. These were pursuits her parents could never have dreamed of, as were the trips abroad for which she eagerly signed up. Building and maintaining friendly links with the former enemy were central to Quaker pacifism, and they arranged trips and working holidays to Germany for those who wanted the experience. Lucie did. In the summer of 1931 she worked as an au pair for diplomats and in 1932 she returned with a group sent to deliver Christmas presents from France for the children of Berlin's unemployed. 'The children were waiting impatiently for me,' she reported in the Quaker newsletter.

They had learnt how to greet me that morning. '*Bon-jour ma-de-moi-sel-le*.' A song and then flowers. Michaelmas daisies that they had bought themselves … 'Long live peace!' they all said. A big girl had written a pacifist poem which she read enthusiastically.

They wanted to know a French song. I wrote Frère Jacques on the blackboard and we quickly learnt it. 'We will never forget this music,' they said.[14]

Germany, like France, was devastated by the Depression, with millions thrown into unemployment. At first Communists and Fascists fought for power democratically, using the ballot box, debate in the Reichstag (the German parliament) and deals with the Centre Party, which held the ground between them. Hitler's accession to the Chancellorship in January 1933 changed all that. Within weeks, the German republic was dead and the first Communists and Socialists had been rounded up, tortured and shot. That year the Quakers in Paris opened an 'international refugee service' for foreigners fleeing the swiftly accelerating political and anti-Semitic persecution in Germany, Austria and Czechoslovakia. Austrians, Germans, Italians opposed to Mussolini, Spaniards opposed to Franco, Czechs and Poles all ended up in France as waves of displaced people sought refuge. In 1933 alone, 35,000 refugees came.

One of them was Joseph Epstein, a man a year or so older than herself whom Lucie met under Communist or Quaker auspices. A square-faced, light-eyed man with the build of a boxer, Epstein was a charismatic Polish Communist Jew. It was a bundle of characteristics which could have been designed to enrage the far Right. Deported from Poland in 1931 for Communist militancy, he had gone first to Czechoslovakia and then to France, where he was soon banned from the city of Tours for attempting to organize immigrant labourers. Moving to Paris to study law, he found a ready audience among students like Lucie for his tutorials on clandestine life. Joseph Epstein taught her a lesson she would fall back on several times: if you need to hide, he told her, hide in full view. He also taught the students who clustered about him a few tricks of the propaganda trade. One day he showed them how to hang a poster from the wires running above a tramway by attaching a length of string to a stone, hurling the stone across and then pulling the string hard from the other side. The fire brigade had to come and get the posters down; 'there was,' Lucie said, 'an element of games-playing to it.'[15]

If they were young people having fun, Lucie and her peers were also learning from Joseph Epstein and other refugees that the real threat was not from France's home-grown far Right, but from over the borders. In 1936, Epstein was one of hundreds who left France to defend republicanism against fascism in the Spanish Civil War, the same conflict which had been swiftly and brutally fought in Germany in 1933 and which would soon be repeated in France. Lucie went on her last Quaker-sponsored trip to Germany that year, and found the atmosphere was changing, and that both public and private life now bore the mark of the Führer's insistence on racial purity and national unity. Three years of violent anti-Semitic repression had changed the look of town and city centres, and public space now belonged only to Aryan males, for Hitler had decreed that a woman's world should be her husband, her family, her children and her home.

Despite the fascinations of her political and social life, her travels, her work and all the activities with which she crammed her time, Lucie had not come to Paris to become a professional politician, but a university graduate and history teacher, and she was struggling to realize that ambition. She was not an intellectual and the demands of studying for first the *baccalauréat* and then the *agrégation* taxed her. By 1934, she had managed to pass all the required courses for the *baccalauréat* except Latin. There, she stuck. It would take three years to absorb this demanding language to the level which allowed her to jump the final hurdle, qualifying to apply to the Sorbonne in late 1937, six years after she had first set her sights on a degree.

The length of time it took Lucie to enter university reflects not only her devotion to political activity and social life, but also her poverty. At times she did not have enough money to feed herself, let alone to heat the little rooms she rented here and there, and it is very difficult to study when you are hungry and cold. Lucie would always talk far more about the excitement and sociability of her young adulthood than its difficulties, but her selective storytelling concealed periods of bare and unglamorous misery. André Marty, who had told her off for wearing trousers, also recorded how he and other older comrades in the Party 'invited her to eat at (their houses) many times when we saw she was on the verge of collapse.'[16] An academic at the Sorbonne, called on for a reference in 1938, painted a vivid picture of her poverty, and the determination with which she overcame it.

This young woman has succeeded in leaving her village, understanding that a primary school education would not satisfy her irresistible appetite for knowledge and obstinately gaining the necessary grades to access further education with a truly admirable will, patience, and disregard for her own physical wellbeing. At times she has gone hungry; she has accepted lowly and exhausting jobs to buy herself the necessary books and pay her university fees. When her over-bright eyes, nervous exhaustion and air of ill health attracted my attention, I persuaded her to speak to me and felt great compassion for what she told me ... I do not know any other child as deserving as this one or who has shown such invincible courage, or more determination to reach the goal she set herself.

These exceptional qualities are matched by an exemplary character: correctness, honesty (a little naïve at times), a sometimes brusque frankness; generosity, the occasional imprudence but always likeability: a lovely nature.[17]

The *baccalauréat* challenged her more than the *agrégation*: a year after entering the Sorbonne, Lucie Bernard achieved her ambition. She graduated in 1938, qualified to teach history and geography in the *lycée* from which she had herself been excluded.

∗ ∗ ∗

When Lucie Bernard got her first teaching post, she was twenty-six. Photos show a big woman, almost awkward, with a face which was not pretty, but deeply attractive in its liveliness, force and intelligence: dark, somewhat flat eyes and a large bony nose; thick dark hair in waves from a side parting in the manner of the day. It was the sort of face whose strong lines would turn more handsome in old age than they were in youth, but one which was always arresting. She had hoped to teach in Paris, but newly qualified teachers had to accept what they were offered. In October 1938, therefore, Lucie travelled to Strasbourg, the largest city in the region of Alsace and two miles from France's border with Germany.

It had been a long hard road to the *lycée* but the superior pay and the relatively few teaching hours at the girls' school where she worked made it worth it. Life in Strasbourg was good. For the first time, Lucie had both time and money enough to amuse herself, and her vivacity and determination to seize her opportunities served her in her new home as they had done in her old. Very soon she had set about recreating her social life and begun indulging her love of sport, skiing in the Vosges and 'riding at every opportunity, giving back my horse at the last moment, and going off in jodhpurs to teach ... a few of the parents went and complained about it and the headmistress told me off. In vain.'[18]

Despite these pleasures, she was already champing just a little at the bit. When a schools inspector came to make his annual report, he noted acerbically that he had not been able to observe Mlle Bernard's teaching because she was off school following a skiing accident. He also recorded his ponderous surprise that such a newly qualified teacher should have simultaneously applied for a post in a Parisian *lycée* and a David Weill scholarship which would take her to the USA for a year, where she wished to study what she described as 'a topic of human and economic geography in the Rocky Mountains of the United States.'[19] (This rather vague research proposal was backed by glowing references from the Sorbonne, and it was probably these, as well as her engaging personality, which won her the grant.) Although schoolteaching would be the only professional activity of Lucie's life – there would be a multitude of non-professional ones – she was not cut out to obey the strictures of a *lycée* timetable any more than she was the demands of a primary-school classroom, the dictates of the Communist Party or the orders of a peasant husband. 'Some Tuesday mornings I bunked off, just to see what was happening in the streets.'[20]

Strasbourg, on the River Rhine, is a beautiful city, the ancient half-timbered houses of the old centre reflected in the placid waters of the canal running through it. Now home to the buildings of the European Parliament, the heart of the project which has prevented war between ancient enemies since 1945, when Lucie Bernard walked its streets it was a place of unrest, rumour, anxiety and furtive hope. Alsace was annexed by Germany in 1870 and remained German until the end of the First World War, only twenty years before Lucie moved there. Many people in the region still spoke German as their first language and the Nazi shadow fell more heavily there than anywhere else in France. A few months before Lucie's arrival, in March 1938, Germany had annexed Austria, and Britain, France, the USA and Russia had done nothing to stop it. As SS officers stepped up the persecution of Austrian Jews, Socialists, Communists, homosexuals and other 'asocial elements', hundreds more refugees were pouring over the Rhine.

One of the people with whom Lucie discussed the growing threat from the East was an old friend from the Latin Quarter who had also moved to Strasbourg to lecture at the university. Jean Cavaillès was one of the most brilliant minds of his generation. A baby-faced, engaging and sociable fellow a few years older than Lucie, Cavaillès had advanced degrees in philosophy, mathematics and the philosophy of mathematics and had also written a sociological thesis on youth groups as a recipient of a Rockefeller Foundation grant. No one could argue with the quality of Cavaillès' intellect, and he brought it to political as well as academic debate. He had told Lucie many stories of his recent residence in Germany, which had been spent partly in amicable communion with German academics for whom he felt both admiration and affection, and partly observing the rise of National Socialism, which he feared and detested.

In May 1939, Lucie's life changed abruptly when Jean Cavaillès introduced her to another clever young man and Latin Quarter alumnus. Two years younger than Lucie, Raymond Samuel had arrived in Paris in 1934 to study at the *École des Ponts et Chaussées*,[21] a prestigious civil engineering college close to the Sorbonne. Like her, he had grown up in Burgundy. His family lived in the prosperous university city of Dijon, about fifty miles from Blanzy, and his youth had been passed in much easier circumstances than hers. A thoughtful, likeable, serious young man, Raymond had also combined his studies in Paris with left-wing militancy, although more discreetly than Lucie, for the students at the *École des Ponts* were heading towards careers in the army, where a Communist past was not an asset. Raymond's group of like-minded students had been involved in fewer street brawls but more debate; where Lucie had enjoyed the rough and tumble of the Communist Youth, Raymond and his friends took a more academic approach, meeting semi-formally to discuss works such as Marx's *Das Kapital* and the writings of Lenin. The Sorbonne, the *grands écoles* and politics had all overlapped in the crowded Latin Quarter, and Raymond had noticed Lucie at one of the many venues where students met. She had not noticed him.

Graduating in 1937, Raymond had won a grant to study at the Massachusetts Institute of Technology in the USA. He had travelled about and enjoyed himself after finishing his studies there, and loved what he saw of the USA. He worked briefly in a patent office and then tried, too soon, to open one of his own in Washington, lost all his savings and arrived back in Cherbourg in August 1938 aboard a cargo ship. After a brief family reunion he headed for the military academy for engineers, hoping to be sent to the South of France after graduating. This ambition was sunk when he discovered photos hung up to develop of his commanding officer's family in bathing suits. He took them down for a good look, failed to hang them back up in the right order and honourably turned himself in when the commanding officer demanded to know who the guilty party was. A posting to Strasbourg was his punishment for over-curiosity.

At the end of his long life, Raymond reflected on the effect his two years overseas had had on him as an impressionable young man. As you go through life, he observed:

> there are some models which you consciously try to imitate. When you have children, you want to turn yourself into a *père de famille*. When you travel, you want to be like the British – pretend not to take anything too seriously ... and the way in which you conduct yourself, even when you are not aware of imitating some vague model in your subconscious, ends by becoming part of your character.[22]

The studious, slightly provincial youth who had gone to study at the *École des Ponts* was still there, but it was a more ironic, even laconic, version, with a touch of the East Coast to him, which returned from America and was introduced to Lucie Bernard.

Raymond would claim with his characteristic dryness that when they first met, Lucie was principally interested in him because she had just been awarded the David Weill grant and thought the newly-returned MIT student might have some useful tips on life in America. She asked him to dinner with Jean Cavaillès and served an excellent *coq au vin*. Whatever her principal motive for inviting him had been, she discovered her guest was a handsome and witty young officer whose louche return on a cargo ship added glamour to his travels. Two days later, on 14 May, he waited for her outside the *lycée* and they went dancing. It was a date which 'had consequences that lasted 68 years,' Raymond said, 'so one shouldn't go dancing too often ...'[23]

Both realized very soon that they had found the person they wanted to spend their life with. Falling headlong in love, they swore 'always to be together on 14 May as long as we lived'[24] and soon they were inseparable, insofar as her teaching commitments and his military service allowed. They loved each other passionately, to the extent that either would have given his or her life for the other. They were physically besotted with each other, and would always remain so. Nearly sixty years later, when Lucie was asked why their marriage had lasted so well, the overriding physical attraction between them was the first explanation she gave. But alongside love, the new couple was fortunate in that there was also liking. There was nothing tortured or star-crossed about their passion: they simply got on immensely well. He fascinated her. 'He was an intellectual,' she said. 'He understood everything. It was lovely talking to him.'[25] And she fascinated him equally. She was perhaps the first working-class woman he had come into social contact with, or at least the first who presented herself to him as an equal. Excited by their attraction and by their differences, Lucie spun stories to enchant him: stories of her father, who had been returned from the war an amnesiac, she said, and only been located by her mother in 1921; stories of her own birth in Paris, by chance, because her parents were up from the Burgundy village where they lived to attend a wedding and her pregnant mother danced too much at the party; stories of the triumph when she passed the entrance examination to the primary-school teacher training college brilliantly and at her first attempt.

Although the differences in background and experience might have added to their own mutual fascination, class and religious boundaries counted strongly in the 1930s. Raymond came from a family of atheist Jewish merchants, exotic and almost alien to Lucie's family of Catholic peasants. His background was moneyed, if not grand, and his childhood and youth had been comfortable. She came from a background of rural or small town poverty. There was also the fact that Lucie had led a life which was by the standards of the majority one of shocking liberty. A young woman living alone in the centre of Paris, mixing freely with young men and foreigners, making her own decisions about where to work and what to do with her pay, and one who was now intending to head off, quite alone, to the Rocky Mountains of America – this was a creature who might entrance some men by her boldness but one whom many would have considered unsuitable as a partner. Raymond Samuel was exceptional in both intellect and character.

On 19 August 1939, only a little over three months after they had met, the couple went to Dijon, and Raymond presented Lucie to his family. She met his parents, Hélène and Albert, the doctor brother, Yvon, who had travelled all the way to Cherbourg to welcome Raymond back from New York, and his sister, Ginette. The Samuels seemed rich to her. Albert managed 'Les Grands Magasins Lyonnais', a large clothing emporium for which Hélène oversaw the design and production of ladies' wear in their own atelier. They danced and entertained and had a big house full of books, with servants, and even a Panhard car, made by the same company outside which Lucie had used to hand out Communist tracts at dawn. There must have been nervousness on both sides: Lucie, torn between her natural desire to please and fit in with Raymond's family and a touchy determination not to pretend to be something she was not, and the Samuels, ready to welcome their son's choice whilst a little wary of how her arrival within the family might change it. In the end, the meeting passed off well. The Samuels were kind and hospitable, and Lucie was not only a university graduate but displayed a reassuring knowledge of the wines her future father-in-law served at dinner. If the elder Samuels ever wondered if this exuberant young woman saw in their son a step on the ladder which led her out of the world of her childhood, they kept it to themselves. Everyone knew in any case that there could be no immediate marriage, for Lucie's application for the David Weill grant had been successful – the first time it had been awarded to a woman. Her ship for New York was booked, and she had the prospect of a year in the Rockies before her.

The couple did not go to visit her parents, although Blanzy was not far from Dijon. Later, Lucie would spin more tales around her relationship with her parents during the difficult first few years of her independent adulthood, claiming that her refusal to take up the teacher training course in 1931 led to many years of estrangement. In fact, Louis and Louise steadily supported their daughter even as they watched, perhaps wistfully but also perhaps with pride, as she moved further from them. The distance between daughter and parents was a natural part of the trajectory which most successful children from humble backgrounds follow: the awkward shucking-off of habits and relationships which sit ill with a changed persona and a different life, and which are difficult to slip smoothly into an autobiographical narrative in such a way that all participants – including the autobiographer – emerge well.

When Raymond saw Lucie onto the train which would take her to the Atlantic port of Saint-Nazaire, her ship to New York was booked for 5 September and the couple did not expect to meet again for a year. In the last few days before Lucie was due to sail, however, everything changed. German troops invaded Poland on 1 September. On 3 September, Britain, France, Australia and New Zealand declared war on Nazi Germany and Lucie had to make a decision which could affect her entire future. She knew what war with Germany might mean: she had fought enough French fascists in Paris and she had just spent a year in a city where Nazi propaganda was efficiently and widely distributed. Only a few weeks earlier, she had been with Jean Cavaillès in a Strasbourg restaurant where they saw a poster in the window proclaiming *no dogs or Jews*. They had torn it down. Raymond was Jewish, and her sister,

Jeanne, was newly married to the Communist leader Pierre Norgeu: both men would be hunted if the Nazis invaded. She cancelled her voyage.

Strasbourg was declared out of bounds to civilians as soon as war was declared, but this did not keep Lucie away. If she was not going to America, she was determined to see Raymond, and an evacuation order was not going to stop her. Inclined by personality and experience to action rather than debate, she made her way across a dislocated and chaotic France and managed to charm army medics into smuggling her into Strasbourg by strapping her onto a stretcher and claiming she needed emergency medical attention. Hopping off as soon as she was left unobserved, she went to meet Raymond, who had managed to get a short leave from his posting just outside the city. Already in love, and now deeply touched – and probably amused – by her act of impulsive devotion, he asked Lucie to marry him that weekend. He was upset, Lucie said, by the thought that tongues might be wagging and her reputation might be soiled. There was an endearing lack of coyness to Lucie. Never inclined to let an opportunity for happiness go unseized, she accepted Raymond's proposal immediately: 'We were very in love. I thought it an excellent idea!'[26] On 30 December, they met again for a hasty wedding in Dijon. His parents, sister and brother were there; her family was not. A first-class train trip to Paris – Lucie's first – followed the Dijon wedding; a stay in a hotel in the Rue Madame – another first for her – and a short honeymoon in a city where the atmosphere was 'unreal'[27] and everyone carried gas masks wherever they went, and only then did they go, briefly and with some misgivings, to visit Lucie's parents. Raymond's uniform confused his new parents-in-law. 'You told us he was a Jew,'[28] Lucie's father hissed in her ear, apparently unable to comprehend that a Jew could also be an engineer, an officer, a graduate and a gentleman. It was not an easy encounter, but a mutual love of pipe smoking offered father and son-in-law a bond in common, and in the end he was, she wrote, 'accepted, despite everything'.[29]

Reading the many testimonies left by Raymond's wife, friends and colleagues, it is easy to see why Lucie fell headlong in love with him in 1939, and why any doubts her parents may initially have entertained crumbled swiftly when they met him. He was an unfailingly courteous and engaging man, who was protective of his ebullient wife without ever seeking to control or reduce her as a man less sure of himself might have done. He made her laugh, he was kind and he had the same unshakeable attachment that she did to friendship, and the same belief that it was morally imperative to identify and speak against oppression.

And for him, Lucie was a fearless, uninhibited, attractive girl; a great gale of fresh air blown into a comfortable life. Some might have pursed their lips and said Lucie had done well for herself, but Raymond always considered that he was the lucky one in their partnership. All his life he remembered the brief glimpse he had first caught of his future wife across some crowded student café or lecture hall in Paris, and found it amusing that she had looked straight past him. Meeting her again in Strasbourg, he had been delighted that she returned his interest, and fascinated by the doors she opened into new worlds. Lucie and Raymond Samuel were an indivisible couple from the moment of their marriage, and to tell the life of one after December 1939 is also to tell the life of the other.

## CHAPTER 2

# LUCIE SAMUEL

LUCIE AND RAYMOND'S marriage took place during the *drôle de guerre*, the phoney war. Hundreds of thousands of Frenchmen were mobilized in September 1939 and sent to the northern and eastern borders, but for nine months there was no fighting. A string of fortifications known as the Maginot Line had been put up in the 1930s along the French border with Germany, and for the best part of a year German soldiers sat on one side of it and French on the other, sometimes in sight and frequently within earshot, while scarcely a shot was fired. Raymond was stationed near a village called La Wantzenau on the banks of the Rhine, where he was realizing the deficiencies of the French army. First he was ordered to build concrete daises for machine guns which never arrived. Then he was ordered back into Strasbourg to blow up a dozen bridges, an operation he considered to be entirely without strategic merit. As winter approached, he watched his initially enthusiastic men sit in demoralizing inaction, shivering through the nights because not enough blankets had been supplied, miserable during the day because their clothes were inadequate and they had no socks. In the officers' mess, he was perturbed by the sympathy expressed for the Nazi regime, and the routine denunciations of the

Jews and Communists whom many believed, or claimed to believe, had engineered France's entry into the war for their own devious ends.

The Samuels spent their first Christmas as a married couple apart. When Strasbourg was evacuated, Lucie had been directed to take up a post in a boys' *lycée* in the Breton town of Vannes, on the opposite side of France to her new husband. Its pupils, deprived of a master who had gone to the Front and displeased to end up with a woman, treated her to such a display of disrespect on her first day that she meted out a sharp slap, then demonstrated her party trick of swiftly tracing the outline of the map of Japan *using both hands* simultaneously on the blackboard. They sat in awed silence. Madame Samuel was not the only unwanted female the boys had to put up with: thousands of people in the North and East of France, as well as those across the border in Belgium and the Netherlands, had begun leaving their homes despite the strange absence of fighting, and were moving south and west towards the relative safety of the Atlantic coast. A dozen girls arrived to share the boys' classes that winter, among them the half-Jewish teenager Simone Kaminker, the future actress Simone Signoret. When Signoret wrote her memoir *Nostalgia Isn't What It Used to Be* in 1978, she remembered her young teacher as 'a marvellous woman'.[1] The two would meet again.

As the French army sat in inaction, enemy forces worked with terrifying efficiency. On 23 August 1939, Stalin's government had signed a Non-Aggression Pact with Hitler's, agreeing that Russia would not oppose German offensives in eastern Europe in return for Germany's agreement not to aid Japan in its attacks on Russia's Mongolian borders. Under a secret clause Russia would feed on the Nazis' spoils, with Romania, Poland, Lithuania, Latvia, Estonia and Finland to be divided into Nazi and Soviet spheres of influence. By the end of October 1939, Nazi and Soviet forces had occupied Poland and carved it up between them, and the Soviets had moved on to the conquest of the Baltic States while Germany fought the Allies at sea, sending out U-boat wolfpacks to hunt French and British shipping. It was not until the spring of 1940 that the Wehrmacht – the German army – pounced again. Denmark fell in April, and Nazi troops moved on to Norway while still the French army waited. In early May, Raymond had a three-day leave and travelled to Paris to meet Lucie. They had not seen each other since their December honeymoon. It was a passionate reunion. The couple was still holed up in Paris when the French government took to the airwaves on 10 May to order all officers to rejoin their regiments immediately. The *drôle de guerre* was over. The Wehrmacht had begun its blitzkrieg invasion of Holland, Belgium and Luxembourg, aiming at a swift conquest of France and a decisive invasion of Britain. It was a catastrophe for the Allies. By the end of May Holland had surrendered, the British Expeditionary Force was scrambling to get out from the beaches of north-west France and the Wehrmacht was just behind them.

Mechanized German divisions had done what no one in the French high command had thought possible, completely bypassing the fabled Maginot Line and invading France through the vast forests which straddle the Belgian border. Paris was bombed on 3 June and the French government and most of its civil service fled piecemeal towards Tours and then Bordeaux however they could, hindering any coordinated attempt to deal with the invasion. The apparatus of the state disintegrated. In what became known as 'the Exodus', between six and ten million civilians fled southwards and westwards under Luftwaffe bombardments, blocking roads and railways as far as the Pyrenees and submerging villages and towns en route. Cars were abandoned when they ran out of petrol; people overflowed from passenger and goods trains which advanced a few metres, then stopped – no one knew why,

or for how long. Thousands of children became separated from their
parents; people looted and fought, and stole each other's cars, bicycles,
petrol, food and water. Order vanished.

France's defeat was swift, utter and humiliating. Within days of the
Germans' arrival on French soil, what was left of the French army was
fleeing hell for leather westwards behind, beside and sometimes even in
front of the politicians and civilians. On 14 June, swastikas hung from
the Arc de Triomphe in an almost deserted Paris. Those residents who
had had no means to get away 'watched the entry in silence' according
to a journalist of the Associated Press. 'Small groups of people still sat
along the terraces and boulevards and in the cafés. Shops were boarded
up. In the Place de l'Opéra stood a solitary motor-car with a big "for
sale" sign. The Paris police still patrolled the streets. Occasionally could
be heard the drone of an unmolested plane.'[2]

The same day, the French parliament, which had come to rest
in Bordeaux, debated the options available. Prime Minister Paul
Reynaud proposed that France surrender, but that the army leave the
country and continue the fight against Germany from abroad. He
was told such a course was unacceptably dishonourable. A plea to
President Roosevelt of the USA brought no concrete promise of aid.
On 15 June, Britain said it would agree to an armistice if the French
fleet was immediately sent to British ports and a Franco-British Union
established, but too many parliamentarians suspected a British plot to
force France into subservience. Unable to find any way of continuing
the fight, Prime Minister Reynaud resigned and the President called
on a hero from the previous war, eighty-four-year-old, white-haired
and walrus-moustached Field Marshal Philippe Pétain. He agreed to
form a government, restore order to the country and negotiate with the
Germans.

As the government debated, the Exodus continued. In Vannes, the headmaster of Lucie's school vanished: as a known Freemason, he belonged to a group at the top of the Nazis' wanted list. The town was invaded first by a stream of terrified refugees, and then, on 21 June, by the enemy. 'A long column of Germans marched, with cars of all sorts following 50 metres behind,' wrote a soldier who saw them arrive. 'The townspeople were in the streets because it was market day. They held up pretty well. [French] soldiers, even officers, were on the pavement to watch.'[3]

All clocks were changed to German time, and a 9 p.m. curfew was introduced. German boomed from loudspeakers. Houses were requisitioned and French flags torn down and replaced with swastikas. Gothic script leapt from the signs which went up overnight: *Keep out! Forbidden! No Civilians!* and worse: posters of smiling uniformed Germans with happy French children in their arms and the slogan *Abandoned populations! Put your trust in German soldiers!* Thousands of soldiers began to gather on the Atlantic coast for the invasion of Britain, and from one day to another, Lucie found herself living in a country which was no longer hers, with no idea of what had happened to her husband.

Half a century later, contempt and anger were still hot in Raymond's mind when he spoke about the frantic days of May and June 1940: contempt for the high command which had failed to put in hand any meaningful plan of defence, failed to predict or respond to the sudden invasion and failed to protect its own soldiers; anger at the inability of politicians and senior officers to hold the line either physically or morally. No machine guns had ever arrived to equip the fortifications his men had spent the winter building. The bridges they had mined to hold back the advancing German army were virtually unreachable because the soldiers had no transport to get there and light the fuses. Raymond was one of the few that managed to make it. With the help of a driver he commandeered an old Citroen, drove towards the river and blew up the bridges. He and the driver then returned to their own position. To his frustration, and the bewildered fury of the young Alsacien soldiers under his command, he was ordered to retreat westwards across the plain of Alsace, without stopping to offer resistance to the invading army which followed two kilometres away.

On 21 June, Raymond's company was attacked by 300 enemy soldiers with machine guns, bare from the waist up. He remembered the detail sixty years later. Throwing himself into a bush, Raymond returned fire, but it was impossible. Every Frenchman there was disarmed, made prisoner, and ordered to march towards a prisoner-of-war camp on what had until hours ago been French soil. Some of them would not return for five years. Raymond wrote his name and Lucie's address on a scrap of paper, dropped it into a ditch for the local people to retrieve and post on, and then walked where he was told along lanes full of defeated, disarmed, trudging soldiers, hedged by flowers which blossomed under the bright summer sun. The following day, he was awarded the Croix de Guerre, although he had no idea of that at the time. After three days and nights of constant action, the first thing he did when he reached the detention camp was sleep. When he woke, he learnt that Marshal Pétain had negotiated an armistice even before he and his men were taken prisoner, broadcasting to the nation 'with a heavy heart' on 17 June that 'we must stop fighting'.

Nearly two million French soldiers were captured in those few weeks of fighting; another 200,000 were wounded and nearly 100,000 killed. But a few thousand civilians and military had managed to get out of France, heading south into Spain and across the straits to Algeria, east into Switzerland or across the Channel to Britain. The then little-known tank commander General Charles de Gaulle left France on 17 June and broadcast a message from the BBC in London the day after Pétain told his compatriots that the fight was over. 'France has lost one battle!' he insisted. 'She has not lost the war! Vive la France!' If today de Gaulle's 18 June speech occupies the same place in French memory as 'We will fight them on the beaches' does in the British, his appeal to keep fighting was heard by very few people at the time, and most of those who did hear him were in no mood to listen to what he said. The nation he addressed, including the vast majority of its military, had been terrified as much by the chaos of the Exodus as by the arrival of the Wehrmacht, and believed that the armistice was the only way to halt the country's slide into anarchy. The First World War was within living memory for the majority. If many – though not all – feared the Germans, everyone feared a return to the horrors of the Somme. In Raymond's prisoner-of-war camp, senior French officers forbade their men to attempt escape, telling them that the terms of the armistice did not allow it. Soothed by the reassurance that soon they would all be sent home and the politicians would begin the work of settling an indemnity and a transfer of territory, just as they had after previous German invasions, most of the thousands taken prisoner simply waited in the camps as they had waited along the Maginot Line, doing as they were told. Raymond was one of the few who refused.

Still in Vannes, Lucie had had no news of her husband for weeks. She passed her first birthday as a married woman as she had done her first Christmas: alone and frightened, not knowing where her husband was, or even if he was still alive. Her parents-in-law knew no more than she did: it seemed nobody had information about their men. Some semblance of ordinary life had to continue, nevertheless, as millions of people waited for news. However bewildered and frightened teachers and pupils were with foreign soldiers in the streets and fathers, brothers and husbands who had vanished, the girls and boys who had been working towards their *baccalauréat* had to sit their examination. Bravely, Lucie contacted the German authorities in Vannes, persuading them to release four French officers from the nearest internment camp to form the examination jury. She was enraged when all four refused to seize the opportunity to escape: had they no courage, no principled determination to resist defeat? Term had ended by the time she finally received a card from the Red Cross at the end of July, with a note that her husband was confined to a barracks in Sarrebourg, converted to a prisoner-of-war camp. He had written the card on her birthday.

Nothing is more monotonous, my love, than life in camp. More than the lack of comforts and the terrible food, it is the false and contradictory reports which weigh on the thousands of poor blokes who are here and who see no hope on the horizon ... when I leave here, I will go to Dijon, and I will find you, and we will choose what must be done, won't we. I hope you are very well, and ready for our future life. And this evening, your birthday, my thoughts will be entirely with you. Raymond.[4]

With most of France lapsing into the stunned inactivity known as *attentisme* – waiting to see what would happen – Lucie Samuel went into action. She had no more faith than her husband that the Nazis would soon let their French prisoners go home, and she knew that if Raymond were transferred to a prisoner of war camp in Germany his Jewishness would put him in terrible danger. He had to escape immediately, and Lucie was not a woman who waited for other people to step in and take care of things. She would rescue him herself.

Once again she crossed France, travelling in even more dangerous circumstances than she had done the previous November, for the roads were blocked not only by refugees but also by the German troops fanning out across a traumatized country, ramming home the fact of their victory as they entered town after town in sleek, grey and green, seemingly endless processions. Single-minded in her determination to rescue Raymond, Lucie had come up with a simple plan: she would engineer her husband's transfer from barracks to hospital, then smuggle in a disguise to facilitate his escape. In Champagne, she stopped off to find Raymond's brother, Yvon, in the military hospital to which he had been posted. Yvon provided her with a drug guaranteed to provoke fever, and on she went, against the current, travelling east as everyone else travelled west, until she reached Sarrebourg and begged permission to see her husband. There was a brief, charged contact between prisoner and visitor – it was the first time they had seen each other since Paris in May – the drug was passed from one to another, time was called and a couple of days later a heavily sweating Raymond was transferred to hospital. Visiting as the anxious wife, Lucie produced the cap and suit of workman's blue overalls in which he would escape. If it was a simple plan, it was also a terrifying one for Raymond, who was more frightened than he had ever been in his life: hiding next to the garden fence was easy enough, but he was all too aware that if the nearby guards saw him during the moment it would take to haul himself over, their bullets would not miss. After what seemed like hours of gut-cramping hesitation, he pulled himself up, threw himself over the top and fell into the street below, where Lucie was waiting.

Obeying the lectures on underground resistance which Joseph Epstein had taught in the Latin Quarter – hide in full view – the young couple took rooms in a hotel where most other guests were German officers. The next day, concealing their nervous exhilaration, they went to the railway station to take a train across the new border, for Alsace had been annexed by the Reich, and found themselves sharing a platform with prisoners from Raymond's camp being transferred that same day to Germany. Lucie had got her husband out just in time. Any one of the men at the station could have recognized the blue-clad workman as Lieutenant Samuel. Among them was a man whom Raymond had tried to persuade to escape with him and for whom Lucie had even brought a second set of blue overalls. He had refused. He would spend the next five years a prisoner.

The Samuels went the other way, with Raymond clinging to the underside of the railway carriage. He was only supposed to stay there while officials boarded to check documents, but he did not manage to come back up before the train rattled off again. He emerged at the next stop 'as black as a coalminer'.[5]

It was Lucie's first rescue. She would carry out many more in the next three years.

* * *

Although Marshal Pétain had initially hoped to govern from Paris, it soon became clear that the Germans would not allow this. Under the armistice signed on 22 June, France was divided into zones. Alsace and Lorraine were annexed and the North-East became a 'Forbidden Zone' under direct German rule, where no civilian personnel were allowed. A small Italian Zone was carved out in the far South-East of the country (Italy having declared war on France on 10 June); an 'Occupied' or 'Northern' Zone covered three-fifths of the country; and the rump, separated by a well-guarded Demarcation Line, was the so-called 'Free

Zone. Unlike the 'racially inferior' peoples of eastern Europe, the French were not officially a defeated people and the establishment of a Free Zone preserved this fiction. In this supposedly sovereign and independent state, Marshal Pétain and the remaining parliamentarians and civil servants established themselves in the spa town of Vichy, persuaded by the large number of hotels, rail links with Paris, the modernity of its telephone exchange (and variety of louche night spots) that this was as good a place as any. The Third Republic of France came to an end seventy years after its inception in the suitably seedy environment of a Vichy casino on 9 July, when 569 parliamentarians voted to give Pétain full powers. Twenty-seven had already left for London or Algiers and only a brave eighty – nearly all Socialists – voted against. Lucie had lost her country twice over: once, when German troops and German tanks invaded French territory, and now again, when the values she believed intrinsic to Frenchness were tossed aside.

The Samuels had wanted to settle in Paris, but Raymond's Jewishness rendered residence in the Occupied Zone dangerous, even if many French Jews did not yet realize that. And even had there not been the threat of anti-Semitic persecution, neither Raymond nor Lucie would tolerate living under direct German rule, where the enemy presence was immediate, intense and visible. Paris swarmed with Germans: Germans working, Germans on leave, Germans taking pictures of each other in front of the Eiffel Tower and the Arc de Triomphe, Germans buying chocolates in the Galeries Lafayette and sipping coffee at pavement cafes. Montmartre and Pigalle by night were full of Germans seeking the capital's other delights, and despite orders to the occupying troops that the French be treated with courtesy, the hard reality of conquest was unavoidable. Lucie found it 'impossible to accept these uniforms which were everywhere; these signs in gothic lettering that no one could understand; this foreign army which was all powerful.'[6] Instead, the Samuels went to Lyon, a few miles south of the Demarcation Line, the most important city of the Vichy Zone and one where they would be near their families. Raymond had aunts, friends and cousins to whom he was much attached in the city itself, Lucie's parents were within reach at Blanzy, her sister, Jeanne, was also heading back to Burgundy with her children, and the Samuels' family home in Dijon was just north of the Demarcation Line.

The young couple found a city in shock. Some of the thousands of refugees who had fled the North in May and June had remained, fearing residence in the Occupied Zone, and Lyon's citizens were still reeling from contact with their conquerors. The Germans had marched into the city on 19 June and stayed until 7 July, the day after the Demarcation Line came into being. Arriving only a month or so after their traumatizing presence, the Samuels found a cowed place where families shut their doors on a changed world whose rules they did not know. One and a half million men had been taken prisoner from across France. Lucie may have snatched her husband back from German custody but innumerable others waited to know if their men would be coming home, when, and under what conditions.

However disoriented and demoralized, Lyon was to be the Samuels' first home as a married couple. At last they were actually living together, after nine months of marriage in which they had been apart for all but a few days, and they approached their new life as any newly-weds did, finding accommodation, employment and friends. After a couple of days spent in crowded hotels, they moved into a two-room flat on the Rue Pierre Corneille in the city's red-roofed and narrow-alleyed old centre, a few steps from the banks of the River Rhône where it slid through Lyon on its journey towards the Mediterranean. A cousin of

Raymond had found the apartment for them, for it had been home to a newly married friend of hers whose husband was a prisoner. She had gone back to live with her parents while she waited for news of him. At first the flat was more an expedient than a home. The owner had left all her possessions there and asked them only to use one room, and 'nothing was to our taste,' Lucie said, 'except the double bed.'[7]

While Lucie adjusted to the demands and delights of marriage, Raymond found work. He was contacted by the owner of a Parisian patent office with whom he had had dealings when he was in the USA and who now wanted Raymond to set up a regional office in Lyon, using his fluent English and contacts to establish business with American clients. It seemed as if the Samuels' immediate needs were taken care of: they had a flat, even if they did not like it much, Raymond had work, Lucie still had access to the generous David Weill bursary which would have supported her in the Rocky Mountains. But just as Lucie was beginning to wonder if a first baby might not be on its way, it became clear that their stability was illusory.

All over France, people recovering from the horrors of the Exodus and the invasion wanted order to return. The twin shocks of civil breakdown and military defeat enabled the emergence of a type of nationalistic conservatism which had always inhabited a part of French society. Pétain's government swiftly cobbled together a soothing narrative based on the need for a return to the old ways and a rebuttal of the new. France, the old marshal told his frightened flock, had lost its way and must rediscover its ancient virtues. If it did so, it could redeem itself, emerging from its trials a stronger, better nation.

The old marshal's message was a popular one, and he was the man to deliver it. Upright and still handsome in his gold-braided uniforms, his moustaches always carefully groomed and his blue eyes bright, he was a walking symbol of French valour. The fame of 'the Lion of Verdun' rested not only on his military success during the First World War but also on his attempts to care for the ordinary soldiers who had been under his command. A humiliated nation could rally to this grandfatherly and morally upright figure. (His enthusiastic womanizing was not yet common knowledge.) What Pétain proposed to France in July 1940 was a 'National Revolution' which would replace the decadent republican values of 'liberty, equality and fraternity' with those of 'work, family and homeland' and – although this aim was given less public prominence – allow the French state to take its place in Germany's New Europe, for neither Pétain nor his First Minister, Pierre Laval, nor the vast majority of those in his government, doubted that Hitler's new order was here to stay for a very long time.

Support for Pétain was almost universal. Clever propaganda positioned his government as the upholder of French sovereignty and fostered a personality cult around the marshal himself, crediting him with having almost single-handedly prevented France from sinking into anarchy.

The marshal might have been displaced from Paris, but he still commanded the French fleet, the 100,000 strong 'Army of the Armistice' which the Germans had allowed him to retain, and the entire French empire: the vast territories of Indochina and West Africa, Syria and Lebanon, the islands of Madagascar, Mauritius and New Caledonia, and the 'French Settlements' in India and Polynesia. His National Revolution had an enormous constituency, appealing not only to the Right and far Right, but to those who espoused the values, or what they believed to be the values, of family, Catholicism and the land. Lucie watched as 'magistrates and senior civil servants [took] the oath to [his] regime ... Only one refused.'[8] Pro-Pétain homilies were preached in church. His portrait appeared in schools and public buildings. He was fêted on the streets and mobbed by a grateful populace during the endless visits he made to craft workshops and veterans' associations, wine cooperatives and dairies, village schools and the newly introduced ceremonies which honoured women enduring multiple pregnancies – any place and occasion which fitted the simple, backward-looking 'blood and soil' version of French nationhood which his government was pushing. Only the tiniest minority yet believed that his administration and the German Occupation of the North were equally abhorrent and equally to be feared. Only the most imaginative – the most able to see beyond their immediate circumstances – could think that any opposition might be offered to the new France and its German protector. Lucie Samuel was one of them.

Refusal. *Le refus*. There was a direct link between the Communist militancy – open in Lucie's case, more guarded in Raymond's – of the Samuels' student days in the Latin Quarter, and their refusal in July 1940 to accept the men – there was little place for women in the new power structure – who ruled from Vichy. For Lucie, that link went even further back: for her, liberty was 'the refusal to accept the constraints imposed on us by others'.[9] It had begun in her childhood, when she had refused to respect what was expected of her gender or her class, and continued when she had thrown up her place in the Boulevard des Batignolles against her family's wishes. Then it had become a fight against those who wished to crush dissent in the Boulevard Saint-Michel. Now it was a refusal to accept not only the National Revolution, but the fundamental legitimacy of the government which proposed it.

Those absolutely determined to contest that legitimacy had already, in general, left France to join General de Gaulle's Free French in London. They, too, were exceptionally few. Among them was a very young man called Daniel Cordier, whom Lucie and Raymond were soon to know well. He realized just how small a group he had joined.

> The first time I saw General de Gaulle was 6 July 1940, we were all civilians, 2,500 of us at most, of whom 800 were from the Foreign Legion. That was what General de Gaulle's army was composed of a month after the armistice, whereas there were 100,000 men in Pétain's 'Armistice Army' … the French were cowards (*lâches*). Very few had any courage.[10]

Daniel Cordier's assessment was not entirely fair. If Marshal Pétain enjoyed huge early support, it was partly because many people who later became *résistants* simply could not see their way clearly in summer and autumn 1940. Another man in whom the Samuels would come to place great trust was Serge Asher, a reckless twenty-two-year-old *polytechnicien*[11] of Jewish ancestry who had also moved to Lyon after the defeat. Serge Asher was one of many who could find neither intellectual nor moral clarity during those months. Despite his later resistance work, he believed in 1940 that Pétain and de Gaulle were working together to offer a united resistance to the Germans, with de Gaulle carrying on an open fight from abroad while Pétain worked against the Nazis from within.

The Samuels were among the very few who opposed Vichy from the very start. Their opposition was rooted in principle, but they also knew that for reasons of both race and politics, they were both personally in danger. French anti-Semitism was different in kind from the insane fundamentalism of Nazism. Nonetheless, it had coloured French political life between the wars on both the Left and Right, particularly during the large influx of Jewish refugees from Poland, Austria, Germany and

Czechoslovakia in the 1930s. French anti-Semitism had always tended to make a clear distinction between assimilated French Jewish citizens, and what one 1930s commentator contemptuously called the 'hundreds of thousands of Ashkenazis, escaped from Polish or Romanian ghettoes ... who detach our compatriots ... from their traditions' and '"encumber" French hospitals.'[12] A few weeks after the defeat, Pétain's government set up a committee to examine naturalizations carried out since 1927. The result was the withdrawal of French nationality from 15,000 people, and their internment in Vichy-run concentration camps. Shortly afterwards, in October 1940, the government brought in the first of the 'Jewish statutes', which proved that if Vichy was not quite ready to *intern* French Jews for no reason, it was certainly happy to restrict and police them. The October statute banned all Jews from working for the military or the press, in commercial and industrial activities, and in the civil service. People trying to prove themselves non-Jewish had to present baptism certificates for themselves, their parents and three grandparents. The result for the Samuels was immediate. From one day to the next, Raymond lost his job. His employer was already travelling every week to Berlin to meet his new clients and, as the man calmly explained, no one expecting a fruitful business relationship with Germans could afford to have a man called 'Samuel' on his pay roll. Raymond told his newly pregnant wife 'in a calm voice, but he was green with rage.'[13]

Raymond found another job inspecting workyards at Bron airport, but the Samuels' situation was precarious, and so was that of many of their pre-war friends who were on the wanted list because of their politics. The French government had begun interning Communists at the outbreak of war because of the pact between Soviet Russia and Nazi Germany. Although that pact still held, Vichy continued their internment under the requirements of 'national security', even offering, to the Samuels' disgust, 'to hand over to the Occupying authorities immigrants from Germany, Austria and Hungary who were sought by their own police force for opposition to the Nazi state'.[14] By the end of 1940, between 55 and 60 thousand Jews and political 'dissidents' were interned in Vichy's cold and unsanitary camps, but the respect and affection in which Pétain was held by the majority had hardly been touched.

The Samuels had realized what the vast majority of French people would not accept for another three years, and some would always deny. They knew that the French 'sovereignty' supposedly incarnated by Vichy was a myth. They detested Pétain, what he had done and what he was doing, and considered him either a *pantin fasciste*,[15] a Fascist puppet, or, worse, a man with a covert far-right agenda. Raymond suspected he had had talks with the Germans when he had been France's ambassador to Fascist Spain in 1939, and that his arrival in government in 1940, and the implementation of the National Revolution, were pre-arranged. Raymond was a man who understood structure, organization and management, and he soon worked out exactly what role the Germans had assigned Pétain's administration.

They had just beaten France, and their policy was going to be to exploit it to the maximum in order to support their war effort. And very quickly … they saw that there was no better way to exploit the whole of France, with its agricultural and industrial resources, than through Marshal Pétain. It was brilliant … [Using Pétain] allowed the Germans to exploit a country at minimum cost and with maximum yield.[16]

In one of the radio broadcasts which General de Gaulle regularly made from London in the months after defeat, he told his nation that 'somewhere must shine and burn the flame of French resistance.' That word, 'resistance', was quickly adopted by those few prepared to fight the Occupiers, north of the Line, but those – equally few – to the south first called their anti-Vichy activities simply *opposition*. On both sides of the Line, resistance or opposition first came as isolated individual acts: the cross of Lorraine, symbol of the Free France, chalked onto houses or German vehicles; swastikas torn down in the night; wanted people hidden in spare rooms and barns, or helped to cross the Line into the Free Zone; *Vive les anglais!* sprayed onto the wall of a *lycée* by a sixteen-year-old girl called Rosa Floch; a telephone cable cut by a young man called Étienne Achavanne. Achavanne was the first Frenchman to be executed for resisting the Occupier. Rosa was later arrested and died in Birkenau. Later these few, isolated individuals impelled by fury or moral outrage to act would be revered as *résistants de la première heure*, resisters from the very first moment. The Samuels would be numbered among them.

Lucie and Raymond's enraged discussions of the illegitimacy of Pétain's government were initially confined to a group of intimates based around Raymond's cousins, the David brothers. 'Fred' David had been a hospital doctor until the October statute restricting Jewish employment in public services. Marcel David was a university student who attended their meetings with his fiancée, Renée Moerel, and his tall, talkative friend André Lassagne, a Lyon-born *lycée* teacher, another childhood friend of the David boys who 'always has a funny story to tell.'[17] And Maurice David, Raymond's particular friend, had managed to escape a German prisoner-of-war camp that summer by pinching a wheelbarrow left on the road and simply turning aside into the fields until his column of prisoners had gone by. Back in Lyon he had taken up management of the business belonging to that branch of the family, a gentleman's outfitters called *Au Roi du Pantalon*. He was to prove himself the staunchest of supporters of the Samuels over the next few years: 'indefatigable Maurice,' Lucie called him, 'so calmly courageous, who in his straightforward way accomplishes the boldest operations, who knows everybody in Lyon, who is trusted by everybody.'[18]

At the same time that the Samuel–David group began meeting for tentative discussions of 'what could be done', Lucie and Raymond were privately wondering if they should stay in France at all. Lucie's grant and visa to the USA were still valid, and American friends had agreed to sponsor Raymond's arrival. In December 1940, the necessary documents arrived from the MIT Graduate School and 'we had to choose,' Raymond said, 'whether to go, or stay.' Should they close this chapter, abandon the country which had fallen on such terrible times and take up their lives again elsewhere? Theirs was not a marriage in which the husband decided and the wife agreed. *À deux* they decided that their life in the United States could wait; that the 'little game' which would 'later be called the Resistance', could not, surely, go on for long – and when it came to an end, they would resume the life they had planned for themselves. America would be there for a long time. Their own country needed them now.[19]

The Samuels' decision – Lucie's second – to stay in France when they could have sailed for American safety was not as insouciant as Raymond painted it. They knew that the first Polish Jews had been deported to labour camps within a month of Germany's invading Poland. Raymond would put himself in real danger by staying in France, but that cut both ways: the young couple were not the only protagonists of their story. Could they abandon his family? They could not.

Very soon the couple began putting heavy pressure on Raymond's parents and his sister, Ginette, to leave their home in Dijon, and move south of the line to Lyon, but their efforts foundered on the absolute refusal of Raymond's father to accept that they were in any danger. Albert Samuel was a decorated veteran of the 1914–18 war and he could not believe that Marshal Pétain would allow such a person to be harmed. 'My family goes back five generations in Lorraine,' Albert Samuel said. 'I fought in the war of 1914, my two sons are officers, one of them an army doctor, at present a prisoner of war. We have nothing to fear.'[20] Raymond knew otherwise. On 24 October, Pétain shook Hitler's hand before a barrage of photographers at Montoire. A week later he declared to the nation: 'I enter, today, into the way of collaboration.' That evening Renée Moerel recorded in her diary that her fiancé's courteous, moderate cousin Raymond had called the nation's hero an 'old turd'.[21] Under their son's constant pressure, the elder Samuels did eventually agree to move, finding lodgings above a grocery shop in Lyon and squeezing in the furniture they had brought from a more gracious home, but Albert Samuel would maintain his trust in Marshal Pétain right up until a very few weeks before his death.

∗ ∗ ∗

When Strasbourg became German, its university was relocated to the city of Clermont-Ferrand, a hot, sprawling place in the Massif Central about a hundred miles south of Lyon. Students and academics gathered uncertainly in October 1940 to start the new term, Lucie's old friend Jean Cavaillès among them. Called up in 1939, he had been captured by German troops in Belgium, had escaped his guards, found a bicycle and cycled south. Shortly after term began, Lucie went to see him in Clermont and he took her to lunch in a city-centre restaurant packed with students, academics and journalists where he introduced her to a man named Emmanuel d'Astier de la Vigerie. For all three, it was a decisive moment. The 'little game' which Lucie and Raymond had been playing in Lyon was about to become something more serious.

Clermont was an early breeding ground of resistance. The city was home to *La Montagne*, a large-circulation left-wing newspaper whose owner had been one of the eighty parliamentarians who refused to vote full powers to Pétain in July 1940. The relocation of Strasbourg University had brought with it another reservoir of anti-Nazi and anti-Vichy activism. Like Lyon, the city housed hundreds of refugees who knew they would be pursued by reason of their politics or their race in the Occupied Zone, and who had scrambled across the Demarcation Line to relative safety. Jean Cavaillès was already playing a central role in the anti-Vichy discussions which had emerged from this mêlée. An archaeological dig out on the plains of Gergovie provided a convenient meeting place for disaffected staff and students discreetly to discuss the same question which Lucie and her in-laws debated in Lyon: what could be done. The man she and Cavaillès met in the Brasserie de Strasbourg had come up with an answer.

Emmanuel d'Astier de la Vigerie was to become one of the greatest heroes of the French Resistance, but he seemed a very unlikely candidate for the role in the autumn of 1940. Everyone who met d'Astier was struck by his *fin de siècle* charm and aristocratic persona: he was the sort of person whom Nancy Mitford might have taken as a model for her French heroes. Lucie found him 'an astonishing character, a Don Quixote-like figure, very tall, very thin, very pronounced features, a hooked nose, thin lips. About forty, he had thick wavy black hair with a little grey, already receding at the temples. I was immediately struck by his large, beautiful hands, delicate and well cared for.'[22] Very few, from any background, could resist d'Astier's charm. It would prove a powerful weapon in the coming fight.

On the face of it, he and Lucie had nothing in common. D'Astier's life had been that of an effete, moneyed writer, playboy, opium addict and lover of the good life from a landed family. There was nothing left-wing in his background but neither had he particularly allied himself pre-war with any of the Catholic, monarchical or otherwise anti-republican factions at whose Parisian representatives Lucie had hurled insults in the Boulevard Saint-Michel. In fact, he had been almost apolitical, and only the shock of defeat had changed him. Commanding troops on the Atlantic coast in June, he had been outraged by the refusal of his brother officers to offer opposition to the German advance. The dumb acquiescence in defeat of his large upper-class acquaintance had awoken him from the life of a dilettante. Having decided not to go to London to join the Free French, he forced himself to break from his addiction (shutting himself alone in a hotel room for eight days during which time he nearly died) and was ready for action. He 'entered the Resistance neither for nationalism nor internationalism, but motivated simply by dignity.'[23] He could not tolerate the ignominy of France's position.

Just before meeting Lucie Samuel, d'Astier had founded *La Dernière Colonne*, the Last Column. It had two aims. First, d'Astier intended semi-seriously to assassinate prominent collaborators and French Nazis. He had his eye particularly on Henri Béraud, the corpulent, double-chinned, English-hating editor of *Gringoire*, a right-wing French newspaper that acted as Vichy's principal cheerleader and was described by George Orwell as 'the most disgusting rag it is possible to imagine'.[24] Second, d'Astier wanted to spread information about the true, treasonous nature of Pétain's regime: that there was nothing free about the 'Free Zone', and nothing sovereign about the marshal's government. D'Astier's niece and nephew had joined him, but the rich friends who had fled Occupied

Paris for their Côte d'Azur villas had almost all turned him down. His recruits when he was introduced to Lucie, apart from his niece and nephew, were only three, but they were remarkable. Jean Cavaillès was one and the others were Georges Zerapha and Jean Rochon. Zerapha, a fifty-three-year-old Jewish businessman noted for his taste in bow ties, his lovely smile and his hatred of racism, had before the war kept the International League against Anti-Semitism going with his donations. He was already actively sought by the Nazis. Rochon was an editor on *La Montagne*, a writer and poet and lover of intellectual freedom. D'Astier's next adherent was Lucie Samuel, who joined the movement there and then, and left Clermont determined to take 'resistance' to Lyon.

Brimming with excitement and purpose, she launched her recruitment campaign in the Rue Pierre Corneille. Imbued by d'Astier's *chevaleresque* personality, the Last Column was almost a game, if one with a serious purpose. That same personality gave it its charm, however. For a couple of days, Raymond was sceptical of this tiny group of adventurers which had charmed his wife and which claimed to be pitting itself against the Wehrmacht. It was hearing the poetry of the chosen passwords, taken from the French poet Apollinaire, which changed his mind, or so he would claim. 'Beneath the Mirabeau bridge!' called d'Astier on arriving a couple of days later and 'Let the Seine flow,' Lucie called back from the kitchen.[25] D'Astier won Raymond over completely by engaging the couple in discussions of music, art, poetry, literature, cuisine and history, as well as the mechanics of opposition.

Now Lucie and Raymond's activities went beyond sharing their anger and frustration with close friends and relatives. They had a mission, and Lucie threw herself wholeheartedly into her new project: she was determined to open the eyes of as many people as possible to the lies they were being told. Her 'entrance into the resistance' was due to 'the need to *inform* people ... when people do not know, they cannot judge and they cannot act.'[26] Vichy's narrative of a hierarchical, God-fearing society where everyone knew their place wrote out independent women like Lucie and men like her liberal Jewish husband, but most of those who could have countered that narrative had been cowed into silence, sent underground or interned. What the Samuels wanted people to know was that their rulers were neither protectors of French values, nor passive resisters, nor benefactors, but ultra-conservatives with a racist agenda who had turned their backs on the Republic – indeed, on the Enlightenment itself. As a historian, Lucie knew all about *La Fronde*, the great seventeenth-century rebellion against the crown which had been incorporated into France's national identity. It was time for a new *fronde*, and Lucie was a natural *frondeuse*.

A typewriter that Raymond had with great trouble brought back from the USA became the group's first weapon; the Samuels' two-room flat became the Last Column's meeting place in Lyon and Lucie Samuel became its heart. Her first clandestine actions have left little trace, for they were a reprise of her days with Joseph Epstein in the Latin Quarter. In the freezing nights of a savagely cold winter, she and Raymond sneaked out into the silent, snow-filled streets to chalk anti-collaborationist slogans on walls: *Collaboration is treachery!* Or *The French who work for the Germans are traitors. We are keeping a list. They will be punished.* At *tabacs* and newspaper stands, they furtively stuck labels onto copies of *Gringoire: Read this and make Hitler happy! Henri Béraud earns 10,000 francs per week for this filth* – signed *La Dernière Colonne.*[27] Crude posters were pasted over the thousands which poured from Vichy's own propaganda machine. A mimeograph was found to boost the output of Raymond's typewriter and tracts were laboriously produced. Some were stuffed into letterboxes and others were delivered by mousetraps placed on icy roofs with a pile of papers on one end and a tin can dripping water dangled from the other. When tipping point was reached, the trap was sprung and sent hundreds of papers floating into the air and down into the street, by which time the person who had set it was long gone. 'We were apprentices,' Lucie said, 'we had to start from scratch ... to invent everything, day after day.'[28]

If action brought joy, it also brought frustration, for the Last Column remained a pinprick of refusal in a vast, suffocating mass of acceptance. Alongside the amateur propaganda, the Samuels' other great task for the Last Column was cautious recruitment: engaging people in conversation as they stood in shop-queues or waited at tram-stops, bringing up newspaper reports, city gossip or what they had heard on the radio, sighing over domestic shortages and furtively gauging reactions. Few people yet gave clear indications of anger. Raymond found that 'the general mood had not yet become defiance'.[29]

Memoirs of what the French call the 'Dark Years' recall them as being like living in permanent night. Acts of resistance and the first brutal responses to them were already happening, particularly in Paris, Bordeaux and the traditionally bloody-minded province of Brittany, but the smothering blanket thrown over French media meant that the Samuels knew nothing of them.

French newspapers had been culled in June 1940, and those which survived had very limited ways to express disapproval, let alone outright opposition. *Le Figaro* published the Jewish statute without commentary, letting its dislike of the measure be inferred; others prefaced compulsory editorials with NC for 'Note Communiqué', but when the newspaper *Le Progrès de Lyon* refused to title a report of a British bombardment of Boulogne 'The English and the Communists agree to assassinate France', it was suspended. Broadcasts were similarly policed. Radio Paris had been handed to eager collaborators who told their listeners that France, innocent and wounded, was victim of a conflict being fought by the Anglo-Saxon nations in concert with international Jewry, from which only Communism could emerge triumphant. There remained film, but Vichy newsreels were surreal. Watching them, 'one might not realize a European war was taking place,' as historian Julian Jackson has remarked. 'They depicted a peaceful and rural France, offering extensive coverage of Pétain's provincial visits, and reports on French traditions and French craftsmen.'[30] Radio broadcasts by the BBC in London gave truer information, but Vichy swiftly banned listening first in public, and then in private, and when these prohibitions were judged ineffective, the signal was jammed.

In Lyon, very few seemed to react to the Last Column's posters and pamphlets, or read their graffitied messages of defiance. And the France which lay across the Line was cut off; even Paris hardly existed any more. Under Vichy, as in the Occupied Zone, a long list of censored writers and artists was circulated and anything which might have an Anglo-Saxon, Jewish, Masonic or otherwise undesirable taint was forbidden. Nor did the cold help. France's first wartime winter was severe, with temperatures falling to minus nineteen in Lyon and most of the country covered in solid snow for several weeks. Everyone locked themselves into their own houses; the streets were deserted and spontaneous public life died. The Vichy message was powerful, and few yet questioned it. The marshal had been legally granted his powers by a parliament which had dissolved itself in July 1940 – and if the marshal went, who would protect them from the Germans and allow the survival, let alone the renaissance, of France? Even the members of the Last Column had no answer to that.

The Samuels were aware that other resistance groups were beginning cautiously to cohere in Lyon itself, but making contact was risky. Serge Asher, the young Jewish engineer who had recently moved to the city, still could not quite accept that Pétain himself was corrupt but he was increasingly repelled by the Vichy administration. He would approach people he thought might feel similarly with cautious comments such as 'You know, the Marshal is badly advised. I'm sure he doesn't know what's really going on ...'[31] Overt criticism was a risky business, for Vichy's early months saw what one prefect (senior civil servant) called 'a veritable deluge of anonymous letters' – over three million of them – from one citizen denouncing another, some motivated by the promised rewards for information, others by politics and a small group by revenge. 'Curés denounced instituteurs, doctors their patients, patients their doctors, women denounced the immorality of POW wives in the absence of their husbands, shopkeepers denounced rivals for trading on the black market, non-Jews denounced Jews, French denounced foreigners, husbands denounced wives.'[32] For people like Raymond and Serge, obvious opposition to the regime was particularly dangerous: a Jew could not afford to be denounced even for a trivial offence.

But step by painful step, a message of defiance spread. As the Samuels discreetly went about their covert work in Lyon, Emmanuel d'Astier was travelling indefatigably, exhorting his friends and acquaintances to rouse themselves and act. Within a couple of months, he had persuaded representatives in the southern cities of Lyon, Clermont, Nîmes, Marseille, Toulouse and Nice to carry out 'dissident' acts, with his valiant niece Bertrande working as courier among them. The number of tracts, posters and slogans chalked on the walls of southern cities grew and by February 1941, about a hundred people belonged to the Last Column. On the night of 27 February 1941, they managed to get identical posters pasted up overnight in eight different towns, a considerable feat of logistics. But the same night their success backfired: four young people were caught red-handed and one of them gave away Bertrande d'Astier. The painfully recruited adherents scattered, frightened, back to their homes, and Bertrande was arrested and imprisoned, badly scaring her uncle. For the central core around d'Astier, Jean Cavaillès, Lucie and Raymond, the message of the 27 February debacle was that the rules of clandestine life needed to be better taught and respected, and that their movement required proper organization if its individual members were to remain secure. 'At that moment,' d'Astier said, 'the certainty was born within me that we could not act as adventurers. We had to forge links with the working classes.'[33] Socialists and Communists, both French and foreign, had spent years fighting repression. The Last Column could learn vital lessons from them, if only d'Astier could make contact, and bring them on board.

*  *  *

The resistance group which emerged in spring 1941 from the ashes of the Last Column was given the simple but compelling name of 'Libération'. It was to become one of France's most famous movements – one of the 'Big Three' in the Vichy Zone – and Lucie Samuel was among its founding members. Liberation's aims were different to those of the Last Column. 'Opposition' had not been an attempt to defeat Nazism, but to expose the hypocrisy of Vichy's claims. 'Resistance' was more ambitious. Libération would be not only larger but more mixed than the aristocratically led and whimsical Last Column. Its Directing Committee, as the group at the movement's heart called themselves, aimed to be politically and socially inclusive, bringing together *opposants* from different backgrounds. D'Astier had another ambition: to produce a proper, literate and well-informed newspaper which would rival *Gringoire* in quality, persuading readers that opposition was serious and well resourced and proving to collaborators that their actions were being recorded.

Underground newspapers had already appeared elsewhere. In the Occupied Zone the *Bulletin de la France Combattante* was produced by two women working a printing press hidden in an abbey; the banned Communist newspaper *L'Humanité* was produced and distributed illegally from various premises in Paris, and *Résistance* was written and printed by ethnologists and anthropologists at the Musée de l'Homme in Paris. In Lyon itself, an underground paper called *Combat* was already being produced by an opposition group with which Serge Asher, future friend of the Samuels, had made contact.

The practical demands of producing a paper were enormous, but so were the editorial difficulties. Was its aim simply to point out that the French people were being lied to? To point the finger at the greatest liars? To show the authorities that consent to their regime was not universal? To encourage adhesion to opposition movements, and if so, how? They could hardly print their names and addresses. Editorial work also required access to reliable sources which might penetrate the fug of Pétainist misinformation. Every evening at nine, the Samuels and whichever friends were in their little flat tuned in to Radio Londres. 'First we had to shut the windows, even in summer, in case we were denounced by a neighbour, or picked up by the police … then, the electricity had to be working, which was not always the case.' They strained to hear the voices crackling through the interference. 'We often took notes to use the information broadcast in an article in our newspaper.'[34] When editorials had been compiled, there remained the seemingly insurmountable practical difficulties of production and distribution. *Libération* was desperately short of money; print and paper were rationed and restricted to approved enterprises and individuals, and they needed access to a press.

Again, the biggest challenge was to penetrate the general apathy and find people who might help. They 'recruited parents, relatives'. Raymond sought out comrades from the *École des Ponts et Chaussées* while Lucie discreetly contacted old friends from the Sorbonne. 'Little by little, it spread like a pool of oil.'[35] Lucie found the process frustrating:

slow and difficult, like building an ant hill ... so much of the work was underground, time consuming and frequently unsuccessful. Any account given of it would not take into account the thousands of kilometres I travelled to talk to someone who might be able to help us, or knew someone who might, etc etc. It was as if we were moving grains of sand around, very slowly. At first, nothing seems to be happening – then there's a mountain. It was work which took a great deal of time and effort.[36]

It paid off. When a press was secretly supplied by the editors of *La Montagne* in Clermont, *Libération* began with an ambitious first print run of 10,000 copies in July 1941. Unlike other early resistance newspapers in the Vichy Zone, *Libération* explicitly placed resistance to Pétain's regime within the context of the international war on Nazism, echoing de Gaulle's insistence that the war was not over. 'This newspaper,' it proclaimed:

will bring you the truths which Germany has ordered our government to hide from us. This newspaper will tell you the tasks incumbent upon all French citizens who have not given up. Our aim is to emerge from the sordid condition of defeat, by action and

through action ... the government of Vichy has lost faith in France
and given up the fight ...[37]

The Samuel household had another birth that spring, for Lucie's growing
involvement with Libération coincided with the last months of her
pregnancy. In May 1941, baby Jean-Pierre arrived after a difficult labour
from which Lucie took some time to recover. Mother and baby were
examined by a local practitioner, Dr Riva, who 'quickly understood
what we were doing', Lucie said:

and he brought me – I was still nursing – a famished baby. The
parents had to flee and were not able to take the baby. They were
German Jews who had been warned, just in time, that the Vichy
police were on the way to their apartment. While efforts were
made to find the parents, the baby had to be fed ...[38]

And Lucie nursed it for a week. It was the sort of fortuitous meeting
which allowed the 'pool of oil' to spread: Dr Riva's support would prove
very useful to the Samuels and their comrades. Neither recovery from a
painful birth nor feeding two babies kept Lucie from her work for long.
A journalist whom she had recruited to Libération found her in early
July 1941 sitting up in bed 'preparing a distribution plan for the tracts
which had just been printed'.[39]

Distribution of the underground newspaper posed its own problems
and part of Lucie's plan involved Jean-Pierre's new pram, for who would
suspect a mother and baby out for a walk? When the fierce heat of the
day died down, off she went into the cool of the evening with her baby
and a few dozen copies of Libération under his mattress. The apartment
buildings of Lyon were not staffed by the legendary nosy concierges of

Paris, and she could nip in and rapidly thrust newspapers into every letter box in the foyer. But if Jean-Pierre's promenades helped distribution within Lyon, copies also needed to be sent hundreds of miles to the other towns where local activists would take over the job. Few civilians had access to vehicles and petrol – the Samuels' little jaunts in their Panhard were a thing of the past – so bales of newspapers were sent by railway, and it was a dangerous business. Emmanuel d'Astier spent one voyage crammed inside a toilet cubicle with four other people, sitting on a suitcase with thirty kilos of newsprint inside, listening for the footstep of the guard. Another day it was Raymond who hid in a goods wagon with a suitcase. He was pulled out somewhere en route by a couple of angry railway workers who probably had him down as a black marketeer. Making a swift judgement, Raymond explained what he was doing. Rapidly they mapped out the quickest and safest route to get him where he wanted to go, and put him back in his hiding place. They soon discovered that nearly all the Lyonnais railwaymen were on their side. When the couriers reached their destination, they needed either to find their contact and pass the newspapers over (d'Astier swapped his suitcase for an identical one just outside the station after his voyage in the lavatory), or to leave them at agreed 'letter boxes', which might be ditches, hollow trees, disused outbuildings or sympathizers' houses. All this, the classic stuff of spy fiction being lived out by ordinary men and women, had to be coordinated by Lucie sitting up in her bed-jacket with her baby sleeping at her side.

Between Jean-Pierre's birth and the first print run of *Libération* in July, the Samuels heard the news that Soviet Russia had finally changed direction, and was now fighting alongside the Allies. It brought them joy tinged by bitterness. Britain had been left fighting alone against Germany after the fall of France because the Nazis' natural enemy,

Russia, had removed itself from the fight just before the German invasion of Poland. News of the Non-Aggression Pact signed by Stalin and Hitler in August 1939 had fallen like a bomb among French Communists, who found themselves split, between the majority who obeyed Stalin, observed the terms of the Pact and refused to make war on Germany even after it occupied France; and those who regarded war on National Socialism as an imperative, whatever Stalin said. Whatever the stance of its individual members, the entire French Communist Party had been outlawed.

Lucie had watched with horror the Soviet occupation of part of Poland in the autumn of 1939, the ultimatums to the Baltic republics and the vicious Winter War on Finland, but if Soviet aggression had led her to distrust Stalin it had not dented her faith in the ordinary members of the Communist Party, nor her belief in communist ideals. And neither Lucie nor Raymond was a member of the Party and therefore bound by Party diktat. Free to act as they wished, Lucie had adopted the same stance she had taken in the Latin Quarter, where years combining Quakerism, pacifism and communism had taught her the value of inclusivity. She was willing to work with anyone 'on the right side', whether they were Communists, Socialists, radicals or apolitical.

Experienced Communist activists performed a vital task in the early days of resistance, by providing means of communication between the many small groups emerging on both sides of the Line. Although some would only work with other Communists, a few of Lucie's former Party comrades had the same pragmatic attitude as she did. André Ternet, former councillor of a working-class district of Paris, editor of the *Avant-Garde* newspapers which Lucie had distributed at dawn in Paris, and now a hunted man, arrived at the Samuels' flat in March 1941 seeking a safe place to hide, and was happy to cooperate with

Libération when they took him in. So was Joseph Epstein, who had returned to France after General Franco's victory in Spain in 1939, had escaped from one of the French camps in which the defeated republican soldiers were penned, and had now taken the anti-fascist fight to Paris. Other Communists, however, toed the Party line even if they expected the Pact to last only as long as expediency dictated. 'We can't join your group,' one told Lucie, 'because the Party will need us later.'[40] When Lucie asked a Communist acquaintance, who had contacts which allowed him to cross the Demarcation Line, to get explosives to Epstein, the man refused on the grounds that he had to 'think about the future': despite Epstein being a Communist, any available *matériel* had to be reserved until Party officials decided what to do with it. Next time the man crossed, Lucie asked him sweetly to take a cuddly toy to Epstein's little boy, and hid a packet of explosives in it without telling him.

On Sunday 22 June 1941, all this changed. Before dawn, and without warning, Hitler turned on his ally with the launch of Operation Barbarossa. German and Italian planes bombarded Soviet-controlled cities in Poland, and three million Wehrmacht troops began crossing into Soviet territory. 'Before three months have passed,' Hitler promised the German nation, 'we shall witness a collapse of Russia, the like of which has never been seen in history!' From one day to the next, Party officials informed Communists throughout Europe that the war was no longer 'imperialist', but instead a crusade against fascism in which it was their duty to participate. For the Samuels and their Libération comrades, the most immediate implication of Russia's entry into the war was that it changed the face of the internal French resistance.

An official blind eye had so far been turned to most of the small manifestations of opposition in the Vichy Zone. This was in contrast to an increasingly brutal repression north of the Line. After June 1941, however, all dissent was linked to Bolshevism, and detection and repression were ramped up throughout France. Eight million German troops were now deployed on the various fronts. Opposition in occupied countries could not be allowed to take fighting men from active service, and had to be immediately and conclusively contained. 'Special sections' were added to French courts to try 'any crime committed with the intention of communist or anarchist activity' and more and more Communists were rounded up.[41] Some were interrogated, tortured and guillotined; others were deported to concentration camps while their families were interned in France. With the resources of the Communist Party released into the resistance, the brutal burst of repression did not succeed in stamping out dissent: indeed, activity became more intense. German officers were assassinated and infrastructure was attacked. In September, a Code of Hostages was announced. Groups of Frenchmen arrested for political crimes were to be held in Vichy internment camps, to be executed in the event of attacks. For every one German killed, fifty to one hundred Frenchmen would be shot. In October 1941, forty-eight hostages were murdered. In December, another eighty-three died. On 11 August 1942, eighty-eight were killed in reprisal for the deaths of eight Luftwaffe soldiers, and in September, three German deaths caused the murder of forty-six more hostages. In November, eighteen Communists were shot by German police in Paris. The barbaric list went on. Scores of men and women, mainly Communists, would be executed in the prisons of Mont-Valérien, Châteaubriant, Nantes, Paris and Martignas-sur-Jalle, and henceforth thousands of *résistants*, both men and women, would be deported to Buchenwald, Auschwitz and Ravensbrück. If 'opposition' had ever been a 'little game', resistance was not.

* * *

A year after the Samuels arrived in Lyon, they had become parents to a baby son, and founding members of a growing illegal organization. Raymond was still working at the airport and in October 1941, Lucie also took up a third occupation. Raymond's employment was insecure – Vichy had just introduced a second round of 'Jewish statutes' further limiting the jobs available to him – and the little family of three had to pay the rent, and put food on the table and fuel in the fire. Lucie therefore sent the Ministry of Education a letter asking to be given a teaching post in Lyon. It was another of her masterly stories: she lived, she claimed, with her parents, 'old Lyonnais' – she did not, they were not – and if she were given a post allowing her to stay in her current accommodation she could count on heating through the coming winter, which was important as she had a young baby. That part needed no embroidering: scores of people had died in Lyon the previous winter because they had inadequate food and heating. Furthermore, Lucie explained, her husband, who 'had just escaped' from a prisoner of war camp, was Jewish and his position particularly 'unstable'.[42] This much was true, although she took a risk in referring to it.

From October 1941, therefore, Lucie Samuel developed a double life: wife, mother, teacher and apparently dutiful citizen on one side; clandestine freedom fighter on the other. Even nursing a baby and helping run an underground newspaper did not use up the energy with which she was blessed. She threw herself into her new job at the lycée des jeunes filles, the inspectors who sat sternly in the corner once a year finding little to complain of and complimenting her on her verve, and on the enthusiasm she inspired in her pupils.

Although she considered it too risky to try to recruit either teachers or pupils at the lycée, Lucie did not leave her secret life at home. She enjoyed her work, especially when the curriculum allowed her to slide some propaganda into her lessons. The new, Vichy-approved curriculum obliged history teachers to show how Marshal Pétain was the 'worthy heir' to Joan of Arc, 'and that the personal qualities of these heroes was identical ... the game began.'[43] Age? she asked her girls. Sex? Profession? Married or single? Enemy or ally? 'As I wrote down the responses, the class kept inventing new categories, and they all laughed until tears came to their eyes.'[44]

A fluent and persuasive speaker, she used geography lessons to show what impact the detention of over a million men in prisoner-of-war camps was having on agricultural production and industrial manufacturing; how farms were starved of fuel which went to the military; and the contrast between the surpluses before the war, and the dearth of food available to ordinary people now. As France headed into its second wartime winter, she noticed how sleepy her pupils became near noon and in the late afternoon: 'the small cup of skimmed milk with a scantily buttered slice of bread and the lunch consisting of a tiny bit of meat and green vegetables'[45] did not keep them awake through the day. There were constant reminders of danger. A Jewish girl abruptly stopped coming, and friends who went to knock on her door found the mailbox overflowing and the shutters closed. 'All my students fell silent at this news.'[46]

However much Lucie enjoyed her new job, her real life was still at home with Raymond and her baby, or with the Libération comrades who gathered in their tiny flat. Her teaching hours were not excessive: four mornings and one afternoon a week left a great deal of time free for resistance work, as well as the necessary drudgery of running a household, for Lucie also had the difficult task of keeping a family going in harsh conditions. As the war continued, the most basic commodities were in short supply, yet 'daily life [had] to be confronted, for a woman more than a man: a household to take care of, a husband and child to feed, clothes to be washed.'⁴⁷ Soaking laundry in water with a few shavings of precious soap; boiling potatoes in their skin because you waste less of them; eating a salad bulked out by dandelions; drinking coffee made from roasted barley; smoking tobacco made from sunflower leaves; soaking coaldust and newspaper together, then drying it in pellets to use when the coal has run out; nailing pieces of wood to shoes when soles wore out, because even bicycle tyres were in too short supply to be used. The immense clatter they made on the streets was a constant irritation and, as Raymond pointed out, 'perfect for a silent getaway.'⁴⁸

The *bon table* of France was a thing of the past and every day there were reminders that the country's bounty was sent straight to Germany. Life was regulated by coupons:

These ration cards and coupons that you have to get every month at the municipal offices are a headache. When are you entitled to what? Unless you consult the announcements posted at the town hall and in store windows, you have to read the newspaper announcements to find out. And what conversations you hear at the stores:

'Do you have a J3, madame?' (J3s are the adolescents.)
'No, but I have two "hard labourers".' (These are also given to pregnant women.)

What labour isn't hard these days, when turnips replace potatoes, when you have to be on intimate terms with the fishmonger to buy even a carp's head without a ration coupon?⁴⁹

Wine, milk, meat and especially tobacco: everything was bartered in

negotiations which were not only enraging but 'degrading. Adults show
the same kind of raw energy, the same serious intensity, as children do
trading marbles or sweets.'[50] Lucie was lucky in having relatives in the
country. When she could, she made the difficult journey by bus and
bike to see parents and aunts in the villages near Blanzy, and came back
with precious eggs and vegetables. In the city, she, like everyone else,
was constantly on the lookout for food. 'I went everywhere by bike with
two paniers: one had my school things in it, the other had empty bottles.
I stopped whenever I came across the chance to buy something.'[51] It
sometimes seemed to her, a woman who loved movement and activity,
that she spent her life 'waiting: for the end of the curfew in the morning;
to have coupons stamped for food distribution, to exchange one's ration
cards every month, for a pass – everything means waiting. On the
pavement in front of the shops, at the tram stop, on station platforms,
at town hall desks.'[52]

In one respect, however, the Samuels' domestic life became more
comfortable during the winter of 1941–2, a development owed to
Libération's first contact with an agent of the British Special Operations
Executive (SOE). Known to the few who were aware of its existence as
the Ministry of Ungentlemanly Warfare, the SOE had been set up at
Winston Churchill's behest in July 1940. Its mission was to 'set Europe
ablaze' by sending secret agents into Nazi-occupied Europe to carry
out acts of sabotage, and to incite and coordinate internal resistance.
The SOE first went into action in France in June 1941, when agents
blew up a power station in Bordeaux and brought work at a U-boat
base to a stop. In July, an SOE agent took back to London Emmanuel
d'Astier's request that a direct liaison be set up between Libération and
Churchill's cabinet. The fruit of this demand arrived at the Samuels'
door in December 1941.

Twenty-seven-year-old Yvon Morandat had been parachuted from a British plane into fields just outside Toulouse on 7 November 1941. His chubby face, short-sighted eyes peering through the thickest of glasses, mop of black hair and schoolboy appearance belied determination and experience. A former union representative from the Jura, a wild eastern region of France which the Samuels would come to know well, Morandat had volunteered to fight in Norway when the Germans invaded that country in April 1940, and had reached England to join the Free French in June 1940. He had not been sent back into France by Churchill, as d'Astier had wished, but by General de Gaulle, who had found himself embroiled in two simultaneous fights: the first, against the Germans; and the second, to maintain his own authority over relations between the Allies, the Free French and the internal resistance. The towering, lonely, visionary leader of the Free French was already planning a post-war French state, and determined that despite constant and overwhelming setbacks his country would not only be liberated, but would *liberate itself*. Persuading his compatriots and the other Allied leaders to believe in that second part was vital. De Gaulle knew that if France were to determine her own post-war trajectory, she had to be seen not as a conquered country liberated by other nations' armies, but as a country which had expelled its occupiers and earned a seat at the victors' table. Yvon Morandat was a soldier in both de Gaulle's wars.

De Gaulle had been impressed as much by Morandat's experience of political negotiation as of fighting and had chosen him to initiate direct contact between the Free French in London and the internal resistance, particularly the workers' movements which Morandat had known before the war. After making contact, Morandat was supposed to return to London to report back to de Gaulle but found himself so impressed by Emmanuel d'Astier (d'Astier's charisma was a recurring motif) that he gave him the full 12,000 francs he had brought from London – thus enabling publication of the December edition of *Libération* – and decided to stay in France and work for Libération. Having rented a large villa in the well-to-do, tree-lined Avenue Esquirol, he found himself under friendly attack. The villa:

> was very good for receiving people discreetly and getting administrative work done. But I didn't keep it very long. Lucie [Samuel] ... managed to persuade me to swap it for her flat in the Rue Pierre Corneille in the centre of Lyon. It was idiotic, because the [Samuels'] ... place was known to too many Lyon *résistants*, but I could not resist Lucie's arguments, particularly when she spoke about her little boy's health, who needed a garden and clean air ...[53]

Having got the villa, Lucie found domestic help. The Red Cross had set up a 'Social Service for Foreigners' to try to improve the conditions in Vichy's crowded internment camps, and get internees out where possible. Maria, a pre-war refugee from Nazism in Austria, who had been interned in a camp in Gurs by the Vichy administration, came to live with the Samuels that winter. It was a gesture of solidarity, but it also gave Lucie relief from housework, and freed her for the resistance work which was making ever greater demands on her time.

The unofficial meeting place for Libération's Directing Committee continued to be the Samuels' home even after they moved to the comfortable villa in the Avenue Esquirol. If their resistance work had sprung initially from political conviction, it had become inextricably mixed with their social life, and indeed their life as a couple. They had lost Lucie's friend Jean Cavaillès that spring, for he had been appointed to a teaching post in Paris, where he had joined the sister organization of Libération-Nord which operated in the more dangerous conditions of the Occupied Zone. Lucie missed him, but the other leaders of what they now called Libération-Sud, or 'Lib-Sud', still provided her with what had been vital to her since her earliest adulthood, 'a network of friends' who:

ate together, sang, recited poems … enthusiasm and solidarity were an important part of how we lived. Each of us could call on the others for help. Anyone wanting to understand our movements during and after the war has to understand this way of life. The history of our organization can only be understood if you grasp the fraternity in which we lived at the beginning.[54]

Fraternity: the French language is relentlessly masculine, but it was also accurate in this case. A dozen men came more or less frequently to the meetings of the Directing Committee, but there was only ever one woman, Lucie Samuel. She made nothing of this in her later writings and interviews, recording neither flirtation from the men who surrounded her, nor any attempt to turn her into a maternal figure to provide a soothing feminine presence among lonely warriors. In all the narratives she created around her life, Lucie would never have assigned herself the role of either coquette or mother hen. If any attempts to sideline her or undervalue her opinions had been made, she would not so much have contested them as simply batted them away. Lucie was supremely confident of the value of what she had to contribute and her bond with Raymond was unshakeable. Their fascination with each other had not waned. She still loved to hear him talk, and he still loved her stories of:

a world he did not know, the world of *les petits gens*, ordinary people. He had never known a two-room lodging where children did their homework on the kitchen table, before it was used for the ironing, and then to eat dinner off. With a well at the end of the yard where you had to get the water! He learnt the existence of all that because he had married me.[55]

And even parenthood and full-time work had not dimmed their physical passion. As an old lady looking back on her younger days, she remembered with touching clarity their kisses and the ecstasy of the marriage bed. She had no need of any other man's flattery, and little interest in what any other man than her husband thought of her, or her way of doing things. The only reproofs she would ever accept came, very gently, from her husband, and, once, from Jean Cavaillès.

Raymond's rebuke was that his beloved wife must stop lying. He had realized that Lucie had the habit of making up stories about herself, indulging in both exaggerations and outright inventions, and he did not like it. The habit was part of her exuberance and sociability, connected to her love of conversation and company. It was also a continuing glimmer of the insecurity she experienced among people from more privileged backgrounds; and, equally, of her pride in both her origins and her success in leaving them behind. But the fibs and exaggerations were misleading and he disapproved. 'Raymond stopped me from fantasising,' she confessed. 'I tended to rewrite my life, to embroider it. He taught me not to embroider things too much.'[56] But not even Raymond's influence cured her of the habit completely, and others noticed. She was, recalled one comrade a little sourly, '*un peu mythomane*'[57] – something of a mythomaniac. It was a characteristic which would come back to haunt her.

That, however, was seemingly the only moment of marital dissension as the intimate and delightful adventure of their marriage ran alongside that of their resistance work. 'The husband is the more temperate,' wrote one of their many visitors, while Lucie was 'intemperate, disinclined to organization, bubbling over, gifted with excessive energy. She is astonishingly brave and takes on a considerable amount of work.'[58] It was an opinion many would echo: Lucie the dynamic, loud, excitable one and Raymond the cooler, moderating voice in the background. Despite everything, 1941 was a happy year for the Samuels. They had each other, and their baby, and their friends, a veritable procession of '*opposants* of different professions and political persuasions'.[59] Every Christmas, Lucie decorated a tree with simple gifts and handed them to anyone who was there. 'You should have seen the surprise of these rough men, committed to underground combat – their emotion and their gratitude.'[60] For the individuals around them who were living lives of fear and risk – under false names, moving from place to place, unable to trust all but a tiny number of people – the Samuels' villa, the home of a family where there was food on the table, a baby in a cradle, armchairs, heating, books, conversation, was 'a little warmth, a breath of normal life in the midst of all the dangers and anonymity'.[61]

\* \* \*

Lib-Sud had expanded suddenly just before the arrival of de Gaulle's representative, Yvon Morandat. Emmanuel d'Astier had succeeded in bringing in the large groups of 'the working classes' which he had identified as being the bedrock of large-scale resistance. The leaders of organized labour had no need to be persuaded to oppose Pétain's government. Daniel Mayer, an Alsatian Jew and long-time Socialist activist, had, with his Jewish Romanian wife, decided not to leave France to join the Free French in London but to stay and fight from within. Since March 1941, he had been rebuilding the outlawed Socialist Party as a clandestine movement, whose members he brought to work with or alongside Libération after meeting d'Astier that spring. In the autumn, d'Astier also met the revered sixty-year-old trade union leader Léon Jouhaux (who would, a few years after the war, be awarded the Nobel Peace Prize) and thousands more workers joined en bloc. This swift numerical and geographical expansion required fundamental changes to Lib-Sud. No longer a group of friends taking ad hoc responsibilities, the Directing Committee was brought face-to-face with the need for security and the separation of roles. The expanded movement was re-organized, with local leaders appointed at regional, departmental and group level and couriers liaising between them.

Within this structure, members found or were allotted particular roles. Many *résistantes* – female resisters – dedicated themselves to social work, in particular to caring for the families of interned or deported men and women, and taking food and clean clothes to internees and prisoners, not easy tasks when everything was scarce. Women also frequently took on the dangerous duties of the courier, weaving the distribution of clandestine messages, newspapers and arms into their ordinary lives: hidden in prams, handbags and shopping bags; disguised by the visits to post office, doctors, school, town hall, high street shops and all the other places their domestic lives required them to visit. On the many visits out of town that women (and some men) undertook to find food in the countryside, the bicycle paniers were full of newspapers or coded letters on the way out, and food on the way back in.

Some women took on responsibility higher up the organizational chain, and Lucie was one of these. She had found two ways to take time off from her teaching work. The first was her son, whom her colleagues at the *lycée des jeunes filles* must have believed to be an uncommonly sickly child. The second was a falsified medical file drawn up by the same invaluable Dr Riva who had brought her a Jewish baby to feed after her son's birth. According to this, Lucie was 'a former tuberculosis patient, with convincing X-rays, medical records with proper dates, and a clinical analysis of my recovery'.[62] Having breastfed for fourteen months on the exiguous diet of wartime, she was certainly skinny enough to carry the diagnosis off, and Dr Riva had added 'decalcification' to her fictional ill-health. 'Decalcification' required frequent periods of rest, which could be backed up with swoonings when she needed to get away fast. The *lycée* became very used to Madame Samuel presenting a doctor's note.

A part of Lib-Sud's increasing 'professionalism' was a new insistence that members' real names must be withheld, and only codenames used. If any member was arrested and forced to give up information, the use of codenames would contain the damage and prevent the strings of arrests which had decimated or destroyed other resistance networks, particularly in the Occupied Zone, and seen hundreds imprisoned, executed or deported to concentration camps. To people who were not among her group of intimates or who had not known her before the war, Lucie was now 'Catherine' in her liaison and courier work. One of 'Catherine's' tasks was to maintain contact with resistance organizations north of the Line.

The Demarcation Line sliced Burgundy in two. Certain underground networks and individual *passeurs* specialized in the business of aiding couriers or refugees to cross from one Zone to another, and some opportunistic 'people runners' took individuals across for money. Lucie had contacts with the railwaymen whom Raymond had earlier discovered were well disposed towards resistance, but she also needed a good dose of the 'astonishing' courage her visitor to the Avenue Esquirol had noted to make her frequent illegal crossings. Lyon is a major crossroads, and its Perrache station was closely patrolled. Once past the first checks and aboard, she steeled herself for the crossing itself, which required skill, agility and nerve. Sometimes false papers could be procured (giving an officially allowable reason for crossing the Line) and produced for the heart-banging moment when first Vichy police and then German guards scrutinized them. Frequently, however, couriers adopted the simple but perilous strategy of clinging to the underside of a train.

Beneath each railway carriage was a large metal cylinder which worked the brakes by means of three long wooden bars lying parallel and close together, and attached to the bogie at either end. A clandestine passenger got out of her carriage at Sennecey-le-Grand, the last station in the Vichy Zone on the line to Paris, preferably at night when lights were dimmed to conserve scarce electricity. She would then slip unobserved beneath the train, crawl into the bed formed by the three parallel bars and lash herself securely to them. As the train moved off, she would lie two feet from the ground with sparks flying all around until the screech of brakes announced the approach of Chalon-sur-Saône, on the Demarcation Line. There she would spend a nervous hour listening to the boots of soldiers stepping in and out of the carriages. The train would eventually creak back into motion and at Chagny, the first station in the Occupied Zone, she unstrapped herself, scrambled back into the train and made straight for the lavatories to wash off the telltale dirt.

As a courier, Lucie was aware that resistance was growing on both sides of the Line. Nevertheless, any idea of offering meaningful armed opposition to the Nazi regime was still unthinkable to most, whatever General de Gaulle continued to insist in his BBC broadcasts. The

Germans seemed victorious everywhere. Greece, Hungary, Romania, Yugoslavia – all had been conquered, or had agreed to join the Axis; the Wehrmacht was pushing ever deeper into Russian territory and U-boats still dominated the seas. There were Allied victories, of course: enormous damages were being inflicted by Soviet troops; the British Royal Navy was fighting back and convoys were getting supplies through to the beleaguered and bombarded British Isles; and the United States was sending more and more aid – at a price – to the British government. But few people in France knew much of that. Radio Paris and all the German- or Vichy-controlled media reported only an apparently unstoppable Axis advance. News of one unpredicted and astonishing event in December 1941 was, however, announced to the French by their rulers. On 7 December 1941, Japanese forces simultaneously attacked the British colonies of Singapore and Malaya, and the American base of Pearl Harbor, where they destroyed 188 aeroplanes and a vast amount of infrastructure, sank or damaged twenty-one ships, and killed 2,403 American citizens and wounded 1,178 others. The following day, the USA declared war on Japan.

Raymond, always clear-sighted, knew immediately that with the Americans in the war 'one could start to think that there might be a chance to fight this Nazi army':[63] that the fascist forces which had crushed France and its European neighbours might not, after all, be invincible. That optimistic scenario was not at all clear to others, however. Future Lib-Sud member Serge Asher felt very differently when he listened to the news, in early 1942, that the Japanese forces were winning victory after victory in south-east Asia just as German forces had in Europe: Guam, Wake, the Philippines, the Gilbert Islands, Singapore, Indochina, Malaysia, Indonesia. He 'had thought the defeat of the Soviet armies was the worst it could get,' but after Japan's entry into the war 'we felt as if we were witnessing the conquest of the world by the united Japanese and German forces'.[64] But Raymond was right. The Japanese attack did what Churchill's appeals had not, provoking America to enter the war, and although the Americans concentrated first on the Pacific, President Roosevelt assured Winston Churchill that his 'view remains that Germany is still the prime enemy, and her defeat is the key to victory'.[65] Six months after Pearl Harbor, in June 1942, General Dwight Eisenhower arrived in London as commander of American forces in Europe. A month later, he was named as head of Operation Torch, codename for a planned Allied attack on Axis troops in the North African colonies which were governed by Vichy France.

It was the start of the fightback; a turning point in the war. For the Free French in London, however, there was one huge obstacle. General de Gaulle was famously easy to detest. His relations with the British were already frosty, but many senior American officers simply could not stand the man. President Roosevelt was determined to replace him with another French general, Henri Giraud, who had escaped from a German prisoner-of-war camp, returned to France and tried to persuade Marshal Pétain to resume the armed struggle against the Occupier. If de Gaulle were to retain his place as leader of the Free French, entitled to a place at Allied councils both during and after the war, he knew he had to demonstrate that the internal French resistance could be considered a combatant, and hammer home the fact that it looked to him, and him alone.

Yvon Morandat's mission to France in November 1941 had been undertaken with this in mind. He was directed not only to contact internal resistance organizations, but also to attach them to de Gaulle: to tell them who he was, what he was attempting to do and how, as Lucie said, he 'incarnated *la France libre*'.[66] Politically eclectic, not bound by ideology to follow another leader, Lib-Sud realized the importance of a figurehead, and accepted de Gaulle as that person. The January 1942 edition of *Libération* announced that de Gaulle was the symbol of France's revival, and the message that he was the one and only leader would be repeated in each subsequent edition. Morandat alone, however, was not solely responsible for the January announcement. It was also made because the man who would become perhaps the greatest Resistance hero of all, and play a lasting role in Lucie and Raymond's life, had just made contact.

* * *

In January 1942, Yvon Morandat informed Raymond that a top-level meeting had been arranged. Raymond knew the man he was to meet only as 'Rex' or 'Max'. He was in fact Jean Moulin, a forty-two-year-old senior civil servant from Béziers.

Like Emmanuel d'Astier, Jean Moulin made an immediate impression on everyone he met: his soft voice, quiet self-confidence, matinée idol looks, likeability and leadership qualities all had an effect. Before the war, he had enjoyed a successful career in politics and the civil service, becoming France's youngest prefect during the 1930s as well as briefly sitting in the National Assembly, and had made a wide and useful network of friends and acquaintances. While working for the Ministry of Aviation, he had helped secretly supply aeroplanes to the Spanish republican armies fighting General Franco in the Spanish Civil War, and on 27 February 1934 he had been one of the few parliamentarians to come out and physically defend the institutions of republican government when they were attacked by right-wing rioters. Moulin fought for two hours on the Pont de la Concorde in Paris that day and never forgot the 'savagery' with which the fascists 'charged unarmed police officers' or how they 'slashed the flanks of the police horses with razor blades'.[67]

When the Germans invaded, Moulin was prefect of the northern Eure-et-Loir department, and one of very few senior administrators to stand up to them. He refused to sign a document which asserted that French Senegalese troops had carried out a massacre of civilians who had in fact been killed by a German bombardment, and was arrested and beaten. Fearing his own ability to withstand torture, he tried to commit suicide by slashing his throat with a piece of glass but survived and was released after the armistice. For a few months, he even went back to his old post, one of those who thought resistance to Nazism might be better offered from within than from without. Within a few months, however, he had realized he could not work within Vichy's administration and resigned.

With most of France frozen before the catastrophe of defeat, Moulin had begun applying the mind and training of an administrator to his country's situation. For several months, he devoted himself to collecting information on the complexion and resources of opposition in both Zones, and in September 1941 he got himself to London via Spain and Portugal. There, he told General de Gaulle that internal resistance could be harnessed to provide military support whenever France was liberated, and warned him that if he did not reach out to the *résistants* soon, then the Communist Party would. De Gaulle was impressed both by the information he brought and the man himself. Moulin was the most senior civil servant to seek him out so far, and his steady assumption that Vichy would end was balm to a proud and isolated man.

Demonstrating that he commanded a large, united, committed 'secret army' on French soil would allow de Gaulle to present himself and his country as he always insisted they were: France, still a participant in the war; and himself, its legitimate leader and an equal to the other Allied leaders. Jean Moulin was even more important to this vision than Yvon Morandat. The immensely difficult mission entrusted to him was to unite the resistance of the Vichy Zone into one body, led by one directing council under his authority; to wrest from it a 'Secret Army', and to persuade both these entities to accept the political and military leadership of General de Gaulle.

Parachuted into fields just outside Toulouse on 2 January 1942, Moulin immediately headed for Lyon, where the three largest resistance organizations in the Free Zone were based. Under the theatre arcades in Lyon he exchanged passwords with Raymond, took him to a private room, emptied a box of matches on the table and handed over a magnifying glass. Raymond found a microphoto of de Gaulle's order identifying the man before him as his representative and heard for the first time the plans to create the 'United Movements of the Resistance' and a Secret Army. A few days later, Moulin met Emmanuel d'Astier and the two men walked for hours on an island in the River Rhône, because 'a chair and table,' d'Astier found, 'gave him a feeling of insecurity.'[68] Both Raymond and d'Astier were impressed by de Gaulle's representative. Moulin 'was already a statesman,'[69] d'Astier said. He needed to be.

Jean Moulin was aware of something which de Gaulle would never fully realize – or, at least, accept: that internal resistance could not be organized like a military force, and that its many representatives must be approached not as soldiers taking orders, but as men and women who, like Lucie and Raymond Samuel, brought personal and political aims to their struggle. He also knew from his long political experience that if it would be difficult to persuade resistance organizations to accept de Gaulle as leader, it would be even more difficult to persuade them to cooperate with each other.

The 'Big Three' movements that Moulin was attempting to unite in Lyon were Franc-Tireur, Henri Frenay's Combat, and Lib-Sud. Franc-Tireur was led by a clever and conciliatory Alsatian Jew of no great political conviction, but Combat and Lib-Sud were led by men who detested each other little less than Roosevelt detested de Gaulle. Combat was the creation of a former army officer called Henri Frenay, but known to his followers as *le patron*, 'the Boss'. It was very different in style and politics to Lib-Sud. Frenay was a complicated character, his reactive militarism tempered by his love for a bewitching feminist and Communist sympathizer, Berty Albrecht, who would end her short, fiercely lived life hanging from the ceiling of a Nazi prison.

Frenay himself loathed Communism and distrusted Lib-Sud because he regarded it as leaning much too far to the Left, and the distrust was mutual. Raymond and Lucie regarded Frenay as a gang-leader, whose followers swore allegiance to him, rather than to any greater cause. They were no more friendly towards Frenay's right-hand man, Pierre Guillain de Bénouville, another officer proud of an aristocratic past he had diligently excavated; he was a veteran of Latin Quarter fights (but on the opposing side to Lucie) and had been a volunteer for Franco's army during the Spanish Civil War. In April 1941, Henri Frenay had already invited Emmanuel and d'Astier to consider fusing their movements, but their personalities and politics clashed, and d'Astier was wary of seeing Lib-Sud swallowed up in Combat's greater numbers, while Frenay's continued belief at that point that Pétain was waging a secret war of 'opposition from within' had made any deal impossible.

Jean Moulin not only had to force unity between the mercurial d'Astier and the ramrod-backed Frenay (and their followers) but also to attempt a rapprochement with the Communist resistance. Lib-Sud was already in touch with the Front National, the organization which the Communists had set up with the similar aim of uniting all resistance under one flag. The go-between was Lucie's friend Georges Marrane, an appealing figure whom d'Astier memorably codenamed 'Vercingetorix' after the Asterix character because of his enormous red moustaches. He had 'a face like a nut-cracker, with brilliant eyes, a bald pointy head' and hands 'calloused, dirty and rough as the wrinkled skin of an old apple'. Lucie had a close bond with Georges Marrane, who was a personal link between her and the Party to which she still felt the tug of allegiance despite her preference for the politically mixed Lib-Sud. Vercingetorix was an utterly decent man '(leading) a clandestine life that is far from easy'.[70] When they could, the Samuels gave him food for his children. Comrades had done it for Lucie during her hungry years in Paris, and now she did the same: the links of friendship and solidarity remained vital to her. However, any rapprochement between Lib-Sud and the Communists had suffered the same 'one step forward, two steps back' as that between Lib-Sud and Combat, and no fusion had been achieved.

Jean Moulin's negotiations would continue for over a year as he travelled back and forth between Lyon, his family house near Avignon and premises in Nice where he ran an art gallery as cover for his travels. A resistance 'press agency' was set up in April to send information to London and diffuse propaganda. A 'General Research Council' followed in July, whose responsibility was to plan for the political and social development of the country after liberation. Raymond was more involved with Moulin's projects than Lucie, for her time was taken up with the courier work which was becoming increasingly dangerous.

Wherever she travelled at the beginning of 1942, Lucie found misery. As France approached its third year as a conquered country, the unrelenting difficulty and unfairness of everyday life was beginning to mobilize larger-scale resistance to Vichy in the South, and the Occupier in the North. The country was staggering under the weight of supporting the Army of Occupation, with a workforce depleted by constant transfers of young Frenchmen to German factories and the loss of over a million prisoners of war. Under the terms of the armistice, the French had to pay for the upkeep of the 300,000 German soldiers who occupied their country, at an exchange rate which so undervalued the franc that the money paid could in fact have supported 18 million men. France was broke. There was little food in the shops and endless queues; clothes had been patched so many times that their original shapes and colours were lost; people wrapped rags round their feet in the winter and burnt their furniture because there was no coal. Women struggled to feed and clothe their families while also carrying out all the tasks their absent menfolk had used to do. For many, life was reduced to survival.

In the northern town of Valenciennes one day, sitting on a freezing open train where rough boards served for seats – the old seats had been taken by the Germans – Lucie found the miners 'undernourished … exhausted and miserable',[71] on their way to quarry coal which would only benefit the German war machine. In the South, she found owners of small vineyards roused to opposition after Vichy inspectors poured heating oil into barrels to make the wine unfit for consumption, thus ensuring what they needed for fuel alcohol would be delivered. Everywhere she found women who watched their children go hungry and saw their families dispossessed while they were obliged to feed and house foreign soldiers who made themselves at home and took what they wished. The winter of 1941–2 was another exceptionally cold one. In Paris, it froze for sixty-six consecutive days, and even in the cities of the South, temperatures again plunged well below zero. Basic services were ceasing to operate because there was no petrol to run the lorries which took away rubbish, or enough medicine for civil hospitals, or workers to keep the streets clean and the sewers in repair, or transport scarce foodstuffs around the country. Only the Germans, and those who could afford the black market, lived well. It was exasperation, Lucie found, that made so many women receptive to resistance: they were infuriated that an uninvited, unwanted soldier 'came to sleep in their beds' (literally, in many cases), 'has a look in the larder and makes himself at home', and outraged by the Germans' simple 'lack of consideration ... by the queues which went on for ever, the empty shops where you were treated like dirt if you didn't have the money to pay inflated prices'.[72]

Vichy's claim to represent a sovereign state within Germany's New Europe was ringing increasingly hollow, and the sham was most evident in two shameful obligations. The first was the sending of ever larger drafts of young men into Germany to act as cheap labour. Although these demands were tempered by promises that prisoners of war would be released in exchange, everyone knew the gross imbalance between the number of 'volunteer workers' sent to Germany and the number of prisoners returning. The second was the increasingly visible and violent persecution of Jews.

The year 1942 saw an increase in popular disquiet over the role of French officials in the mass deportations to eastern 'labour camps'. No one in France knew the truth of the Final Solution yet; there was a general vague belief that some sort of agricultural colonies or 're-education centres' were being created for the Nazis' unwanted in eastern Europe, but the manner of the *rafles* – the round-ups – and the transportation out of France of those arrested had become distressingly brutal. Internment had begun before deportation, with the Nazis less concerned to send Jews to concentration camps than into the Vichy

Zone, for Marshal Pétain to deal with. That policy changed in 1942, when the Nazis and their Vichy helpers began rounding them up for deportation from France. On 27 March, 1,112 Jews were detained in the Northern Zone, and sent to Auschwitz. (Twenty-two were alive at the end of the war.) On 1 June 1942, the yellow star was introduced, and no Jew was allowed to be in public without this symbol of their race stitched and clearly visible on their clothing. In July 1942, 10,000 Jewish men, women and children were arrested in Paris and taken to the *Vélodrome d'hiver*, a huge sports stadium, and made to wait there for several days in dreadful conditions while they were processed for deportation. A former Communist deputy denounced the atrocity on Radio Londres: 'you can hear the heartrending cries of mothers whose children are being torn from them,' he told his listeners, still few, 'even newborn babies – to be sent without any mark of identification to the cursed Reich's re-education centres.'[73] That horror provoked public outrage and even protest from the generally silent Catholic Church, but to no avail. In the summer of 1942, the hard, visible reality of Jewish deportation – French policemen forcing French citizens onto trains heading into an unknown future – hit the Vichy Zone, too, when 6,500 Jews were arrested in mass round-ups orchestrated simultaneously between 26 and 28 August.

It was while on courier work that Lucie received the reproof she remembered all her life from Jean Cavaillès. Raymond had identified in his wife's character the tendency to fantasize and embroider but Cavaillès saw an even more dangerous one. Lucie was, as she herself admitted, 'crazily optimistic and confident', and those characteristics could lead her to take stupid risks. 'Very brave,' another would say of her, 'even reckless, but very excitable.'[74] Sometimes her character was *too* large, particularly in circumstances where discretion and coolheaded planning were vital. Sent north during the Easter holidays of 1942 to meet representatives of Lib-Nord, Lucie managed to get herself briefly smuggled across the border into Belgium before the meeting. It was an adventure, nothing more, and she happily told her story to Jean Cavaillès when she arrived in Paris. As a friend of both Lucie and her husband, and a man who ran daily risk of death, he was furious.

Resistance in the North had always been more dangerous than in the South. Just before Lucie's adventure, the leaders of the group at the Musée de l'Homme in Paris were executed by firing squad and another 113 loosely connected 'terrorists', thirty-five of them women, had been arrested in another operation and were in prison awaiting torture, internment, execution or deportation to concentration camps. Jean Cavaillès had the precarious cover of his teaching job, but Lucie's other regular contact in the capital, Joseph Epstein, was now commanding a detachment of the Communist resistance and living a completely clandestine existence with his young family. Had he been identified and arrested, he would have been tortured and shot, and had Lucie been linked with him and tracked down, she would have been deported to Buchenwald or Auschwitz. And if interrogators had beaten information out of her first, it could have led to the arrest and death of countless others. Jaunting to Belgium was a stupid thing to do, and Cavaillès let her know it, his fury at her irresponsibility reducing her to tears. 'You frightened me, Lucie,' he said when they met, passions cooled a little, the next day. 'Don't play stupid games, you have a husband and a child.'[75]

\* \* \*

In the Vichy Zone, Jean Moulin continued his patient negotiations through the spring, summer and autumn of 1942, attempting to persuade warring factions to bury their differences and present a united front to the enemy. Every so often he was picked up by a British plane and taken to London to confer with de Gaulle, leaving his secretary, Daniel Cordier, in Lyon to maintain contact between him and the internal resistance. Cordier, only twenty-one and living a doubly clandestine life as a *resistant* and a homosexual, adored his boss and was passionately committed to his mission, but found himself at times overwhelmed by the forceful personalities of the men in charge of Combat and Lib-Sud, some old enough to be his father, who attempted to sideline him in communications with London during Moulin's absences.

The leaders of Lib-Sud, Combat and Franc-Tireur had agreed to form a united military force even though political agreement between them would take longer. Forestalling fights between the three leaders, Moulin decreed that an outsider must be given command and appointed sixty-five-year-old General Delestraint, who was untainted by any association with Vichy. Under Delestraint's command, Franc-Tireur, Lib-Sud and Combat were invited to appoint senior representatives to the Secret Army.

Unlike Combat and Franc-Tireur, Lib-Sud had no existing paramilitary wing to contribute, but if it wanted to exert influence on the newly united resistance, it had to create one. Among the intellectuals, writers, journalists and academics who made up Lib-Sud's fluid Directing Committee, Raymond Samuel stood out as a man of practical bent and rigorous training as both an army officer and an engineer. The responsibility fell to him. In the autumn of 1942, he attended Delestraint's secret briefing as Lib-Sud's paramilitary chief. Addressing his new senior officers, Delestraint explained how the Secret Army would work. The more an army is motorized, he said – and the German army was heavily motorized – the more vulnerable it is to commando attack and sabotage: those, therefore, would be their principal tasks.

Again, Raymond began the dangerous job of targeted recruitment, identifying which of the men under his command were most suitable for armed combat and asking them to organize themselves into autonomous groups of six. Each group appointed its own leader, and was trained in the rules of clandestine communication. These were the *groupes francs* – autonomous units – which would be the shock troops of the emerging Secret Army. Slowly, Raymond built a trusted team around him. Serge Asher joined Lib-Sud that autumn and, after some perilous courier work, was permanently attached to Raymond's staff, his engineering studies giving him common ground with his boss. Brought into the Samuels' inner circle, Serge Asher – or Serge Ravanel, as he was now known within the resistance – was seduced by the tone set at their villa. He had previously floated on the edge of resistance groups which were coloured, like Frenay's Combat, by the militaristic personalities and training of their leaders and in which divergent political views were discouraged. In Lib-Sud, and particularly on the Avenue Esquirol, he found Catholics and freemasons, Communists and republicans, Socialists and radicals, bosses and workers refusing to allow friction and difference to divert them from their common goal. He was particularly fond of the Samuels themselves, admiring them for their different and complementary capabilities: Raymond 'calm, with a remote humour, liberal in the sense the eighteenth century (*le siècle des lumières*) gave that term ... Her, crackling with life and authority.'[76] Despite his youth, he was well travelled and could hold his own in the Samuels' confident and cultured circles, and Lucie came to regard him almost as a younger brother.

A second man to join was Maurice Kriegel, who had plucked his codename, 'Valrimont', from the classic French fairy tales, the *Contes de Perrault*. Although ill-health had prevented his fighting in 1939, his brother had been posted to La Wantzenau as a military doctor, where Raymond was stationed in 1939, and the two men had become friends. The Jewish Kriegel family had been forced to leave their home in Strasbourg and had reunited in Toulouse, where they were visited by Raymond on one of his clandestine journeys. He invited Maurice, who had experience of left-wing militancy from before the war, to move to Lyon to help create and command Lib-Sud's contribution to the Secret Army.[77]

Recruiting a paramilitary force was only the first step: then they needed to train and arm it, all in strict secrecy. The new Secret Army was almost entirely without means. The men in its ranks regarded themselves as equals, working together side by side as comrades, pooling their resources and seeking solutions together. Raymond, with his military experience, was nevertheless aware that what they most needed – after guns – were good officers. Raymond, Maurice and Serge knew that many of the officers who had resigned or been demobilized in June 1940 had kept their weapons and even hidden caches of ammunition and guns, but contacting them to negotiate handing these over was immensely risky. Raymond was 'always asking myself, "am I not about to recruit a 'sheep', a spy?"'[78] Few officers, even non-serving ones, were yet prepared actively to aid an illegal force whose declared aim was to depose the head of state. Nor were these the only challenges the Samuels and their comrades were facing as resistance stepped up a gear.

Quite apart from the constant risk of exposure and arrest, the Samuels – still working and looking after their son – found that living two lives was exhausting.

Always be on the lookout. Know how to check if we were being followed. Write nothing *en clair* in our diaries. Do not send uncoded messages. Be discreet, do not speak to just anyone in public places. Do not go to places where we are known or where the police may be waiting. Don't get into habits. Don't often go to the same restaurant.[79]

Added to the endless waiting in queues were other long, nerve-racking waits 'for a liaison agent, for a friend coming from afar',[80] for the arrival of illegal newspapers, for the start of a military action – the fabric of daily life riddled with dangers. Serge Asher-Ravanel found the strain made people tense, irritable and tired.

Lucie was shouldering ever-greater responsibilities, and taking longer and more frequent absences from her work at the *lycée*. The increasing repression in both Zones had led to huge numbers of men and women being held in internment camps, military prisons and police cells. And as the underground resistance spread and armed, the information each detainee might give up under torture threatened more people and larger plans. While continuing her courier work, Lucie was therefore moving into another area of specialization, that of rescuing imprisoned *résistants*.

The techniques of rescue, like those of disseminating propaganda, had to be learnt from scratch: however lively her past, Lucie was a history teacher, not a commando. Occasionally she worked solo, but more frequently she operated from within one of the new *groupes francs* being formed by her husband. These were overwhelmingly male, but prison breaks required a female lead as females were more likely to be allowed to see prisoners. It was expected that wives, mothers or girlfriends would bring food and take away dirty laundry; they were often allowed brief visits and guards were likely to be more moved by their distress and induced to pass on messages. Lucie's preferred method continued to be that which had got Raymond out of Sarrebourg in the summer of 1940. She would pretend to be an imprisoned man's fiancée, gain access to him and pass over whatever circumstances allowed: a weapon, a file, a suit of civilian clothes or drugs to provoke fever. A favourite was a packet of cigarettes composed of compressed aspirin which, eaten in one go, caused palpitations and sweats. The man was then transferred to a prison hospital where the second stage of the rescue could take place: either male comrades disguised as Vichy police turned up and demanded the man 'for interrogation', or a sympathetic guard would be persuaded to look away while he escaped. At the worst, a resistance-friendly doctor (there were many) would prolong the illness so the man did not have to return immediately to prison.

Sometimes the rescues succeeded and sometimes they did not. In August 1942, Lib-Sud was devastated to hear that Jean Cavaillès had been arrested and imprisoned while visiting Montpellier, and Lucie went into action. Visiting him at the prison with her wedding ring removed, she kissed her old friend chastely through the bars and passed over files and a sleeping powder for the informer who was known to share his cell. She waited all night in the heat under the prison wall, starting at shadows, just as she had done for her newly wedded husband two years before, but Cavaillès, unlike Raymond, did not come: the informer had been too vigilant. She returned home anguished for her friend.

Behind the façade of normality which the Samuels presented to the world, their home continued to be both a political headquarters and a safe house for people on the run. Anyone surveying the villa in the Avenue Esquirol would have thought it was home to a very sociable couple, as indeed the Samuels were. Friends constantly knocking on the door, the sound of conversation and laughter from the garden, candles lit – when they could be bought – well into the evening. What they would not have known was that the guests were resistance fighters, men and women on the run, leading lonely and dangerous lives from which a meal, a night, a few days in the Samuels' villa was their only respite. Lucie's sister, Jeanne, had settled nearby with her two little girls while her husband Pierre, who had escaped a prisoner-of-war camp in Germany, went about his own dangerous resistance work for the Communists. Pierre Hervé, an old Latin Quarter Communist friend of Lucie's, arrived with his delicate wife Annie, who had helped him escape from a Parisian police office after his arrest and had the memorable characteristic of sudden and spectacular fainting fits. In March 1942, the Jewish politician Max Hymans – one of the brave eighty who had voted against handing powers to Marshal Pétain in June 1940 – was hidden there. Bored, unable to leave, he devoted himself to studying Raymond's old engineering texts to give himself something to do.

Pascal Copeau, son of a famous theatre director, was another to join Lib-Sud that year. A journalist a little older than the Samuels, he had lived in Germany before the war and spoke the language well. He lived entirely undercover, devoting himself to resistance work, and spent much time at the villa. At parties in the garden where little Jean-Pierre staggered about, he drank large quantities of wine, told dirty stories and entertained the company with impressions of Hitler. In January 1943, Pascal Copeau's parents were met at Lyon station by 'a cart pulled by two skeletal horses' which took them to the Samuels' villa. 'We stayed twenty four hours,' Copeau's father recorded:

in this little villa in an atmosphere of mystery and conspiracy. The friend who had lent it to us is a likeable and very intelligent Jew. His wife … was absent. His child, a big baby known as Boubou sucks his thumb and wees everywhere. Cooking and cleaning are carried out by an Austrian saved from a concentration camp, whose Jewish husband was deported, no one knows where ... The house is extremely untidy. Salad servers in the bedroom. Hair products in the lavatory ...'[81]

Lucie was absent that weekend because she had gone to Paris, where Jean Moulin had finally succeeded in pulling together a 'United Movements of the Resistance'. It was a success, but it had taken a terrifying turn of events to bring it about.

*  *  *

On 8 November 1942, Allied troops commanded by the American General Eisenhower landed in French North Africa. General Giraud, de Gaulle's rival, was smuggled out of France and brought to Gibraltar in a rather farcical operation which involved a British submarine masquerading as an American one, because Giraud had said he would only take part in Operation Torch if there were no Brits involved. The Americans had intended him to be commander-in-chief of French forces in Africa, but when Giraud demanded to be commander of *all* Allied forces in the operation they refused, so in the end he remained in Gibraltar as 'a spectator in the affair'.[82]

In North Africa, the Allies were aided by local Resistance forces, among them fighters commanded by Emmanuel d'Astier's brother Henri. With Giraud out of the game, Allied commanders parleyed with Admiral Darlan, the highest ranking French officer in Algeria, who broke with Pétain, threw in his lot with the Allies and ordered French forces to cooperate. French soldiers were now among victorious Allied troops on French soil, a fact which greatly boosted General de Gaulle's status at Allied councils, even if the Americans continued to favour Giraud. Allied landings on the Mediterranean coasts had become a real possibility and the German response was swift. On 11 November, Wehrmacht troops crossed the Demarcation Line; the Free Zone no longer existed and Lyon was an occupied city.

Serge Asher-Ravanel stood among the fearful Lyonnais who watched the Germans enter their city that day, watching 'one convoy after another: open lorries transporting helmeted soldiers, sitting, guns between their knees, cannon towed noisily on the pavements, lorries carrying food underneath tarpaulins. A couple of days later, the tanks were taken off trains, dozens at a time.'[83] Within days, Pétain's Army of the Armistice had been dissolved and disarmed, and the admiral of the French fleet was ordered to blow up his ships to prevent their falling into Allied hands. Only three submarines got away, their commanders determined to join the Allies. People cried in the streets when they heard.

Overnight, the city which had become the Samuels' home changed as the citizens of Lyon experienced what their compatriots north of the abolished Line had lived with for over two years: the brute fact of occupation. German soldiers patrolled the streets, a six o'clock curfew was brought in, buildings all over the city were requisitioned and the French had to find a way of cohabiting with their conquerors. In the summer of 1940, when Paris was struggling with the new Occupation, a Socialist called Jean Texcier had produced a 'manual of dignity' which was secretly passed from hand to hand. Included in his 'Advice to an Occupied Population' were semi-facetious suggestions – soldiers asking for directions in the street should be courteously sent the wrong way, for example – but Texcier's message was a serious one. 'Husband your anger,' he wrote, 'for you may need it [and] have no illusions: these men are not tourists.'[84] Now *Libération* began to write its own editorials on how to deal with the conquerors in their midst. Whenever Germans arrived in cafés or restaurants, all French should ostentatiously rise and leave; swastikas should be chalked on buildings belonging to industrialists or merchants who worked with the invader, and patriotic bunting should be hung in the streets on the anniversary of the Battle of the Marne, when French troops had soundly beaten the Germans in 1914.

Among the German institutions arriving in Lyon in the winter of 1942 was the feared Geheime Staatspolizei, the secret police organization better known as the Gestapo. One of its senior officers was a slight, mild-faced twenty-nine-year-old whose brutal efficiency at a previous post in the Netherlands had impressed his masters. Obersturmführer Klaus Barbie, later to be known as the 'Butcher of Lyon', established his first headquarters in the elegant Hotel Terminus opposite the Perrache railway station, with twenty-five officers working directly for him and two principal tasks: to crush the resistance, and to rid the city of its Jews. Barbie's weapon of choice against the resistance was infiltration, 'turning' captured *résistants* by torture or threats to harm their families, and sending them back into the field as double agents. He personally interrogated and beat many of those his men brought in. Survivors said he enjoyed it.

Persecution of Jews, Communists and *résistants* was stepped up even further in January 1943, when the French paramilitary force *la Milice Française* was created to help the Gestapo. Its founder, former army officer Joseph Darnand, declared that its mission was to save France from Bolshevism. The pride of the French nation, he said, could not allow the fight against Communism to remain in the hands of foreigners. The *miliciens'* knowledge of language, dialect and local geography made them even more effective than their German counterparts in hunting down the Gestapo's wanted. Again, Lucie and Raymond begged the elder Samuels to allow resistance contacts to get them out of France and into nearby Switzerland. Again they refused: despite the changed circumstances, Albert's belief in the protection of Marshal Pétain would not be swayed.

It was now more important than ever that all *résistants* respected the rules of clandestine life. No more than two people to meet in public. Never be late to a meeting. Never speak of secret business on the telephone, not even obscurely. Don't shroud yourself in mystery, don't provoke people's curiosity, make small talk – stay away from serious subjects; don't change anything in your daily routine, don't start buying things you don't normally buy or clothes you wouldn't normally wear. If anyone was arrested, or disappeared, 'we had to change the mailboxes, the passwords, organize new hiding-places, find new refuges, switch liaison agents, change our people's identities and even their appearances.'[85]

In particular it was vital that real and assumed identities were kept completely separate, and in this Lib-Sud was aided by an invaluable new recruit. Pierre Kahn was known as Pierre Farelle to Vichy in order to hide his Jewishness and as 'Pierre des Faux Papiers' – 'Pierre the Forger' – to his resistance comrades. Lucie was impressed by his remarkable ability to remember the list of communes whose records had been destroyed during the war and could not therefore be checked by suspicious police or soldiers, and his meticulously kept files of people who had gone abroad or were prisoners of war. Pierre the Forger would manufacture false papers on an almost industrial scale, 'employing' twenty-five people and producing 18,000 stamps and about 100,000 false records during the course of the war.

Active *résistants* now had three identities: their real name, their codename, and whatever was stated on the papers furnished by Pierre

the Forger. Lucie was still 'Catherine', and carried false identity papers
in the name of Lucie Montet, a childless spinster, or her own identity
papers from her student days in the name of Lucie Bernard. Raymond
was codenamed 'Balmont' and carried papers in the name of 'François
Vallet', which would not only prevent links being traced to his family and
comrades if he were arrested on resistance business, but also conceal
his Jewishness if he were stopped during one of the terrifying *rafles*.
François Vallet's parents were dead, he had no police record and he lived
alone in a tiny apartment in the Croix-Rousse area of Lyon, where the
Samuels were careful to stash a few personal belongings, and enough
food to make residence credible if it were searched. If Lucie was in her
element creating stories for their new identities, it went against the grain
to back them up by leaving edible goods in an unused cupboard on the
other side of the city, but they knew such precautions were vital. Pierre
the Forger also made identity papers for Hélène and Albert Samuel.
After the war, they would be found pushed between the pages of a book,
unused.

With the heavy-booted patrols in every street, and the overbearing,
ubiquitous presence of *miliciens*, Vichy police and German guards, the
Samuels were forced to curtail their social life. In these new conditions,
it was too dangerous to have people banging on the door at night, or to
throw parties in a garden into which curious neighbours might peer,
and report their suspicions. Just before the Germans crossed the Line,
Lucie had triumphantly come home with a live goose, meaning to fatten
it for a sociable Christmas feast. (The beast had proved a menace: it
never stopped eating, it honked all night, it rummaged in the coal and
bit little Boubou.) Defiantly, they killed it for a Twelfth Night dinner (6
January, a Catholic festival), and Lucie spent hours on the foul job of
plucking it, carefully saving the feathers. D'Astier and Pascal Copeau

came secretly to celebrate, and as the new curfew deadened the city, there was a furtive tap at the door. It was Jean Cavaillès, who had evaded his guards and escaped prison. Jaundice had turned him yellow, and he had suffered an attack of impetigo with which he had been treated with blue chloride. The Samuels' unexpected guest was an astonishing shade of green, and his appearance a flash of joy in the new darkness.

The Allied invasion of North Africa and the Germans' invasion of the Free Zone gave new impetus to Jean Moulin's negotiations for unity among resistance groups. In January 1943, the MUR (*Mouvements Unis de la Résistance*, United Movements of the Resistance) was finally created at a meeting in Paris with Henri Frenay of Combat, Jean-Pierre Lévy, leader of Franc-Tireur, and Emmanuel d'Astier its signatories. Lucie had accompanied d'Astier to the capital in order to see Jean Cavaillès, who had, with extreme courage, resumed his clandestine life there after his unexpected arrival at the Samuels' villa. She and d'Astier stayed in a resistance-friendly brothel near the Opéra until the mirrors on the ceilings disturbed her too much and they fled to her sister's mother-in-law in the very working-class area of Belleville, which the aristocratic d'Astier had never visited. Madame Norgeu was valiant: they asked her to print and distribute Lib-Nord's underground newspaper from her print shop and she immediately agreed. Flushed with this success, the pair met Jean Cavaillès to eat oysters, then went on to a night club, 'as happy as high school students', with d'Astier, as ebullient in his way as Lucie, laughing that 'all the Gestapos in the world could not throw a cloud on our happiness.'[86] Coming out of one of the few metro stations still open, Lucie was delighted to bump into her old friend Joseph Epstein and walked a little with him on the boulevards, exchanging news of their families. Both were parents of a young child, and both were married to a fellow-*résistant*. They understood each other, through years of friendship and a common devotion to a cause. It was the last time Lucie would ever see the old friend who had taught her so much.

As Raymond, Serge Asher-Ravanel and Maurice Kriegel-Valrimont and their counterparts in Franc-Tireur and Combat struggled mightily to bring a Secret Army into being, the French government gave them a powerful recruitment weapon. Until 16 February 1943, administrations on both sides of the now-defunct Line had managed to scrape together enough 'volunteers' to meet German demands for French labour on their farms and in their factories. When a further quarter of a million was demanded, however, and voluntary take-up failed to come anywhere near this figure, STO (*Service de Travail Obligatoire*, Compulsory Work Service) was introduced throughout France. In February, the French government announced that all men born between 1920 and 1922 were to be conscripted, but even that number was not enough to satisfy Germany's insatiable need for labour. Millions of Wehrmacht troops were bogged down in Russia, and now thousands had to be sent to North Africa and the Mediterranean coasts. In March, Germany demanded another 220,000 labourers from France, and this time the nation revolted. Thirty-seven thousand young men did cross the border, but tens of thousands of others left their homes and hid with relatives or friends, or camped out in forests, mountains and isolated regions such as Savoy and the Jura, east of Lyon. It was the start of what came to be known as the *maquis* and for people like Raymond, attempting to create a paramilitary force from scratch, it gave the Resistance great hope, but also an enormous task: young rebels, some of whom had never held a weapon, had to be turned into trained combatants.

The Secret Army still had few officers or guns despite the fact that the Army of the Armistice had been practically pushed into the arms of the resistance. After the Germans crossed the Line, the French army was ordered to hand over its military hardware. Most officers had complied, but for some this had been a step too far, and they had hidden their arms for the day when the military tide would turn and they could fight for their country. Some of these disaffected officers had already formed the ORA (*Organisation de résistance de l'armée*, Armed Resistance Organization) but that did not mean they were ready to cooperate with Jean Moulin or his Secret Army representatives. The ORA's leader was General Giraud, still preferred to de Gaulle by the Americans despite his refusal to take command of French forces in North Africa. General Giraud's plan was for the ORA to provide a resistance army which, unlike de Gaulle's Secret Army, would not engage in guerrilla warfare against the Occupier, but would wait, only going into regular action at the moment of the liberation of France. Jean Moulin gave Raymond the particular task of persuading demobilized officers to hand over their weapons to the Secret Army instead but most refused to help, partly out of loyalty to Giraud, partly because they were convinced that any weapons handed over would end up in the hands of Communists and partly, Raymond believed, because the military has a horror of arming civilians.

Scarcity of weapons made it almost impossible to arm the *maquis*. Raymond toured groups of prospective paramilitaries in the Jura with the one gun he had at his disposal, showing it off to them in an attempt to excite their interest. Nor did the Free French or the Allied command in London or Algiers seem to grasp the immense new possibilities which lay just out of reach. Jean Moulin was in London when STO was announced in February 1943, and his young secretary, Daniel Cordier, found himself besieged by angry men demanding he hand over the funds he was believed to have at his disposal, and arrange immediate

arms drops into the areas where the *maquis* was gathering. Cordier
would remember the fury of Libération leaders against 'the London lot':

'What are you waiting for?' they asked.

'I'm waiting for instructions.'

'You lot are always the same. You let the *résistants* collapse, you
don't understand what's going on. What's the point of you if you
don't give us money and arms in circumstances like these? Are you
here to fight a war or run a savings bank?'[87]

In an odious position of responsibility without power, Cordier begged
London to fast-forward the checking procedures necessary to identify
safe landing-grounds for parachute drops, sending the coordinates
which the *résistants* themselves had marked for him on a Michelin
map to show where the *maquis* was gathering. In mid-March, Jean
Moulin authorized the distribution of one million francs to arm and
train the *maquis*; while in London, he and General Delestraint, leader
of the Secret Army, insisted to the dubious British cabinet that arming
50,000 civilian *résistants* who would be ready to rise up at the time of
the landings could only be to Allied advantage. In France, the young
men and women in the hills, who were attaching themselves in growing
numbers to resistance organizations, were also demanding action:
enough newspapers, enough propaganda, they said, telling Serge Asher-
Ravanel they were 'impatient to fight', and criticizing the resistance 'for
not being active enough against the Germans and against Vichy'.[88] On 12
March, Maurice and Serge arrived, singly and with all due precautions,
at the Samuels' villa to discuss how best to organize this new force.
Maurice arrived last, and immediately addressed Raymond.

'The police have seized some papers which had your codenames on them. You have to change them.'

Sitting in his library, Raymond was smoking a pipe. He turned round, pulled out a book at random: 'I'll take the first proper noun I find.' That's how Raymond Samuel became Raymond Aubrac.[89]

'Balmont' no longer existed. At the end of their brief meeting, 'Aubrac', 'Ravanel' and 'Fouquet' (Maurice Kriegel-Valrimont's Secret Army codename) arranged to meet at a fifth-floor flat in 7 Rue de l'Hôtel de Ville in central Lyon on 15 March, hoping news would have come from London that arms drops were imminent. Instead, they walked into a trap.

* * *

Two days earlier, an inexperienced liaison agent had been arrested by German soldiers who searched him and found a list of addresses hidden in his sock. One of them was 7 Rue de l'Hôtel de Ville, where Raymond, Serge and Maurice arrived separately for their meeting on 15 March and found armed French police waiting for them. Serge Asher-Ravanel arrived last, saw what was happening, made a run for it and was caught and beaten up. All three men were bundled into the notorious black Citroens used by Vichy police and taken to the police station in Quai Perrache for questioning. It was 'heaving with people', and they realized they 'had been victims of a dragnet operation. About twenty men and women had been arrested.'[90]

Later that day Raymond and Maurice first gave the story which they would tell innumerable times over the coming weeks. They had gone to the Rue de l'Hôtel de Ville, they said, to discuss selling sugar on the black market. The police inspected 'François Vallet's' papers, and took him to the flat in the Croix-Rousse district. There they searched the cupboards and found the supplies the Samuels had carefully left, including a few kilos of sugar which Raymond told them had been the object of his negotiations with the other two. He knew, however, that his story was weak and that the police would not have bothered surveying Rue de l'Hôtel de Ville if they had not suspected resistance activity. As the officers were poking about, Raymond slammed the door on them, dived into the twisting narrow alleys that criss-cross the old city of Lyon, and ran for it. He was young and fit, and he would have got away had he not cannoned into an old lady and sent her tumbling into the gutter. 'Someone must, during my infancy,' he joked much later, 'have dinned into me the principle that whenever one knocks down an old lady, one must stop and help her up again.'[91] A pistol was pressed against his temple as he did so and he was taken back to the cells.

Although the French police were certain the three men they had arrested were somehow mixed up with the resistance, they suspected they were small fry. 'The leaders,' they reported in frustration:

> have not been arrested … those accused are merely liaison agents, whose tasks are to go and pick up the messages left in various letter boxes round the city and take it to another agent with whom they had an appointment at certain times of day, sometimes in the street, sometimes at a café, and take back other post to put in the letter boxes … [92]

But Raymond, Maurice and Serge were not the only *résistants* arrested that day, and when the door to their cell was opened that evening and another four men were thrust in, they knew the evidence against them was mounting.

Intelligence had also led the French police to the leader of Combat's paramilitary wing, François Morin (codenamed Forestier), who was seized along with his secretary, a courier and an entire suitcase full of coded documents on the Secret Army. Caught with three identity cards in his pocket, François Morin-Forestier knew he would be suspected of resistance activity even before the Germans deciphered the Secret Army documents. He was rescued by the French judge who brought his case to trial. Lucie would reflect that one never knew which French officials were decent and which were not: they were lucky with Judge Cohendy, who was a secret Gaullist and, from his position within the Vichy administration, was doing what he could to protect arrested *résistants*. Hearing Morin-Forestier's garbled and feeble story about a fiancée sending him identity cards from Paris 'just in case', Judge Cohendy informed him he had, in fact, been 'living in sin' and required these cards to hide it from his upper-class family, knowing the story would be swallowed more easily by both French and German police. But not even the judge could release him then and there. That night Morin-Forestier slept in the same cell as Raymond, Maurice, Serge and a very young Socialist called Raymond Hego who had been scooped up on a different raid. When Hego told the others that his arresting officer had been Klaus Barbie, they realized how dangerous their position was. After two and a half years of clandestine life, it seemed the Samuels' luck had run out.

News that 'Aubrac', 'Valrimont', 'Ravanel' and 'Forestier' had all been arrested sent shock waves through Lib-Sud, Combat, the entire Secret Army and the villa on Avenue Esquirol. Lucie and Raymond's cousin Maurice David were the first to react. Maurice took the considered step of engaging a lawyer, Maître Fauconnet, who was known to be pro-resistance, but Lucie was already planning escapes beyond what a lawyer could manage. She had done it before: her audacious journey across France in 1940 was part of the story of their marriage, a brick in the protective edifice which husband and wife had built about themselves. Each knew that he or she could count on the other absolutely. The night of Raymond's arrest, Lucie presented herself at the police station and, although she could not see her husband, a sympathetic policeman told her how the arrest had happened. The following day, the five men were transferred to the vast Palais de Justice – the court – which stands on the west bank of the river, and shut into basement cells which 'gave off the sour smell of piss'.[93] Waiting to be brought before the magistrates, Raymond found himself approached by a man whose rather sinister looks led him to turn down a quiet invitation to follow the man down the corridor. He would later realise that he should have: the man was a police inspector recruited by Lucie who had agreed to try and spirit the arrested men out. Lucie's first attempt had failed, but when she and her comrades heard that Morin-Forestier had been taken with a suitcase full of incriminating (when decoded) documents on him, she knew she had to get her husband out by any means, and whatever the risk.

Those close to Lucie at the time were unanimous in recalling that she was brave, daring, audacious, but also very excitable. Her personality was large and dominant; she attempted to carry others with her through volubility and sheer conviction of her own rightness. Where some might use impersonal calculation in planning rescues, Lucie threw her courage and her emotions at the task. It was the way she had fought in the Latin Quarter; it was the way she fought in wartime Lyon; but it was not everyone's preferred method. Other comrades were angered by her insistence that 'everything else must stop, and the entire forces of Lib-

Sud ... be put at the disposal of a rescue attempt.'[94]

During the week after Raymond's arrest, Lucie orchestrated at least two dangerously under-planned attempts to get him out. The cool courier, who had negotiated the Line countless times, carried arms and packed a teddy bear with explosives, had disintegrated, replaced by a woman made careless by fear. On 21 or 22 March, she persuaded a comrade to get himself shut into the Palais de Justice overnight so he could saw through the bars which led to the basement cells, but the saw made too much noise and he had to wait it out until he could slip away the following morning. On 23 March, she even induced three men from a Lib-Sud *groupe franc* to mount an attack on the vast and well-armed Palais itself. It never stood a chance of success. Indeed, when the members of the *groupe franc* met that morning in a nearby church, they saw immediately that it was hopeless, but could not get away before they were detected (or informed upon) and their leader was arrested and imprisoned. Furious, he would describe Lucie's plan much later as 'a farce'.[95] She was acting like a wife, not a comrade, and her credit within parts of Lib-Sud and the wider resistance was being damaged by her single-minded insistence on rescuing Raymond.

Shortly after the aborted attempt to attack the Palais, all five of the arrested men were moved to Saint-Paul prison, a grim nineteenth-century gaol a short drive away. Raymond and Maurice had to physically support Serge, for he was unable to walk after the beating he had taken at the Rue de l'Hôtel de Ville. A sympathetic guard made sure they were all put in the same cell. From here they would be brought back to the Palais each day for interminable interrogations, for if the police still did not realize the importance of those they had captured, they were sure they knew more than they were telling. French officers led each day's questioning, but a small, unidentified man 'came and went'.[96] Raymond did not know it at the time but the man was Klaus Barbie. He would learn his features intimately some months later.

Not all the questioning was hostile. Left to themselves, some of the French officers displayed a distinct lack of zeal. Their position was an unenviable and complicated one. Serge Asher-Ravanel had already been arrested once, while on courier business in Marseille, and told his comrades that an arresting officer in that city had set up an escape opportunity for him which only his own naivety had stopped him from taking. They knew that there were some men and women in the police, the prison service and the judiciary who thwarted German demands whenever they could: not all, but many, and their number was increasing – but there was only so much they could do.

Towards the end of March, the tone of the interrogations suddenly changed. The police had finally decoded some of the documents discovered in the suitcase that Morin-Forestier had had with him when he was arrested. They appeared to give a shocking picture of a massive, armed and organized resistance of which the Occupiers and their Vichy collaborators had been unaware. When the arrested men realized what their interrogators believed they had stumbled upon, they did not know whether to laugh at their credulity or fear its consequences. The 'information' described a very different force to that which actually existed, for Morin-Forestier, a reserve army officer and the son of an admiral, approached his resistance work as if he were a conventional commander of a conventional army, drawing up grandiose organigrams which Raymond and the others knew were 'a dream, a utopia'.[97] But if the men in the cells knew just how exaggerated a picture of the Secret Army's resources was given by Morin-Forestier's documents, their captors did not. So alarming was the apparent evidence that the case passed from French to German police, and the cars picking the five men up from Saint-Paul now headed not to the Palais de Justice, but to the new Gestapo headquarters at the School of Military Medicine, where Klaus Barbie was to become personally involved.

Gestapo interrogations, the men discovered, were very different from those carried out by the French police: focused, lengthy and vicious. Between beatings, the same questions were shouted over and over again. *Who is Bernard?* (the codename of Emmanuel d'Astier). *Where are you getting the guns from? Who is helping you?*[98] The small, mild-looking man whose name Raymond still did not know came more frequently and watched. The questioning went on every day for weeks, with fists suddenly lashing out when the men asking the questions were frustrated, and throughout it all Raymond and Maurice stuck to their story of black marketeering. Raymond's fury at his compatriots lasted longer than his injuries, for although the French might have been deliberately lax in the early stages, they cooperated fully with German demands when they were made. The first thing Serge Asher-Ravanel saw on the table when he went to Gestapo headquarters was his French police file on a German officer's table. And if the beatings were being delivered by Germans, it was Frenchmen who ferried them back and forth to Gestapo headquarters. When the Germans were around, 'French inspectors behaved like doormats,' Raymond said. 'They escorted us to the officer of the Gestapo, saluted, and left.' At the end of each interrogation Raymond was disgusted to find they 'had been waiting downstairs, by their car, like obedient children'.[99] Lucie swore she would never forget these men and these events: 'French policemen, government employees, not just fascist rabble like the Milice, obeying German orders as a matter of routine'.[100]

When they were not being interrogated, the five bruised and battered men shared a cell measuring two by three metres. Each was tortured not only by the threat of violence, but by their lack of knowledge. They had been cut off completely, and knew nothing of what was happening beyond Saint-Paul prison, or even in its other cells – only that a summons to court, a beating, another violent interrogation, a train to an eastern European camp or a death sentence could come at any moment. To sleep, four men lay side by side on the floor while the fifth lay crossways at or on their feet. There was one uncovered bucket, infrequently emptied, to use as a lavatory, and soon they were crawling with lice. Perhaps worst of all, every one of them knew that the police might have already made the link to loved ones, and that comrades, spouses, children or parents might be enduring the same treatment. During these dark hours, they turned to each other for support.

Suspicious of hidden microphones, for eight weeks they talked of anything but their resistance activities. Political differences were not allowed to cause friction. Morin-Forestier, an upper-class type typical of Combat's senior ranks, 'whistled entire symphonies'[101] and declaimed Baudelaire by the yard. They recited the classic tales of French literature which they had learnt at school. The two mathematicians set tricky maths questions, the two who had studied some law (Raymond one of them) recited statutes. They set up a debate: 'Goethe said, in the beginning there was the verb. Kant said, in the beginning there was action. Which was right?' They scratched out a chess set on a piece of paper and played games. They even prepared for interrogation with one taking the role of judge and another of accused man, a pantomime which gave Morin-Forestier 'more belly laughs than I have ever had in my life'.[102] Raymond's cellmates nicknamed him Napoleon for his habit of standing with his weight on one foot and one hand on his breast as he debated, or played his part in the interrogation charade. Raymond recalled that Raymond Hego, the youngest, seemed to appreciate the opportunity to complete an education his class had denied him. 'I am very lucky', the young man burst out one day, forgetting the possibility of microphones, 'to have met men as educated as you. I'm a worker, I would never have met you without the Resistance. For me, resistance means hope for a life where workers will no longer be rejected by society'.[103] All five stayed strong. As long-time *résistants*, they had lived 'in expectation of being arrested', as Raymond said. 'And that is very important ... it is a surprise, but not an insurmountable shock. It's not the end of the world. All *résistants* expected to be arrested, and not only that, they had prepared their reactions. It was very important, psychologically. We didn't lose our heads'.[104]

On the outside, Lucie had also forced herself to consider the situation coolly. She knew she could not afford to dwell on what might be happening to her husband: that she had to compartmentalize her mind, lock the horrors away from herself and maintain the pretence that life was normal in case anyone made connections between an absent Raymond Samuel and the man in Saint-Paul prison. She could never visit him, even disguised, for 'François Vallet' was a bachelor with no family, but she queued at the prison gates with dozens of other women to collect dirty clothes for all five men in the cell, knowing that the others had no one in Lyon to do it for them. She had to boil the laundry for hours to kill the lice which collected in the seams: they went 'transparent, completely bloodless but still moving'.[105] The toughest had to be killed with a hot iron. She berated herself for feeling uncomfortable about waiting with the rest of the women coming to see their men, who were not *résistants* but ordinary criminals. She thought they realized her situation, for the signs were there – a woman doing laundry for five men, none of whom she ever saw – but she did not go so far as to try to recruit them, unsure of the networks and loyalties in what she now saw as a 'marginal world'.[106] She had come a long way from her childhood.

As Raymond's refusal to change his original story gradually began to persuade his interrogators that he was, after all, nothing but a black marketer caught at the wrong place and wrong time, Lucie was working towards another rescue, but this time with greater sense and greater caution. Chagrined by the arrest of the *groupe franc* leader whose help she had sought in March, she had decided to go outside the confines of Lib-Sud. Instead, she asked for help from the ORA, the resistance organization set up by demobilized officers who had frustrated Raymond's recent attempts to get French arms into the Secret Army. Travelling back to Clermont-Ferrand, where her resistance journey had begun, Lucie contacted two ORA members who knew Judge Cohendy, the French magistrate in charge of Raymond's case, and who promised to contact him. This was only one of her plans, however, for she had not given up hope of rescuing her husband by direct means and had also recruited a pharmacist neighbour in the Avenue Esquirol who secretly supplied her with doses of the drug ipecac, which produces immediate and – taken in the correct quantity – spectacular vomiting.

In Saint-Paul prison, the men in the cell were one day passed a secret message. It told them that Lib-Sud's Directing Committee had decided to extract Raymond, Maurice, Morin-Forestier and Serge. They were to be sent 'chemical products' and instructions as to which symptoms they should describe to the medics to get themselves suspected of contagious disease and transferred into medical care. First Raymond and then the other three swallowed what was brought in by an 'obliging prison guard'[107] who was told it was medication, gave the doctors the right answers and were transferred from Saint-Paul to the 'disciplinary section' of Antiquaille hospital. The first stage of the rescue was complete.

The order of events, and which events, finally brought about

Raymond's release from Antiquaille hospital, is still not clear. In later years, Lucie spoke and wrote about what happened many times, remembering her desperation to free her husband in time for the fetishized May anniversary of their meeting. In her version, Judge Cohendy asked his senior, the Attorney General, to release Raymond provisionally but the Attorney was *un salaud*, a bastard, and refused. At that point, Lucie intervened personally: rather than the more prudent course of letting Judge Cohendy make arrangements behind the scenes, she went into action.

Her plan was based on Radio Londres' daily broadcasts of brief, surreal and deliberately enigmatic messages to *résistants*: 'Aunt Emily likes her coffee.' 'Clarisse has blue eyes.' 'Jean has a very long moustache.' French and Germans alike were aware of the practice. Lucie had 'heard from a radio operative the text of a personal message which would be broadcast in the next two days.'[108] The words were *Continuez de gravir les pentes!* – continue to scale the mountains! – and her new plan was to use the broadcast to threaten the Attorney General into releasing her husband.

'I presented myself, alone, at the attorney's house. I explained to him that he had a man called François Vallet in prison, that I was a representative of General de Gaulle, and that it was imperative that the prisoner be released before the morning of 14th May.'[109] If he heard the words *Continuez de gravir les pentes* on the BBC that evening, he could take it as the resistance confirming what she had just told him. 'If he is not freed,' she finished, 'you will not see sunset on the 14th.'[110]

The archives suggest a different, or additional, story: that on 10 May 1943, Judge Cohendy signed an order for the provisional release of François Vallet on health grounds, and that on that day or the next Raymond was sent home. Haggard, grey and unsure, he appeared at the gate of their house in Avenue Esquirol and Lucie experienced such intense, visceral relief that she almost fainted.

> About nine-thirty in the morning, I catch sight of Raymond from the window of my room ... there he is, holding a strange bundle at arm's length. I recognize it at once: tied by the coattails and sleeves, it is the overcoat he was wearing the day he was arrested. I wait for him at the garden gate. Once the door is closed, our initial effusiveness is cut short.
>
> 'I need to wash.'
>
> ... Holding the coat in my fingertips I spread it on the fence in the end of the garden ... looking up at it close, I see a round hole right through the shoulder pad ...
>
> Later, inside our house, stretched out on the bed, our longing for each other satisfied, I say nothing, but I already know: we will have that second child that I have been wishing for for months ...[111]

Their precious fourth anniversary on 14 May was celebrated together.

When the couple visited Maître Fauconnet, the lawyer engaged on Raymond's behalf by Maurice David, he was furious with Lucie for disrespecting the due process of law. 'You can't do this!' he shouted. 'It's simply not done! You have threatened an officer of the court, and that's a very serious matter. What would become of the independence and dignity of the law if everyone acted like you?'[112] Lecture given, he then toasted the couple warmly with a precious bottle of liqueur.

Raymond was free, but Kriegel-Valrimont, Asher-Ravanel and Morin-Forestier were still in the Antiquaille hospital and at any moment could be returned to the horrors of Saint-Paul prison and the beatings at the School of Military Medicine. Raymond's deep remorse at finding himself free while his friends were still in Antiquaille hospital was assuaged when Lucie announced that she had organized their escape.

On 23 May, Serge Asher-Ravanel was lying in a hospital bed guarded by gendarmes when a food parcel was brought in. Discreetly investigating when the gendarmes' attention was elsewhere, he found a hidden message telling him to be ready for escape the following day. More notes were smuggled in to his comrades, each kept separate and under guard. From dawn on 24 May, Serge 'was on the alert. The hours passed. Nothing. But the message had been clear. Suddenly, a loud argument in the hall ...'[113] Serge could not see what was happening, but two cars had pulled up outside the hospital and Raymond had got out, accompanied by a group of experienced Communist fighters in Gestapo uniform, among them a Luxembourger who spoke perfect German. They had two guns between them, one of which was 'the last pistol we have', the *groupe franc* told Raymond, with 'no hammer, so it's useless.'[114] While Lucie stayed in the car, for the presence of a woman would have given the game away, Raymond ran to the office where he covered the telephonists with the defective pistol to prevent them giving the alarm. The voice which Serge had heard raised in argument in the hall was that of the Luxembourger, who had a machine gun and was demanding that the three *résistants* recently brought in from Saint-Paul prison be handed over. The gendarme charged with guarding Serge was terribly distressed. "*Mon pauvre monsieur*," he whispered to him, "they're armed and they have orders. What do you want us to do?"'[115] Unable to see anyone he recognized, hearing a native speaker of German barking his orders, Serge himself was convinced that the Gestapo had got wind of the rescue attempt. He dressed, composed himself, shook the other patients in the ward by the hand and only then noticed that the Gestapo officer's machine gun was a British Sten.

In the car, they laughed wildly as they recalled how the hospital director had nearly caused the whole thing to fail by refusing to give up his patients until the Luxembourger had thrust a gun in his ribs. The rescuers and their three rescued comrades all 'imagined the joy of those who had wanted to stop our being taken away'[116] when they found out the whole thing had been orchestrated by the resistance. Serge Asher-Ravanel was dropped on the embankment and the car was parked in the garage where several of the *groupe franc* worked as mechanics. Raymond 'stuffed his hat into a pocket of the gabardine raincoat, which he carries over his arm. Hand in hand, we take the tram home.'[117]

Once again, Lucie Samuel had ridden to the rescue. Her husband and his three comrades were free.

\* \* \*

Despite the exhilaration of his own and his comrades' escape, Raymond was exhausted and weak, and before him now lay only strain and increased risk. His face was known to a lot of dangerous people in Lyon, and he and Lucie had no way of knowing exactly what the Gestapo had learnt of 'François Vallet's' contacts and other identities. Did they know he was Raymond Samuel? Did they know he was also 'Aubrac'? Did they know he was married, with a child? Again, and again *à deux*, the Samuels conferred. Morin-Forestier had been smuggled to London, for it was judged too dangerous for him to stay in France after his records had been seized and his secretary had gone on the run. For one thing, the Samuels could not leave their families behind as possible hostages. For another, they knew that Raymond's work in the Secret Army had never been so important. It was dangerous, even terrifying, but it was also deeply, perilously exciting. 'The MUR command,' Pascal Copeau told Raymond just after his rescue, 'is going to use you to inspect the secret army. So here you are inspector general for the whole southern French zone'.[118]

Much had happened during the two months that Raymond was held in Saint-Paul prison. The spring of 1943 was a turning point both for the resistance, and in Allied fortunes outside France. The number of people resisting the Occupation, fascism, unfairness, misery, the loss of a son to the STO or a brother to the *maquis*, or whatever else it was that finally drove them to disobedience, had suddenly increased, and the network of tiny, far-flung threads held together by the lonely work of couriers had within a few vital months developed into a widespread and viable movement of passive and active resistance. This growth had been not only fuelled by disillusionment or despair, but boosted by the realization that the Germans did not, after all, deploy an invincible force against which armed resistance was a risible dream. The all-conquering German army of 1940 to 1942 was suffering a string of reverses, and the BBC and the underground newspapers were doing everything they could to make sure the French public knew about them. The German 6th Army had surrendered in February after the Battle of Stalingrad, and the juggernaut of the Russian war machine had been firmly on the offensive ever since, with the Wehrmacht being pinned down or pushed back at enormous cost to life. Allied aircraft were using new radar devices, beginning the destruction of the mighty German U-boats, and, best of all for the prospect of liberating France, a swift Allied campaign across North Africa had led to the surrender of the German Afrika Korps in May, with 275,000 Italian and German soldiers taken prisoner.

This was no moment for the Samuels to give up the fight. From now on, they decided, they would manage on Lucie's salary alone, even though she had been put on half-pay during the extended sick leave she had taken during Raymond's incarceration, and Raymond would dedicate himself fully to the Secret Army. When he offered his resignation at the airport, he gambled on telling his boss the truth. The boss revealed himself staunch: he would continue paying Raymond's salary, he said. He need not turn up to work, and he could even use one of the company's cars when it was free. All the boss required was a certificate of baptism in case police suddenly descended to check no Jews were being employed. Despite the resolve to continue, however, Raymond's close call had shaken both him and Lucie deeply. It was perhaps only when he came out of prison that they realized how drained they were by the endless fear and subterfuge and distrust. The answer was a holiday.

There is an element of the bizarre in the idea of two people immersed in deadly serious underground action heading off to the seaside in Occupied France, but Vichy itself wanted to project the image of a stable and prosperous nation in which all the natural rhythms and activities of family life were no less possible than they had been before June 1940. Within the constraints of travel permits, food coupons and all the other restrictions, those families who could afford it still took holidays, ate in restaurants, attended theatres and cinemas and gave themselves what meagre treats they could.

Lucie's leave of absence from the *lycée* was extended still further after a visit to Dr Riva, and the family left for ten days at the Riviera, in the Italian Zone. The journey south was stressful. They could not risk leaving from Lyon's Perrache station, for too many police and soldiers were on the lookout after the escape from Antiquaille. Instead, they took a tram into the suburbs, then a bus thirty kilometres to Vienne. It was slow, because a shortage of petrol meant that buses now ran on wood-gas engines, and overcrowded because few people had private

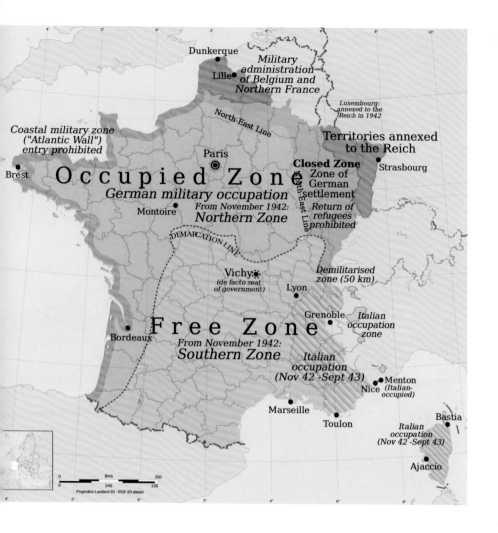

The armistice of June 1940 divided France into four areas: the Occupied Zone in the north, a Closed Zone near the border with Germany, a small area of Italian Occupation in the south-east and the so-called Free Zone where Marshal Pétain's government ruled from Vichy.

ABOVE: Lucie and Raymon
Samuel as a young married
couple, when their legal lives
an engineer and a *lycée* teach
ran alongside their clandestir
work as leaders of the Lyon-
based resistance organization
*Libération-sud*.

LEFT: Jean Cavaillès, the
brilliant mathematician,
philosopher and Sorbonne
professor whom Lucie
befriended when she was a
student in Paris. A *résistant
de la première heure*, Cavaillè
was among the leaders of the
twin resistance organizations
*Libération-Sud* in Lyon and
*Libération-Nord* in Paris
before dedicating himself
to the sabotage of German
submarines.

**ABOVE:** Fear and distress on the faces of Parisians as they watch German troops enter their city on 14 June, 1940. Paris was almost deserted, most of its population having joined the chaotic exodus of between six and ten million people who had fled the Nazi advance.

**BELOW:** The handshake between eighty-four-year-old Marshal Pétain, president of Vichy France, and Adolf Hitler, which took place on 24 October 1940 just outside the station of Montoire-sur-le-Loir.

**LEFT**: Emmanuel d'Astier de la Vigerie, alias 'Bernard', the charming, whimsical and courageous aristocrat whom Lucie met in December 1940, and whose charisma brought recruits and funds into the Resistance.

**RIGHT**: Eighty-four-year-old Marshal Philippe Pétain, a First World War hero, was leader of Vichy France and loathed by the Aubracs and their comrades. Image © ADAGP, Paris and DACS, London 2015.

REVOLUTION NATIONALE

Lucie Aubrac aged about thirty. She was still known by her legal name of 'Madame Samuel' when this photo was taken of her outside the Lyon *lycée* where she taught history and geography between 1941 and 1943.

**POPULATIONS**
**abandonnées,**

*faites confiance*
**AU SOLDAT ALLEMAND!**

**LEFT**: One of the most famous of the German posters which appeared after the conquest of France in June 1940, exhorting a population 'abandoned' by their own rulers to place their trust in German soldiers This image was part of a huge propaganda drive to persuade the French that the Germans were a benign force whose mission was to restore order.

**RIGHT**: The Resistance hero Jean Moulin, alias 'Max', pictured a couple of years before his meeting with the Aubracs in 1943. The scarf around his throat hid the scar left from an attempt at suicide when the Germans arrested him in 1940.

When the Aubracs escaped from France to London in 1944 aboard an RAF plane, Lucie was catapulted into celebrity. One of the more entertaining spins on her story came from the American publication *True Comics*, which turned it into a brightly coloured tale of derring-do to entertain and inspire the troops.

**LEFT**: A 1944 photo of Oberstürmführer Klaus Barbie of the Gestapo, later known as the 'Butcher of Lyon', who received 'Lucie Montet' in June 1943 and told her that her 'fiancé' (in reality her husband) had been sentenced to death.

**RIGHT**: Lucie and Raymond Aubrac in October 1991, nearly forty years after their wedding in Dijon and shortly after they had confronted unfounded accusations of wartime treachery.

transport anymore. At Vienne, they changed onto the Côte d'Azur train: 'a horror! It's jam-packed. People in the compartments, the corridors, even in the toilets and between the cars! ... We sit on our backpacks in the corridor.'[119] At every change and halt policemen boarded to check documents and each time there was the danger that Raymond would be recognized as the fugitive François Vallet. Alighting exhausted at Saint-Raphael at dawn, they went finally to the little town of Carqueiranne, where they obeyed the same Epstein-taught rule of hiding in full view as they had after Raymond's first escape, and took rooms in a *pension* largely occupied by Italian officers.

The small Italian Zone was a very different place to German-occupied France: calmer, slower and less threatening. Raymond grew a moustache in an attempt to change his appearance. Unfortunately it grew out a startling red which, as he said to Lucie, was just the thing to go unnoticed. Before leaving Lyon they had visited a resistance-friendly barber who gave Raymond 'two tiny flasks, one containing bleach, the other black dye. As soon as a millimetre of red hair appears, he shouts: "My roots!" [and] sets to work like any coquette with dyed hair.'[120]

In other respects, the holiday was a second honeymoon. They lay for hours side by side on the beach – touching was out of the question in the Vichy era: 'how he stirs my senses ... I feel our two bodies as strongly united as if we were making love.'[121] Slowly he told her the more humiliating details of his imprisonment. The toilet bucket, the strip searches, the infestations. In the *pension* dining room at lunchtime, Italian officers in white gloves sent orderlies with ripe peaches or plates of lasagne for Boubou. In the afternoon, the child slept and they 'make love until we fall asleep.'[122] Lucie told Raymond she was pregnant with their second child. They wondered if they might be able to come back the following summer, with the new baby.

The holiday was brief. On 6 June, they left to make the long journey home. Boubou 'takes along a few shells and some sand from the beach. "Bye-bye, sea," he says. "Hello, train."'[123] The following day, the family was back in the Avenue Esquirol, where the grass had grown, the flowers in the garden were blooming and the apple tree was covered with small green fruit. Later that week, they visited Lucie's aunt and uncle and came back with food and wine, and invited Raymond's parents to dinner. As always, the elder Samuels refused their son's pleas that they should leave France.

Furtively, the couple resumed their lives. 'Raymond Samuel' had disappeared, but Madame Lucie Samuel continued to lead a legal existence, her name attached to a *lycée* which in reality she hardly ever attended. 'François Vallet' was also buried, for Pierre the Forger had brought papers proving Raymond to be a demobilized soldier from Tunisia called Claude Ermelin. A photograph showing his new, dyed moustache was inserted and a new backstory created and learnt. Armed with his papers, Raymond resumed discussions with his comrades on how to arm the ever more numerous *maquis*. Every time he left the house, Lucie did not know if he would return. Three days after their return from the seaside, they learnt that the Secret Army had been betrayed.

CHAPTER 3

# 'LUCIE MONTET'

WHILE THE SAMUELS were on holiday in Provence, Jean Moulin had travelled secretly from his base in Antibes, in the South-East, to Paris and finally chaired the inaugural meeting of a 'National Council of Resistance'. It was the pinnacle of his achievement, a political union which represented not only the 'Big Three' Lyon movements that had formed the United Movements of the Resistance, but also five northern resistance movements, five political parties and two trades unions. De Gaulle's claim to represent the internal resistance was now founded in fact, but it had been a struggle. Henri Frenay of Combat refused to attend the Paris meeting and there was little warmth among the rest, but they were present, and they voted a motion that de Gaulle be recognized as the single head of a French provisional government. On 30 May 1943, armed with this news, de Gaulle arrived in Algiers. The proof that he did indeed have a united and armed resistance behind him had persuaded the Allies that he and his rival General Giraud could jointly preside over a new French Committee of National Liberation, a French government on French (colonial) soil.

The Samuels heard of it on Radio Londres, recognizing the voice which read out the news as that of Pierre Brossolette, a former

Sorbonne student and *résistant de la première heure*. 'For all of us and henceforth for all of you,' Brossolette announced, the Committee of National Liberation was 'the basis for legality, that's where the flag flies, that's where your duty lies – outside of it, there is only usurpation and violence.'[1]

*Résistants* and Germans alike knew that with the defeat of the Afrika Corps, Allied landings must soon be made on the Mediterranean coast of Europe, in France, Greece, Italy or elsewhere, singly or simultaneously. General Delestraint, commander of the Secret Army, was drawing up plans for his troops to rise and support the anticipated arrival of Allied troops in France. On 9 June, he headed for La Muette metro station in Paris to meet Henri Aubry, a senior officer in Combat. The object of their discussion was a nationwide derailment of trains planned for the day of the Allied landings. What Delestraint did not know was that Henri Aubry, indisposed, had arranged to send in his place the sabotage expert René Hardy; or that Aubry's letter to Hardy organizing this had, against all the rules, been written in uncoded language, left in a 'burnt' ('blown' in British intelligence slang) letter box and intercepted by the Gestapo; or that Hardy himself had been arrested by Klaus Barbie's men three days earlier, and released after interrogation. Who did know any or all of these things is still a matter of bitter controversy. Certainly Jean Moulin did not, nor any of the heads of the United Movements of the Resistance or the new National Council. What is incontestable is that this trail of negligence, deceit or both could have only one ending. Gestapo officers were waiting at La Muette.

Jean Moulin was in London when he heard that General Delestraint had been arrested. He immediately parachuted into France to hold a top-level meeting with Secret Army officers to decide who should replace him. 'Aubrac' was instructed to meet 'Max' – he and Lucie still did not know Jean Moulin's real identity – on Sunday 20 June at the Tête d'Or Park, on the banks of the Rhône and in the outskirts of Lyon. It was a green and airy place with a zoo, a lake, botanical gardens and playgrounds where city families took their children, and both Boubou and Lucie went with Raymond for relief from the hot city streets and to provide extra cover.

Raymond had met Max once under the theatre arcades of Lyon, but it was the first time Lucie met the man she knew to be de Gaulle's representative. On the lawns where children played and mothers picnicked, she found herself face to face with 'a very charming man, very handsome, with glowing eyes, a wonderful smile, elegant features'.[2] She could ask him almost nothing about himself for they both knew the rules of clandestine life. 'We talked about me for a bit, while he played with the little one.'[3] She asked him about de Gaulle. What was he like? 'Tall,' Max replied.[4] They took Boubou to see the Punch and Judy show in which:

> a mean drunkard is forever clobbering an ugly, stupid, ignorant gendarme. These skits strike home nowadays, and the grown-ups laugh just as hard as the children. When the show is over, my two conspirators laugh and applaud with all their might. For a brief instant, they have recaptured the joyous, carefree feeling of their childhood.[5]

Then there was a handshake, Max told Lucie he looked forward to meeting her again tomorrow at a dinner arranged for after the meeting, and left. 'There was never a tomorrow,' she would recall half a century later. 'All I knew of Jean Moulin was two hours in my life. A handshake when I met him, and two hours later another handshake when he said goodbye.'[6] Despite the brevity of their contact, Moulin was to have a lasting and profound effect on her life.

Among the Secret Army leaders invited to meet Max was André Lassagne, the old, lively friend of the David brothers who had come to the Samuels' very first discussions, back when they were still *opposants*. Max had asked Lassagne to find a place for the meeting and he had suggested the premises of his old friend Dr Dougoujon in the northern suburb of Caluire. Before her husband left that Monday morning, Lucie drilled him on all aspects of his new identity. Where was Claude Ermelin born? How old was his father when he died? His mother? What was the exact date of his demobilization? What wounds had he sustained, what illnesses had he suffered, what was the date of his first communion, the name of his primary school, his first teacher, his aunts, cousins ... every detail had to be perfect. 'Goodbye, my darling, see you tonight at six-thirty, place Tolozan. Don't be late, but not too early either. There are too many people meeting by the river.'[7] After giving Boubou a ride on his shoulders upstairs for his nap, Raymond left.

In Dr Dougoujon's waiting room that afternoon, nine *résistants* found themselves sitting with a few genuine patients. The password was 'I have come for the special treatment.' The first few to arrive exchanged wary glances, waiting for Max. The only man who had not been expressly invited was Combat's René Hardy, who turned up with Henri Aubry. Jean Moulin arrived forty-five minutes late and as he took a seat next to Raymond, a Gestapo patrol led by Klaus Barbie burst in, smashed the place up, spread round the house and handcuffed everyone they found. Max reacted fast, asking Raymond to take a paper from his pocket and get rid of it. As the Gestapo officers broke the furniture and shoved everyone out, he ate it. Outside, where they gathered in the sunshine, pushed and kicked by the soldiers, they saw that only one man had not been handcuffed. He made a run for it, the Germans fired a few desultory shots, and although one wounded him, none brought him down. That man was René Hardy.

In the Avenue Esquirol, Lucie dressed, did her hair, kissed her son goodbye and left him with Maria. At half past six she entered the restaurant in Place Tolozan. A quarter of an hour passed. Twenty minutes. Half an hour. She knew that something was wrong. Raymond never kept her waiting, it was not his way of doing things. Quietly she left the restaurant, and then rushed to the house of Cousin Maurice, who told her what he had just learnt himself: that Max and all the men meeting him at Caluire had been arrested by the Gestapo. Lucie 'didn't have time to be afraid,' for she knew she 'had to warn everyone immediately'.[8] Both she and Maurice were aware that the stakes were higher than they had been when Raymond was arrested in March. The Caluire meeting could not be explained away with stories of black marketeering, and if Max were forced to talk, then every detail of de Gaulle, every name on the United Resistance Council, every password and secret meeting place and plan might be given up. The coolness which had deserted her in the days after Raymond's first arrest did not desert her now. Only when she and Maurice had warned everyone connected to the arrested men whom they could find did they turn to checking every place to which Raymond might have gone if he had escaped. He was in none of them. It was late when Lucie returned alone to the silent house where Maria and Boubou slept and took 'Raymond's pyjamas [from] under his pillow. I hug them to me. Breathing in the smell of the man who wears them, I finally break down. I cry and cry without stopping. Exhausted, I fall asleep with my grief.'[9] The following day, grief was replaced by determination.

When the Gestapo released Dr Dougoujon's maid, she gave

resistance contacts the first eyewitness account of what had happened, telling them that eight men had been arrested, and one had got away. Rapidly, Lucie and her comrades ran through the men they thought had been invited, and came up with eight names. Who could the ninth have been? But identifying the mystery man was less important at that moment than finding out where the eight others were being held. Were they in one of Lyon's prisons? In the School of Military Medicine? Or had their identities been discovered and they had already been sent by a triumphant Barbie to his superiors in Paris? Daniel Cordier, Max's secretary, refused to panic. 'We'll figure out some way to help them escape … Max has a chance of remaining anonymous with his false identity card and his tight cover. If there's a traitor, he doesn't know Max.'[10] But no one was coming up with any ideas for contacting the arrested men.

Lucie took the initiative. She filled in some of the clues on a newspaper crossword, left the others blank and tore out the page. Rolling a shirt, trousers and clean socks in it, she made her way to Montluc military prison, the most likely place for the men to have been incarcerated, told the guard that they were for Claude Ermelin and waited. When the guard came back some time later, he had not only a bundle of dirty washing which confirmed her husband was here, but it was wrapped in the same page. Raymond had understood. MAXWELL had been written into one part of the grid, and LEONIE into another. Max was well, and Leon – from the March nickname, Napoleon – is denying everything ('*Léon nie*' – 'Leon denies'). It was little enough, but Lucie knew her husband was alive, and Raymond knew his wife had not been arrested.

This time, Lucie did not insist that resources be deployed to rescue her husband for she knew that rescuing Max had to take priority. She did not yet know that Raymond had been mistaken in believing that 'Max was well', or Daniel Cordier over-optimistic in thinking his cover could hold, for Klaus Barbie had discovered his true identity and was savagely and systematically beating him. When Raymond squinted through a hole in the door of his cell a few days after Lucie's visit, he discovered the truth when he saw Max being carried down to interrogation, covered in blood, his clothes filthy and ripped.

For just over a week the other seven arrested men were interrogated at the School of Military Medicine. Barbie led the questioning, beating Raymond so severely that many times he fainted and was kicked back into consciousness by the guards for the questioning to begin again. Who is Bernard? (d'Astier). Where is he? Who is Charvet? (Henri Frenay). Where is the resistance getting its arms and money? *I had an appointment at the doctor's*, Raymond said, *I know nothing of the resistance.* They told him they knew Claude Ermelin and François Vallet were one and the same. They told him they knew that Vallet was a senior officer in the Secret Army. *I had an appointment at the doctor's*, he repeated. They beat him again and told him his comrades, Max included, had been transferred to the Gestapo in Paris, and that Henri Aubry of Combat had cracked under his beatings and talked. He repeated his story, and they told him he had been sentenced to death. Each night he was taken back to his cell in Montluc prison, knowing the torture would begin again the next day, and the next. He knew that if he had the cyanide pill which many *résistants* always carried with them, he would have taken it. Worst of all, he dreaded to hear that Klaus Barbie had made the final link between Aubrac, Vallet, Ermelin and Raymond Samuel – and what would happen to Lucie, Jean-Pierre and his parents when he did.

On the outside, everyone seemed paralysed: neither the Directing Committee of Lib-Sud nor the National Council of the Resistance had come up with any rescue plan. Liberating men from the custody of French gendarmes in a French hospital in May had been audacious enough, but now they were dealing with the Gestapo. If the heads of the resistance seemed unsure what to do, however, Lucie was already putting together a desperate scheme. She had no more idea than her comrades how Max or any of the other men might be rescued, for the plan forming in her head would rescue her husband alone, but that was no reason to wait for someone else to act. With no one higher up taking charge, 'I will arrange it,' she told Serge Asher-Ravanel. 'I have the time. I am going to organize the operation. I will need the help of the *groupes francs*. Will you help? … Still today,' he would write forty years later, 'I wonder why I accepted. The danger of the operation was out of all proportion to our resources. Our enemy was the head of the Gestapo for the whole of the Lyon region, the most powerful in France after Paris.'[11] It was Lucie's sheer force of will which persuaded him. Consulting the fifteen *groupe franc* comrades whom he commanded, some of whom had taken part in the Antiquaille rescue in May, Serge explained that Lucie would be in charge of planning, and that the rescue operation would be extremely dangerous. Every one of them agreed without hesitation.

Lucie's plan would begin, as it had done before, with the pretence of being the pregnant fiancée of a jailed man, but this time it would go further. This time, she could not simply beg gaolers to be allowed to visit and then pass the man drugs or a file: a man suspected of serious resistance activity was not allowed visitors, and any request would risk revealing 'Ermelin's' true identity. Instead, she would make her approaches further up the chain of command, to the Gestapo itself. As Lucie Montet, the name on her false identity papers, she would claim that Claude Ermelin was the father of the unborn baby which was beginning to show, and whom she was desperate to legitimize. If

Raymond had been claiming that he was an innocent patient caught up in the raid, then Lucie Montet's story would back him up. If his identity as a senior officer in the Secret Army had been uncovered, then release was an impossibility, but staging a last-minute marriage to legitimize the baby would allow the *groupe franc* to ambush the vehicle which carried him between prison and wherever the marriage was performed. As Serge's *groupe franc* comrades exclaimed when he explained this elaborate plan, '*Elle a un culot fou!*' (She's got a nerve).[12] Few people could have persuaded them to undertake it but Lucie's indefatigable spirit inspired confidence. 'Our men liked to tease her,' Serge said, 'about her unpredictability, but they liked her way of plain talking, her directness. More than one of them envied Raymond for having her as his wife.'[13] '"We will succeed!" she told them. The possibility she might fail never entered her mind.'[14]

Only with her sister, Jeanne, did Lucie give way to her terror. She and Raymond had planned to travel to Vichy, where Jeanne and her family now lived, for her thirty-first birthday. Instead, she took the crowded train alone, and blurted out the terrible story to the sister who shared not only blood but an intimate knowledge of danger, married to a leader of the Communist resistance and living under the enemy's nose. The sisters shared a bed that night, Lucie's brother-in-law banished to the children's room, and Jeanne 'lying close to me, holds my hand'.

'Calm down, Lucie dear. Tomorrow, I'll go to Lyon with you and I'll take Boubou to the children's home at the foot of the Vercors mountains. He'll be in lovely company and well fed. With one less worry you'll be able to think straight.'

'I don't want to live if Raymond dies. It's impossible. I'll give you my child, and then ...'

In my imagination, I already see myself in a suicide attack on the
Gestapo, dying in an apotheosis of carnage of German policemen.
Why shouldn't I blow them all up, in the School of Military
Medicine? I know where their leader is and I won't chicken out.[15]

They returned to Lyon together, and Jeanne took Boubou away so his
mother could dedicate herself to the task of rescuing his father. Calmer,
her determination rediscovered, Lucie embarked on her plan. 'Don't let
yourself be cut off from your friends,' she lectured herself. 'Show them
that you are still part of the action, that you share in the fight. They must
not get into the habit of thinking of you as a wife who is overwhelmed
by what has happened, a mother expecting a second child, a weak
woman who has to be protected, who has to be spared.'[16] Carefully
she assembled a disguise appropriate to the age and character of Lucie
Montet, a well-to-do *vieille fille*.[17] 'I put on a very pretty checkered rayon
suit, big white porcelain daisy earrings, and a tiny pillbox hat with a
little veil. If Raymond saw me now, he'd say: "You're looking mighty
olé olé, honey!" I hope I look like a society girl.'[18] Her backstory was
basic but compelling. A rather naive young lady of good family, 'Lucie
Montet' had recently met the charming Monsieur Ermelin at Saint-
Paul de Vence in Provence and was now carrying his child. Painted,
earringed, documents in hand, wedding ring left at home, on 23 June
'Lucie Montet' walked into Gestapo headquarters and was taken straight
to see Klaus Barbie.

All her life, Lucie remembered with chill clarity the details of that
meeting. It was the first time she had laid eyes on the man who was
torturing her husband. 'Behind the desk, a man is putting on a light
beige jacket over a pale green shirt. This man, about my age, with blue
eyes, light hair and complexion, gets up and greets me coldly … "I'm

Obersturmfuhrer Barbie. You know how to read, it's on the door. What do you want?'"[19]

Timidly and politely, I answer in an even tone of voice as if sure of my rights: 'I haven't seen my fiancé since Monday and I found out what happened. He had left me to go and see a physician. Some time ago, he had a bad bout with TB and he has to have a checkup. I was very worried when he didn't come back. I was afraid there'd been an accident, so I went to the police station, where I was told you had arrested a lot of people at that doctor's in Caluire ... I came to ask you to let him out quickly, his health is so frail ...'[20]

When she told him Ermelin's name, Barbie smiled, pulled open the drawer in front of him, took out a wallet and threw it onto the desk. 'The wallet opens and out tumble papers, cards and a little photo of me in a bathing suit, on a beach with a baby by my side.'[21] Her Lucie Montet disguise must have been superb, for Barbie did not realize that she and the woman in the photo were the same. Smiling, he told her that Claude Ermelin had deceived her; that her 'fiancé' was in fact François Vallet, a criminal, a Gaullist and from the look of it married with a child as well, and showed her the door.

Barbie's contemptuous ejection was only the first check to Lucie's ambitious rescue plan. *Résistants* had been keeping constant watch at Perrache station ever since the arrests at Caluire to see if the men were being sent out of Lyon. Just after Lucie's visit to Klaus Barbie, the watchers reported that a large group of prisoners had been put on the train to Paris. Was Raymond among them? They did not know. Five days after her first visit, therefore, 'Lucie Montet' returned to Gestapo headquarters to find out if her husband was still in Lyon. Again she was shown into Barbie's office. 'Today he is alone, with a magnificent dog. The door hasn't even closed behind me before he has crossed the office with the dog at his heels – "You again! I have nothing to say to you – get out. Your fiancé is ready for his last cigarette and his last glass of rum, as you say in France," he adds, grinning.'[22]

Serge Asher-Ravanel found her 'traumatized' by the news. Putting aside the Lucie Montet costume, she embarked that day on a grim routine of visits to the city's morgues. Every day for a month, the morgue assistants took her bribes and opened the drawers where the corpses lay, some so mutilated by torture and torn by bullets as to be scarcely recognizable. Even she, immersed in the resistance as she was, had had no idea of the scale of Gestapo repression in her city.

* * *

Her loneliness was immense.

> Right from the start, our movement consisted of a group of deeply united friends ... until [now] I had had the good fortune to see us as a couple, our baby and our friends all remain intact. Today, the couple is apart, our little boy is far away ... and our friends – no one comes to the house anymore. I set up meetings through [Cousin] Maurice. I have no right to endanger the safety of those who are still free.[23]

Most of her resistance comrades had dropped her. It was a rule of clandestine life, but it left her desolate, and a little bitter. Even Emmanuel d'Astier would not meet her, but at least sent Pascal Copeau as an intermediary, dear Pascal 'on whose shoulder I can cry without restraint when I cannot stand it any more.'[24] Serge Asher-Ravanel, too, stayed in close contact despite the rules: 'the younger brother I never had … few people I know have such *joie de vivre*, such reserves of physical strength.'[25] Even Serge could not spend much time with her, however, for he was immersed in the tasks which Raymond had assigned him just before the arrests at Caluire. The construction of the Secret Army had halted only briefly: the arrested men had been replaced and their replacements were urgently continuing the plans for risings to coincide with the anticipated Allied landings. Raymond's job had been taken over by a former naval officer who believed the resistance must begin actively fighting the Occupiers, not simply wait until the Allies landed before it rose. How, he asked Serge, were they going to 'enthuse the men' if they told them 'your only activity will be preparing to help the Allies when they land'? He knew they were, as he said, 'joining the resistance because they want to fight now!'[26] Ever more young men were arriving in the *maquis* hideouts of Savoy and paramilitary chiefs were badgering London for arms drops. Sabotage of infrastructure, attacks on military outposts and the assassination of German soldiers were becoming an almost daily event in the southern cities as they had in the North, and with them the execution and deportation of *résistants*. Lucie, still making the rounds of the morgues in search of her husband, discovered that more people were being killed than even she and her comrades had guessed. 'Every day they brought new corpses. No one knew. The newspapers said nothing.'[27]

At the same time as coordinating the increased paramilitary activity and attempting to locate Max, heads of the southern resistance organizations were investigating who had betrayed the meeting at Caluire, for it was clear that Klaus Barbie had been acting on information. Lucie and Serge Asher-Ravanel were among many 'convinced that the

Gestapo had been led there by René Hardy'.[28] Hardy was the only one who had not been specifically invited. He was the only one who had not been handcuffed. He had made a run for it, and the Gestapo had fired a couple of badly aimed shots, and taken no other steps to prevent his escape. When he was arrested some days later by Vichy police, he was taken not to Montluc prison but to a German military hospital to have the bullet wound in his arm treated. Although some of Hardy's comrades defended him, Lucie agreed with 'those of our leaders who have decided to eliminate him,'[29] and was cold-bloodedly arranging the means.

Her plan, concocted with Serge Asher-Ravanel, was to send a food parcel to him – 'we know how precious food is these days, especially in prison'[30] – including a pot of jam poisoned with enough cyanide crystals to 'kill all of Lyon.' The pot had to be small enough that it would not be worth sharing with cellmates, for they did not want any innocents to die. Lucie prepared it, left it at the hospital reception and:

> for days and nights afterward, the idea of what will happen tortures me. It's one thing to decide, but quite another to execute such a decision. Now that I'm sure I have inside me a new promise, a child, life takes on even more value. Even when the man's a dirty rat! Three or four times a week I go to greet the anonymous dead at the morgue. But I wouldn't recognize him [Hardy] if he showed up – I never saw him.[31]

She would find out a little later that the plan had failed. It was a relief, perhaps, not to have his death on her conscience – although given what was to happen many years later, she might equally have come to regret not trying harder.

Still no one had any plan to rescue or even contact Raymond and the other arrested men. The weeks dragged on and every night, Lucie went weeping to bed, clinging to her fetish, the pyjamas which still smelt of her missing husband. She knew a third visit to Klaus Barbie would be too dangerous. He had shown Lucie Montet the door twice. A third time and he might ask himself more questions about the persistent young woman who showed such interest in his prisoner. The hot days passed without news or hope – until suddenly a chance presented itself when Serge Asher-Ravanel learnt that another convoy of prisoners was about to leave Lyon for Paris. Could the Caluire men be among them? Immediately he alerted comrades near a station where the train must stop, and a plan for derailment and rescue was sketched out. The *résistants* staked out the station, but the train never arrived. Claude Ermelin seemed to have vanished.

It was Pierre the Forger who finally found a way to make contact. Six weeks after Raymond's arrest, Pierre came to find Lucie and told her about a strange, twisting, improbable network of acquaintance which might just get her the new entrée she needed. He had met a young Jewish woman who was working as translator for the Abwehr (the military secret service) at the Hotel Carlton in Lyon. There she had met an elderly colonel who had been friendly with her family in Germany many years before and was serving in some way as her protector. It was enough. When Pierre introduced 'Lucie Montet' to the young woman, 'we hit it off at once. I don't mention escape attempts, I just talk about my anguish as a pregnant fiancée. I want to know the fate of my baby's father. She agrees to introduce me to the colonel. The time of the meeting is set for August 17, at 6 p.m.'[32]

Three months pregnant, drawn and sick from her weeks of tension and distress, 'Lucie Montet' had no difficulty in portraying herself as a pitiable figure when she went to meet the old colonel, 'a fat, white-haired man – not at all impressive'.[33] Her respectable family, she told him, and in particular her officer father, would never recover from the dishonour of a grandchild born out of wedlock. This was a language the elderly officer understood. Accepting the box of cigars Lucie had brought him – nothing was done without a bribe – he agreed to find out where Claude Ermelin was, and to pass on to him her request that he marry Mademoiselle Montet to legitimize the child. Lucie left with a faint hope blossoming, but when another meeting followed soon after the first, it was dashed, for the colonel gave her terrible news. Barbie's black joke about the glass of rum and cigarette had been true. Claude Ermelin was still in Montluc prison, but he had indeed been sentenced to death.

Sentenced to death – but still alive. That was Lucie's stance when she had recovered from the shock. Serge Asher-Ravanel found her 'indomitable … Animated by her immense love for Raymond … [t]he sort of love you might think only existed in romantic novels',[34] she simply refused to give up. Raymond was under sentence of death – well, she would force this horror to make her plan work even better. French law allowed individuals on the verge of death to contract marriage 'in extremis'. This, Lucie decided, was what she would now tell the colonel in order to force a meeting with 'Ermelin' before the sentence was carried out. But just as she had reworked her plan with new hope, the colonel went quiet. The expected summons to another meeting did not come. The young Jewish translator could not be contacted, the colonel was away and the dreadful fear bore in that she was too late and that Raymond had already been shot.

Throughout it all, Lucie was presenting to the world the face of a mother, teacher and wife whose husband happened to be away, keeping her grief and fear only for Serge, Maurice, Pascal Copeau or the privacy of the house where she now lived only with Maria, in whom she could not confide. The façade had to be maintained even before Raymond's parents, for she and Maurice had decided to spare them the anguish of knowing their son was in Gestapo hands, and had told them instead that he had gone to join de Gaulle in London. Again she made the rounds of the morgues, her heart stilling in terror each time a drawer was opened and another broken body was shown. None of them was Raymond. Still no one managed to get messages in or out of Montluc prison. Still there was no word from the colonel. She was tortured by the constant fear that Raymond's body had been dumped in an unmarked grave. And then something strange happened.

Lucie was sent a message by the secretary of the *lycée* that there were history books waiting for her at one of the city's bookshops. She had ordered none, she was on extended sick leave and did not know what the message could mean. When she presented herself warily at the shop, she found an elderly bookseller whom she had never met, but who ushered her quickly into a back room. There, curtains drawn and door shut, the man astonished her by producing Raymond's wedding ring, and telling her that he had shared her husband's cell for two weeks. Impossible, she said sharply. Her husband was in London. He must have met another man. The bookseller shook his head gently. 'After your wedding,' he said, 'you spent a ten-day vacation in Paris, in a hotel on the Rue Madame. Your favourite aperitif is a porto-flip. Your sister's oldest daughter's name is Martine. For your wedding your brother in law gave you Paul Geraldy's *Toi et Moi* ...'[35] He had left Raymond only two days before, alive. If her relief and her gratitude to the bookseller were immense, there was still no word from the colonel.

Lucie did not know it, but Pascal Copeau and Emmanuel d'Astier were also doing everything they could to help. At the same time, they and others who had known Max were dealing with the horror of what had happened to him. Tortured almost to death by Barbie and his men in Lyon, he had been put on a train to Paris, where Barbie's superior was to take over the interrogations. That officer, realizing the importance of the Caluire meetings – although not from Moulin, who gave away nothing despite the barbarities to which he was subjected – slung him on a train to Berlin for Hitler himself to question. Max had died of his injuries en route. His death was a shattering blow: he was not only the lynchpin of de Gaulle's united resistance, but a man whom his comrades had admired and deeply respected. His secretary, Daniel Cordier, would never completely recover from the loss of the man he had come to love.

Many of the others arrested at Caluire had also been transferred out of the city, but Raymond was still in Montluc prison and d'Astier and Copeau, picking up the pieces of the broken network, were sure that if anyone could get Raymond out it was his wife. 'She will succeed,' d'Astier told Copeau, 'she doesn't give up, it's just a question of time and means. We have to help her as much as possible.'[36] One day in early September, therefore, Lucie opened her door to Pascal Copeau who had brought the enormous sum of 350,000 francs, authorized by d'Astier to buy weapons, informants, gifts to bribe German personnel and whatever else was necessary for Raymond's rescue. It was a gesture of solidarity and faith.

After a wretched month, things now began to move as another piece fell into place: on 10 September, the elderly colonel was back in touch. This time, he told Lucie he would introduce her to another German officer who was in a position to arrange a meeting with Claude Ermelin. On the day of her meeting with this new German who held her fate in his hands, Lucie Samuel left the Avenue Esquirol, her clothes, hair, make-up and demeanour no different to those she presented to the gaze of her neighbours every day, and once again presented herself to Gestapo officers as Lucie Montet. She was keeping her disguise in the little flat in the St Croix district which 'François Vallet' used to rent, and whose owners asked no questions. With a newly acquired blond wig, 'which I attach with two tiny clips above my ears. It really gives me quite a different look,' a smart dress and 'sandals with extra-thick soles' to make herself taller, 'Lucie Montet' once again confronted the enemy.[37]

'Sir, I come from an officer's family. I know what order and discipline mean. I'm not here to beg for mercy for this man. But I'm expecting his child. For my family's sake and for society's, I absolutely cannot be an unwed mother. And this child is entitled to a father. In French law there is an article, permitting marriage on the eve of death. It's called marriage in extremis. Since you have sentenced him to death, please grant me the possibility of marrying under these circumstances. My child will then be born the son of Mr and Mrs Vallet – since you say that is his real name.'[38]

The officer listened, considered and told her to come back on 21 September. As she left, he kissed her hand. Not only had he believed her, but she had caught his sympathy! That night, once again Lucie Samuel and hugging her husband's pyjamas in bed, she felt her baby's first tentative movements inside her. 'I cry with joy. She is there, really alive, my little girl to be, this Catherine who is helping me to save her daddy.'[39]

The meeting at which 'Claude Ermelin' would be asked if he wanted to marry 'Lucie Montet' would take place in a week's time. If he agreed, the wedding itself would take place shortly after that, giving Lucie and Serge's *groupe franc* a second shot at rescue. Now everything was geared towards 21 September, when a Gestapo van would bring Raymond to and from Montluc for his meeting with Lucie. Serge's *groupe franc* began reconnoitring the route the Gestapo van would take through Lyon when returning to Montluc, to determine the best point at which to mount their ambush. The *groupe franc*, many of whom were mechanics at a city-centre garage, set about procuring vehicles to ambush the van and use as getaway cars. All of them met at cafés and restaurants to go over and over the details, Serge with a map in his hand, the others wolfing down their meagre lunches or dinners, Lucie listening, asking for clarifications, and directing. At the same time, she set about procuring something to slip into Raymond's hand in case the wedding was vetoed at the last moment and this was the only chance they got. She knew that mere sickness was no longer enough to get a *resistant* out of Gestapo custody: the Germans had stopped observing Red Cross conventions long ago. Only the threat of contagious disease would work and Dr Riva, she found, 'has exactly what I need: the German health services have sent specimens of Argentinian meat that their physicians judge responsible for a great epidemic of dysentery to the (local) laboratory … Dr Riva took a culture from these epidemic agents.'[40]

In Montluc, emaciated, stunned and bruised from three months of beating, Raymond knew nothing of all this. On 21 September he was collected from prison as normal and expected nothing except another brutal interrogation. Instead he was pushed, handcuffed and stinking, into a room where he was horrified to see his wife. Thinking she had been arrested he declared immediately that he had never seen her before, 'but then I saw she was wearing a lovely hat and a new dress. The Gestapo officer was very polite to her and I realized then that something was up.'[41] As the Germans looked politely away, 'Lucie Montet' asked the father of her unborn child to marry her. 'He looks me straight in the eye. He has understood. "Of course I stand by my word; I'm very sorry to have put you in such a difficult situation."[42] After an interview lasting only minutes, Raymond was taken away, Serge Asher-Ravanel's *groupe franc* prepared for the planned ambush, Lucie rushed to change her clothes – and everything failed, for the Gestapo van headed back to Montluc so fast that they missed their chance. It was a severe blow, but Lucie's grief and disappointment were indulged strictly in private. Assuring her comrades they would succeed next time, sending them off with cheerful words, she got home late and exhausted, and shut the door on the world. 'How quiet my house is tonight, and how large the bed is! Luckily I am not alone. As soon as I stretch out, the baby unfolds, turns over, cuddles up, and finds a good place to spend the night.'[43]

The following morning, she began new preparations with new hope. Another possibility of arranging meetings had occurred to her: having presented herself as the daughter of a wealthy family, she was within her rights to have drawn up a contract stipulating that her groom had no right to her family property. It was absurd, and when she returned to the Gestapo officers to ask for a date to see her fiancé for him to sign this contract, they told her as much, remarking sarcastically on the irritatingly legalistic nature of the French. In the end, however, they allowed her to go ahead with the plan. Waiting for the German officer to send her a date for the next meeting, Lucie returned to the grim tour of the city's morgues to see if any dysentery patients had been brought in, but there were none. With the baby tumbling inside her, she ticked off tasks on the strangest of to-do lists: apply for a marriage licence; source silencers for the *groupe franc*'s guns; have a fictitious property contract for a fictitious bride and her equally fictitious bridegroom drawn up by a notary. She was in her fourth month of pregnancy when finally, on 19 October, she was told she could present it to her fiancé on 21 October.

The rescue was on again and this time, she told her comrades, they would assuredly get their men! Then, at dawn on 20 October, she found Serge Asher-Ravanel on her doorstep, having just escaped from arrest after a failed sabotage operation. He was too beaten up to take part in Raymond's rescue. Lucie would have to direct the *groupe franc* herself.

On 21 October, she left her home on the Avenue Esquirol knowing she might never see it again, for in a few hours' time both she and Raymond would be dead, in prison or on the run. What did a woman take with her in such circumstances? In the end she chose a tapestry bag her mother-in-law, Hélène, had embroidered for her, a bottle of rum, some pipes and a twist of tobacco for Raymond's first smoke.

On her way to the meeting with her 'fiancé', she called for the last time at the garage where her *groupe franc* comrades were preparing the old Citroen van they were going to use. 'They have removed the window, which didn't slide down completely inside the door; that would have made it difficult to steady the sub-machine gun aimed at the German driver.'[44] Although the smell of oil and gasoline made her stomach heave, she stayed with them as long as she could, deriving strength from their skill, their determination and their loyalty to the woman they still only knew as 'Catherine'. She told them she would see them at five thirty, and left.[45]

At her safe house, she turned herself one last time into Lucie Montet. She did not know it, but 'Lucie Samuel' had just ceased to exist. Walking the last stretch of road towards the Gestapo headquarters where the meeting with 'Claude Ermelin' was to take place, she was amazed not to find herself nervous. As she told herself, 'action is the best tranquilizer.'[46] Raymond was already waiting for her, handcuffed, his hair long and unwashed, and his skin pale where it was not bruised. This time the Germans present seemed nervous, urging them to hurry their conversation along, a little less courteous to Mademoiselle Montet than they had previously been. Both parties duly signed the marital contract but Lucie was 'barely able to talk to Raymond. He risked only a quick wink when I looked at him while the other [the German officer] peeked out into the corridor.'[47] She was ushered quickly from the room and as she went downstairs was startled by a thunderous noise behind her: was she being followed? Had she been found out? Had Raymond misunderstood and made a run for it? ... Thank heavens, just a soldier running past ...

There was a dreadful hour to fill before the prison van carrying Raymond would be heading back to Montluc. The hunger of pregnancy propelled Lucie towards a tea room where she drank what passed for hot chocolate, a 'concoction of cocoa husks sweetened with saccharine.'[48] She resisted the temptation to have a second, in case another physiological imperative of her condition caught up with her. 'That would be the height of irony, to be obsessed by a terrible need to pee later on when we go into action.'[49] In her safe house, she took her make-up off, removed her wig, changed her clothes and, once more the 'Catherine' her *groupe franc* were expecting, took the tram to the spot where the driver and gunman were parked in their Citroen above the Boulevard des Hirondelles. One of the mechanics had a sub-machine gun on his knees, and handed Lucie a pistol.

All three in the car gazed at the gates of the School of Military Medicine, where Raymond's van was due to emerge in five minutes' time. A few minutes early, two German soldiers came out to halt the traffic outside, and then the prison van itself slowly came into view, swinging into the avenue. From the moment that the driver started the car, everything happened with extreme speed. The prison van appeared from the courtyard of Gestapo headquarters, and Lucie's driver nosed the Citroen van out behind it. A sharp left turn, and they were down on the Boulevard des Hirondelles where the driver suddenly accelerated until they were level with the prison van. Daniel the mechanic raised the sub-machine gun, fired a silent shot and the van slowed, veered into the kerb and came to a halt. For a second, the three in the Citroen sat, paralysed, thinking Daniel had missed, before they saw guards handcuffed to prisoners leaping from the van's back doors as the rest of the *groupe franc* sprang from their hiding places on the boulevard and shot the guards in the head. Lucie, unusually diffident, did not record whether she had herself fired, but only that 'within two minutes we have emptied our clips, and so have the Germans.'[50] Certainly, she was carrying a loaded pistol. After a brutal two-minute exchange of gunfire, the one surviving German guard raised his weapon, a *resistant* fired a final shot and his bullet caught Raymond in the cheek.

Some of the unknown prisoners, bewildered by their rescue but seizing the opportunity of escape, scattered into the twilit streets. Other resistance prisoners were shoved into the back of the Citroen van and Raymond was taken into a getaway car standing ready. By ten past six, the only men left by the prison van were dead German soldiers.

Later that night, Lucie came to Raymond in the safe house Maurice had arranged. Although desperate to see her husband, she had had to go with one of the *groupe franc*, railwayman Julien Chevalier, who had received a bullet wound in the skirmish, to a resistance-friendly doctor. It was not until nine o'clock that she went to find Maurice, who took her to the safe house where Raymond had been taken. They had not seen each other for five months. 'We can't stop looking at each other. "But, look, it's true," he said, "you're pregnant! In less than four months we'll have another child."'[51] They talked and talked, lying on the bed while Raymond smoked the tobacco she had brought in her tapestry bag and

Lucie, utterly exhausted, dozed off to the sound of his beloved voice.

I open one eye when I feel the soft touch of his lips on my stomach and a lukewarm moisture. Is he crying? No. His wounds are bleeding from all the talking; the dressing on his cheek is all red, completely soaked in blood. We don't wake our hosts. I fall asleep next to a man who looks like an Easter egg, with a towel tied round his head.[52]

A telegram sent to London announced:

*in the middle of Lyon Gestapo van attacked by patriots stop three boche dead stop Aubrac repeat Aubrac liberated with 16 unknown others has whole city in uproar stop more to follow ...*[53]

## CHAPTER 4

# 'LUCIE AUBRAC'

RAYMOND WAS FREE, but both he and Lucie were in mortal danger, and a risk to everyone connected to them. As the reunited couple shut themselves in for a precious day in the safe house, their friends were already beginning the work of getting 'the Aubracs', as the resistance now knew them, out of the country. Their destination was London, for which they required a pickup from a designated point by an SOE pilot, to take place during the two or three days of full moon each month. No one knew how long the wait would be. Until all the conditions were right they would have to live 'from hiding place to hiding place'.[1]

The first stage was to get the couple out of Lyon. The next safe house had already been arranged at a private clinic in Pollionnay, about twenty kilometres away, where Raymond's bandaged face could be explained away to any curious parties with the off-putting explanation of 'infected boils'.[2] It was while they were at the clinic that Lucie began to realize just what damage her husband had sustained, for though the bullet wound in his cheek could be mended, the trauma would take longer. He was tormented by memories of the beatings meted out with particular viciousness by Barbie and his creatures, and Lucie was distressed by his insistence on having a gun always within reach, for if he were retaken he intended to shoot himself. 'He won't let go of it. He takes it apart, oils it, checks the mechanisms, puts the cartridge clip back in, and puts a bullet in the barrel. At night, he slips it under his pillow.'[3] He talked ceaselessly about his imprisonment, exorcizing the horrors of the recent past, while Lucie tried to divert him by talking about the future, the new baby, Boubou, the family life to come. She removed the gun when he fell asleep, terrified it would go off in the night and kill them both.

The ambush of a Gestapo van, the release of *résistants* and the shooting of German guards had caused a sensation in and around Lyon, and a manhunt had immediately begun. The Germans had discovered that François Vallet and Claude Ermelin also had something to do with a Raymond Samuel who lived on the Avenue Esquirol, or that Lucie Montet had something to do with a Lucie Samuel at the same address. A few days after the ambush, they banged on the door. Maria told them only what she knew – that Monsieur was in London, and Madame had disappeared. But lying waiting on the table for Lucie's return was a letter from the director of the children's home in the Auvergne to which Jeanne had taken Boubou, asking his mother's permission to carry out an inoculation. 'We've got her! We'll use the child,' one Gestapo officer said to the other.[4]

Two weeks into the Aubracs' stay at the Pollionnay clinic, therefore, Maurice and Pascal Copeau arrived with the news that Gestapo officers were on their way to snatch their little boy, and that although other comrades had already set off to save him, no one knew who would get there first. For Raymond, 'it was the worst night of my life'; for Lucie, 'the longest and most terrible.'[5] Hours of desperate waiting passed, and then there was a knock, 'Raymond opened the big door, and our son ran into his arms.' They did not yet know that although their son was safe, Raymond's parents were not.

The couple could not stay safely in the clinic with Boubou for the presence of a young child was too odd. 'In those desperate times,' as Lucie knew, 'there was always the risk of jealousy, of enmity, of denunciation.'[6] They had no idea where they were being taken as they were driven away. 'We had a driver, and a co-pilot who told him where to go. I had the impression we had completely lost control of our own lives. From now on others would be deciding our fate.'[7] The only thing they knew was that they had to listen to every Radio Londres broadcast, for at any moment one of those strange little messages could be aimed at them: *Ils partiront dans l'ivresse* – 'they will leave joyfully' – would let them know their flight was imminent. Until they heard it, there was nothing they could do.

They were heading into the Jura, the hilly, thinly populated region between Burgundy and Switzerland where massive wooded hills ascend towards the snow-covered peaks of the Alps and the *maquis* was gathering. Under the very upper-class name, as Lucie remarked (*'un nom très comme il faut'*[8]), of Monsieur and Madame St André du Plessis, they were about to embark on a tour of safe houses which would continue for the final three months of Lucie's pregnancy, sheltered and cared for by a network which showed just how far the size and complexity of resistance had grown.

Their first host had been dismissed from the mayoralty of his small town by Vichy. The man who had replaced him was thoroughly decent, he told Lucie and Raymond, and the *résistants* of the region gave him what support they could, Vichy man or not, for fear a worse person would take over if he went. The Aubracs rarely stayed more than a couple of nights in one place, moving on to families, single men, old couples, retired policemen, women tending lonely farms because their husbands were imprisoned and their sons had fled to the *maquis*. Heartening news came from BBC broadcasts, when it was safe to listen to them. The first of the anticipated Allied landings had been made in Sicily in July, since when Allied troops had pushed north whilst Italian *résistants* rose to clear their towns and cities of German troops. On 3 September, Italy surrendered. In Russia, the Red Army was retaking city after city, and in Germany itself thousands were fleeing Berlin as the Allies bombarded Hitler's capital. On 11 November, General de Gaulle took the salute at a parade of Free French forces in North Africa, and a few days later the Aubracs heard the message they were waiting for: *ils partiront dans l'ivresse.* Lucie was seven months pregnant, tired, breathless and clumsy. They packed their few belongings, and were moved for the final few hours to a farm close to the isolated landing strip. Then fog descended, and the SOE pilot who had been sent to collect them could not make out the lights and was forced to return to England. All three of them 'slept that night on straw, next to the pigsty. A thin partition separated us from the pigs, and we could see and smell them.'9

From there, the little family was driven to stay with a postman; then someone came to take them to the isolated small town of Cuiseaux, where they spent a fortnight hidden on a farm. They left accompanied by a downed English airman called John Brough, who had been given a deaf-mute identity card in case they were stopped as he spoke not a word of French. Lucie's pregnancy advanced inexorably, and still they heard no message. Over the next few days they and John Brough spent nights with a retired gendarme – an officer of the Secret Army – and his family, and then a still-working gendarme who had come to the conclusion that when the law itself was illegitimate he must break it. Lucie's eighth month approached. They scanned the leaden winter sky and tuned in to the BBC and as their hopes rose with the growing moon, they had a visit from Cousin Maurice, heartbroken, who told them that Raymond's parents had been deported.

All the efforts they had made to bring Hélène and Albert Samuel over the Line from Dijon to Lyon; the hours they had spent begging the couple to leave France; the identity papers constructed by Pierre the Forger; Raymond's efforts to convince his father that Marshal Pétain was not the protector he seemed – none of them had saved the elder Samuels. Like 72,000 other Jews in France, they had fallen victim to the combined insanity of some and cowardice or indifference of others. The Aubracs would later learn that Hélène and Albert Samuel were among the 1,153 people of 'Convoy 66', which left for Auschwitz in January 1944. The sadness, and the feeling of guilt, would remain with them all their lives.

On 8 December, the grieving Aubracs and John Brough were moved again, this time to the little town of Villevieux and a freezing chateau owned by three elderly sisters known as 'les dames Bergerot', the last of their family and left husbandless by the previous war. The sisters had been *résistantes* since 1941, when they had risen from their seats in church in patrician reproof to a priest who hailed the virtues of Vichy. They had renamed the oldest and most incontinent of their dogs Marshal for the pleasure of snapping orders at him. 'Down, Marshal,' they shouted. 'Filthy boy,' and 'Marshal, be quiet!' The Aubracs and John Brough were the latest of many who had been hidden in their unused rooms, protected not only by the sisters but by the complicity of the town beyond the walls of their neglected park.

In the final stages of pregnancy, caring for a toddler, and with her husband distracted by sadness and guilt, a mountain winter bearing down and a countrywide manhunt underway, Lucie's situation was pitiable. The worst of it was that 'I had no control over my fate.'[10] From her earliest childhood, she had needed to control her own life and her own decisions: to present to the world whatever version of herself she chose. All that had been taken away from her, and 'I could not bear it.'[11] While Raymond worked in the garden and practised his English with John, Lucie spent her days lying in her room. They passed the evenings in the sisters' vast, gloomy library, playing cards or reading, and tuning in to the BBC at 9.30 p.m., desperate to hear 'their' message. 'I lived an almost vegetative life, as if in slow motion. I felt as if I were regressing.'[12] The solidarity of the village women touched her. In those times when almost everything was lacking, they took apart sheets to make a layette for the baby, cut up old shirts to make maternity bras for Lucie and unravelled jerseys to make blankets. There was a little of everything in what they brought her: curtains, coverlets, towels, napkins. They also brought fresh rabbit skins as blankets for Boubou, for the chateau was freezing. He received his gift less graciously than his mother: 'it stinks!' he announced.[13]

Christmas approached, and still they were in Villevieux. Chatelaines and villagers rallied themselves to make the best of their fourth Christmas since the defeat. John and Raymond decorated the house, and Lucie even accompanied the sisters to Midnight Mass. On their return to her Jewish husband and his English Protestant companion, they exchanged gifts. John offered the sisters his stripes and for Lucie he had fashioned a miniature machine gun from barbed wire. They broke open a bottle of wine and John 'became very merry'.[14] Last Epiphany, they had killed the goose and Jean Cavaillès had turned up with a green face. This time, the BBC suddenly broadcast their message and sent them into a flurry of hope and activity.

Their escape had been taken over by a local *résistant* known as 'Colonel Rivière', who was in charge of coordinating incoming British flights. On 7 January, he gathered Lucie, Raymond, Boubou, John

Brough and a couple of passengers, whose identities they did not know and did not ask, on a freezing landing strip until it was clear that the pilot was not coming: the flight had been aborted at the last minute because of information that German soldiers coming from the Russian front had been sent to recoup their strength at Lons-le-Saunier, only fifteen kilometres away. The little group returned desolate to the Villevieux chateau, Lucie resigning herself to the fact that their daughter – she was still convinced she carried a girl – would be born in hiding in France. Then, in the first week of February, 'their' message came over the radio again with new dates: '*de Carnaval à Mardi gras* (between Carnival and Shrove Tuesday), *ils partiront dans l'ivresse*'. On 8 February at midday the message was repeated; when they tuned in at seven that evening, they heard it again, and when it was broadcast a third time at nine, they knew the aeroplane had left London and was on its way.

The temperature had risen a little since the last attempt and the ground was no longer frozen, but the little family, accompanied by John Brough and Colonel Rivière, still left for the landing ground with newspapers stuffed inside their coats as insulation. Nobody knew how long they might be waiting or where they might have to sleep. They looked, Lucie said, 'like Michelin men – especially me'.[15] Loaded aboard a tractor, they ground their way ten kilometres into the ever-wilder countryside, with everyone praying Lucie would not go into labour. At just after eleven they heard the sound of an engine, and at half past, Lieutenant Affleck of the RAF landed his massive Hudson on the sea of chopped-up mud left by the recent thaw. Affleck jumped out, assessed the situation with Colonel Rivière and within minutes a ground crew of *résistants* and eleven waiting passengers had their shoulders to the aeroplane's wings and were pushing. Lucie could do nothing. At one in the morning, the passengers climbed in. Finally, after months of danger and inaction, they were away! But when Lieutenant Affleck started the engine, the wheels were stuck in the mud.

Again, all Lucie could do was watch, paralysed, sitting on the muddy ground with her little boy asleep across her knees as the landing strip became a field of frantic, hushed activity. Everyone had got out. The plane had to be moved, even if the passengers did not get on, for the Germans were nearby and hunting parties were sent out against the *maquis* every week. Colonel Rivière's men sprinted off to a score of surrounding farms, and very soon there were farmers with teams of horses and oxen to pull the plane clear, a crowd of people watching and even a couple of gendarmes to control them. Once again the Hudson was hauled out, the passengers got in and this time the pilot took off – but could not gain enough height and had to wheel around and land again. A third time Affleck dismounted and inspected the damage. Lucie had given up hope, but just before two in the morning there was a sudden call for her, Raymond, Boubou and John Brough. Concerned about the weight of mud on the belly and wheels of his plane, Affleck would allow no one else to come. For the third time, the Hudson climbed into the air, and this time the plane did not turn about to land again, but steadied into a westward course.

There was no immediate feeling of triumph. The three adults knew too well what the men and women left behind on the landing strip must be feeling as they returned to clandestine lives or safe houses. Lucie was 'shaken, dazed and nauseous. A nightmare. Boubou was the only one who could sleep.'[16] Nor were they yet out of danger themselves: they had to fly across the whole of France, and the plane's radio had broken so Lieutenant Affleck could not contact the ground crew in England, nor identify himself to British air defences. He kept to himself the knowledge that the mud-covered wheels might freeze solid and he would have to

land without them. When they finally bumped and screeched onto a
London runway at seven in the morning, the British ground crew had
given them up as lost. On the ground, the waiting English commander
translated the pilot's worries for Lucie and was amused by her reaction.

> Having exhausted all my potential for worrying, I nonchalantly
> reply, 'Bah, we've seen worse,' to everyone's astonishment.
> The pilot has a request. He would like to have the wooden clogs
> our little boy is wearing. 'They'll be our mascot,' he says. I gladly
> give them to him, which is why Jean-Pierre arrives in London
> wearing only his socks.[17]

\* \* \*

The Aubrac family arrived in London on 9 February 1944, exhausted,
confused, still numb with distress over the deportation of Albert and
Hélène Samuel, with Raymond's wound not yet healed and Lucie on the
point of giving birth, all their possessions in one suitcase and spattered
with mud. Raymond was taken immediately to the 'Patriotic School'
where all incoming French were questioned but Lucie's interview was
deferred. She was taken instead to Free French headquarters in Hill
Street in Mayfair. 'The office where I was received was crowded, I
was bombarded with questions and nearly fainted – I was exhausted.'
A female officer rescued her, taking her to the Savoy Hotel where she
took 'the longest bath of her life with Boubou'[18] before going out to
dinner with Emmanuel d'Astier, briefly in London from his post at the
Committee of National Liberation, the provisional French government
in Algiers. The restaurant was underground because the full moon
which had allowed the Aubracs to leave France also allowed German

air raids, and in the dim light she was shocked to see people leaving food on their plates. She could not get used to the idea that she did not have to watch what she said, nor shake the habit of glancing over her shoulder, nor stop herself making instant evaluations of people and situations and the number of exits and who was looking her way. Later during that exhausting, surreal evening Raymond reappeared, although 'accompanied by a guard'.[19] Too many double agents entered Britain for even the celebrated Raymond Aubrac to be let loose before he had been thoroughly investigated. The couple spent their first night in freedom apart, she in the Savoy and he in the courteous but insistent custody of MI5.

On her third night in London, bombs again rained on the streets and Lucie rushed into an air-raid shelter where she promptly found herself in labour. Raymond was still not with her. It was another Frenchman, a *résistant* also recently extracted by the RAF, who held her hand and argued with her when she insisted on fetching her suitcase of baby clothes before she went to hospital. 'Given the scarcity of wool, it was a treasure. And it had a yellow bra which I had knitted myself!'[20] As when her son was born, she suffered a difficult labour for she was emaciated, and the baby weighed over ten pounds but the English matron was unimpressed by her patient's roars and screams. 'Be quiet!' she ordered. 'There's a war on!'[21] As Lucie had known from the moment of her conception, the baby was a girl. The following day, while little Catherine slept in her cradle and her mother lay stunned and exhausted on the bed beside her, a uniformed Free French general appeared on the ward with Raymond, read a citation and pinned a medal on her nightie. A few days later, Radio Londres broadcast the message *Boubou has a little sister, Catherine.*

Lucie had little time to recover from Catherine's birth, for her 'situation had changed from one month to another. Now, I was a celebrity!'[22] Aware of the plan to get the Aubracs out, and of the public relations value of Lucie in particular, Emmanuel d'Astier had been talking her up for months in both London and Algiers. The media interest was intense. While coping with the legacy of months on the run, a still-traumatized husband, a two-year-old and a newborn, the woman known as Lucie Aubrac was catapulted into the spotlight as a very marketable representation of the Resistance. Her story was wrested from her as quickly as possible and put to service. Radio Londres talked of her in terms both magnificent and calculated: as a patriot who could snatch captured *résistants* from the claws of the Gestapo, but also as a wife and mother.

*The Times* presented her to its readers in similar terms.

Not long ago, Mme Aubrac was the only woman member of an underground group that has rescued 71 people from the Gestapo, among them her own husband who, under sentence of death, was liberated with 13 other prisoners in an ambush. She is a university graduate, a teacher of history, and the mother of two small children – the last person, it seemed, likely to have handled a sub-machine gun against the enemy and to know the risks and rigours of the maquis. Yet, in her own words, there are many other women in France like her: indeed with millions of Frenchmen in enemy hands, there are probably more women than men in the resistance movement.[23]

The most unsubtle reworking of her image came in the Allied series of *True Comics* in 1944, although the Aubracs themselves would not see it until 1946, when a friend brought the comics back from the USA.

These propaganda magazines for the troops reproduced sensational and uplifting events as strip cartoons, and Lucie's story had been too appealing to resist. An improbably coiffed and crimson-coated heroine is seen marching, head down, shopping basket over her arm, past a 'Wanted' poster bearing her own name. *The story of Mme Lucie Aubrac, brilliant agent of the French underground, can now be told. A skillful planner and daring actress, it was through her courageous efforts that many loyal Frenchmen sentenced to death by the Gestapo lived to fight again ...*

Lucie's circumstances made her perfect for human interest stories but there was a more serious side to her interviews. Telling the right sort of stories was now the best contribution she could make to the resistance: she might have left France, but she still had a job to do, and she threw herself into it. As the date for Allied landings in France grew nearer, it was vital that she enacted what de Gaulle had always aimed at: credibly presenting her country as a combatant, rather than as a conquered nation whose interests would be determined by its liberators. Proving the existence of a united and strong resistance was vital to achieving this, and Lucie was the person to hammer home the fact that exactly such a body existed. What the journalists who respectfully interviewed her for Allied papers and broadcasts wanted was stories: anecdotes of bravery and romance, nuggets of true-life experience, eye-opening accounts of cruelty and fortitude, and Lucie obliged. An experienced raconteuse, used to holding forth to groups of men and confident of her own authority, able to turn out entertaining tales in which was embedded a discreet political message, she was the perfect interviewee. Over and over again she stressed 'the deep admiration of General de Gaulle felt by the whole of the resistance movement,'[24] and produced hair-raising, heart-warming tales to show that all classes, both genders and all political parties were united in their resistance to the Nazis.

Lucie's 'united resistance' theme was not only shaped by Gaullist pressure. Inclusivity had been a hallmark of Lib-Sud and of Lucie's pre-war political engagement. If insistence on solidarity came easily to her, the other old characteristic of *le refus* also cropped up in London, where she had to resist the attempts made by various different factions to co-opt the power of her name and write her story as *they* wished. The press wanted to constrain her within the marketable but limiting image of 'housewife and teacher'. General de Gaulle wanted her to don a uniform and join the Free French military, but she knew she was not cut out for the role and refused. In particular she was irritated by the French who had left France in 1939 or 1940 and seemed unable to recognize the work of those who had stayed and resisted. She disliked the striding about in uniform and the insistence on military honours and military hierarchy, and was enraged by some people's expectation that they could return to a liberated France and pick up exactly where they had left off in 1939. Reinstatement of the old elites was not what she and her comrades had fought for, either in the Latin Quarter in the 1930s or Lyon in the 1940s, and she let people know it. Sometimes she refused to meet individuals who asked to be introduced to her, impatient with their politics and their posturing; French people who had escaped in 1940 and now invited her to dinner to express their dislike of de Gaulle over oysters and champagne – she had no time for them. Resentments were created which she would later regret.

Emmanuel d'Astier and Pascal Copeau had made another plan for 'Lucie Aubrac' even before she and Raymond landed in England. She was to be the 'representative of the domestic Resistance with a seat in the Advisory Assembly' – the National Committee of Liberation sitting in Algiers, which was the French provisional government. 'You'll shake them up a little,' Copeau had told her the last time she saw him, at the clinic in Pollionnay, 'all those survivors of the Third Republic who are among us.'[25] Shortly after her arrival, she was appointed the first female delegate to the National Committee at a time when Frenchwomen did not even have the vote. Sensible of the honour, she chose nonetheless to delegate her seat to Raymond, and remain in London. Action was always more appealing than debate, and it was clear that Allied landings must very soon take place, and the resistance would move into its final phase.

For both Aubracs, the spring of 1944 was a strange period of waiting. Again they were separated from each other. In Algiers, Raymond was frustrated by the pomposity of the National Committee, which seemed to be full of people principally interested in their own career advancement. He shared a villa with Emmanuel d'Astier, appointed Minister of the Interior by de Gaulle but equally disenchanted with an assembly which should have been planning reconstruction, the building of post-war unity, social reform and the enfranchisement of men and women who had resisted fascism, but instead proposed motions on titles and salaries. Absenting themselves from sterile debate, Raymond and d'Astier discussed how civil war might be prevented after the Allied landings in France which both knew were imminent, and the vast Communist and Socialist resistance found that Allied and Free French plans for a post-war state had no room for them.

In London, Lucie spent the months without her husband as a sharp-witted and valuable addition to the Radio Londres team. Having found a nursery for the children in Ascot, she devoted much of her time to the BBC. Sometimes she broadcast, sometimes she was asked to verify incoming information, but the particular task she allotted herself was to check the messages broadcast by others to make sure the tone was right. 'People living in London since 1940 had hardly any idea of what daily life was like in Occupied France. I had to prevent gaffes.'[26] She was breakfasting with her children on 6 June 1944 when she learnt that the day so long anticipated had arrived and the Allies had landed on French soil. Rushing into London, she took the microphone of Radio Londres to tell 'the women of France' what was required of them in the last moments of the fight against the Nazis. 'The hope and the future of our country are in your hands: protect the children, organize their evacuation to the countryside. Protect the children and help the men: you are part of the Patriot Army. You must be everywhere: supplies, liaison, medical care, advice, you must give all this and you must give it everywhere.'[27]

After massive bombardments on German batteries along the coast of Normandy, the first paratroopers had been dropped south of Caen, 155,000 Allied troops were stepping onto the Normandy beaches and the largest amphibious military operation in history had begun. Hundreds of thousands of French people, inside and outside France, had been awaiting their day of vengeance and liberation for years. But if the Nazis were about to meet their reckoning, there was furious competition between the Allied leadership, Free French leaders and the resistance organizations in France about how exactly that reckoning was to be meted out, and what would happen now that Allied boots were on the ground. For the huge left-wing resistance, including Lib-Sud, it was vital that groups such as the army officers' ORA – right-wing, tardy in its opposition, overly connected with disgraced pre-war regimes – be prevented from seizing command and manoeuvring themselves into the position of 'official resistance representatives' in the eyes of American commanders. For de Gaulle, it was equally important that the Free French seize control of civil government. Fully aware that the Americans intended to set up their own administration in France, AMGOT (Allied Military Government for Occupied Territories), de Gaulle knew it would be a race to claim control of his country. Therefore, even while allied troops were still fighting their way hedge to hedge and street to street out of Normandy, de Gaulle and his ministers were already sending in emissaries to resurrect civil government in their name. D'Astier, as Minister of the Interior, despatched Lucie Aubrac among others with written orders to 'participate in the setting up of Committees of Liberation in the freed areas, which would reflect the National Council of the Resistance.'[28]

No arrangements had been made to actually get Lucie into France, but assuming a convenient identity was child's play. Piggybacking on the Canadian Health Services, Lucie set foot on French soil at the end of July, dressed in the uniform of a Canadian worker, and made her way slowly south towards Nantes, entering that city while the battle for liberation was still in course. Nantes presented her with the first painful attempt to distinguish degrees of guilt and innocence. D'Astier's orders required her immediately to replace the 'collaborationist' town governor with one who had actively resisted. She was perplexed to find that the proposed replacement was the wartime governor's own son-in-law, who was unprepared to humiliate his wife's father, whom he considered a decent man. It was one of hundreds of thousands of similar cases which France would soon have to confront.

As Lucie struggled with the rebirth of French government, the battle went on around her. The various elements of resistance which Jean Moulin had worked so hard to bring together had finally united, temporarily and more or less willingly, to support the Allied landings. The French Committee of National Liberation, presided over by Generals Giraud and de Gaulle, had asked the Allied command to recognize about 200,000 French soldiers – Secret Army *résistants, maquis* fighters who came down from the mountains and other remote areas, members of the army demobilized in 1940 and a few thousand surviving Spanish Republicans, men of extraordinary valour whose story is one of the greatest tales in the anti-fascist canon – as the new FFI (*Forces Françaises de l'Interieur*, French Forces of the Interior). The Allies placed the FFI under General Marie-Pierre Koenig, a native of Normandy despite his German surname, whose task it was to coordinate and direct attacks on the enemy in order to support the advance of regular Allied troops across the country. The value of the FFI was recognized by the American commanders General Patton, who said his speedy advance across France would have been impossible without them; and General Patch, who estimated they were worth four full divisions in aiding the second Allied landing, which took place on the Mediterranean coast in August. In Paris, the FFI were behind the anti-Nazi uprising which began when rumours reached the city on 19 August that the Allies were almost there. For five days the Parisian FFI fought the Germans from street to street, until first soldiers of the Free French Forces and then Patton's American troops arrived. On 25 August, the German garrison in Paris surrendered,[29] and Lucie was among the huge, jubilant crowds on the Champs-Élysées when General de Gaulle gave his magnificent speech: 'Paris, martyred but liberated! Liberated by its own efforts, liberated by its people with the support of the armies of France, with the strength and support of all France – of the France which fights ... *la seule France* ... *la vraie France* ... *la France eternelle.*'

\* \* \*

With the second round of Allied landings in France, those on the Mediterranean beaches in August 1944, the German armies found themselves almost encircled. Allied troops were working their way up the Italian peninsula, having taken Rome in June. After the liberation of Paris came Operation Market Garden, when thousands more soldiers were dropped into the Netherlands by parachute or glider. The Soviets had just inflicted massive losses on the Germans in Poland, and the Allied troops who had landed in Normandy were rolling eastwards towards the Rhine. Hitler's war was being brought home.

As the Occupiers retreated before Allied advances, France found itself liberated but shattered, its industries and agriculture dislocated, its people traumatized and dispossessed, its resources scattered and depleted. Town centres had been destroyed, entire villages razed. Railway lines were torn up, ports had been bombed to pieces and left mined. Main roads were impassable. Electricity, gas, communications – anything which depended on physical infrastructure – was damaged. Food could not be carried from where it was produced to where it was eaten. Fields had been burnt; schools were rubble, or the roads which led to them rendered too dangerous by mines for the children to take. There was nothing in the shops. There was no petrol for cars or tractors. During their talks in Algiers, preparing for reconstruction, Raymond Aubrac and Emmanuel d'Astier had feared civil war might break out. It had not, but it still could. When Lucie set off with d'Astier on a tour of France, she found 'apocalypse. Alongside the roads for hundreds of kilometres the German army had abandoned military equipment half-destroyed by bombardments. Wrecked tanks, armed cars, burnt-out lorries.'[30]

When Lucie crossed the Channel to France late that July, she did not know where her husband was. In fact, he was trying to get from Italy to the southern port of Marseille. General de Gaulle's plan to take control of France rested on eighteen 'Commissioners of the Republic' whose task was to restore and enforce the authority of the Republican state. Raymond Aubrac was the youngest of these, appointed at his request under his resistance name because, as he told de Gaulle, the war was far from over, his parents were still in German hands and any link made between them and the new commissioner could be fatal.

Raymond's five-month stint as Commissioner in Marseilles would give rise to accusations which followed him throughout his life. The American captain asked to take him across the Mediterranean delayed his passage, unhappy about transporting a man of known left-wing views and who was the representative of a government his country had not yet endorsed. When he finally arrived in Marseille on 18 August, Raymond found a desperate situation. The Germans had not yet surrendered, there was still fighting around the port, de Gaulle's own mandate was far from secure, and the American commanders were alarmed by the largely Communist resistance which had risen en masse to liberate their city.

Raymond's fluent English, quiet self-confidence and authority over the unruly resistance reassured them to some extent, but the problems the Commissioner and his American 'guests' faced were still enormous. Vast amounts of infrastructure had been destroyed, the bombed port had to be repaired for the American fleet to get in, and a population living among ruins had to be fed and housed. Determined not to appeal to the Americans for help, Raymond took action. First, he created a police force to prevent looting and banditry, and second, as permitted under his instructions from de Gaulle, he authorized the takeover of large industries and services, particularly those whose owners were known to have collaborated with the Nazis during the Occupation, or had gone abroad to sit out the war in safety. His solutions were pragmatic and left-leaning, and had been thoroughly discussed with d'Astier, Minister of the Interior. He encountered opposition almost immediately. Chilly political breezes were already blowing. As soon as it became clear that Germany would be beaten, Allied planning had switched to containing the Communist threat presented by a victorious Russia and a Red Army on its way to Berlin. The Cold War was underway even before the Second World War was won. Allied commanders and the Gaullists were desperate to prevent Communism taking hold at local, regional or national level anywhere in Europe and this made Commissioner Aubrac a threat.

As Raymond and other Gaullists attempted to get an executive grip in the immediate aftermath of liberation, Lucie Aubrac took up the place in the legislature which she had previously delegated to her husband, sitting in the National Assembly when it transferred from Algiers to Paris. It was not a role in which she felt comfortable, for Lucie was a problem-solver, not a politician. She also felt torn between her duty to her country, and that to her husband, whom she knew to be still damaged by his arrest and torture. She travelled from Paris to Marseille several times during Raymond's five-month tenure, attempting to combine the requirements of an Assembly delegate with those of the wife of a senior official and a man in need of support. If she managed the second part, she was not always successful in the first. Despite the insurrection, chaos, uncertainty and Communism of Marseille, Raymond's rank carried with it an important element of ceremony and protocol, for de Gaulle believed that respecting these was vital in the re-establishment of France as a legitimate and self-governing country. Just as Lucie had found herself transformed into a celebrity in London, now she found herself having to play the role of 'a lady with duties to fulfil and protocol to observe.'[31]

Among the most important ceremonies she had a hand in arranging were those to mark the arrival of General de Gaulle himself in Marseille. The general was making a tour of France to celebrate victory, and to emphasize to the Allies his grip on a united and functioning country which needed no political interference from outside. As in other liberated cities, he was to take the salute at a victory parade of FFI troops and then attend an official dinner. Responsibility for the dinner fell to Lucie in her role as Commissioner's wife, and she gave it her usual vigorously nonconformist touch. Whereas de Gaulle wanted ceremonial events which demonstrated discipline and a return to normality, Lucie, Raymond and many of Raymond's advisors were determined that the resistance – particularly the Communist resistance – should be honoured for its wartime courage and the part it had played in liberating the city. This determination had been strengthened by de Gaulle's recent ungracious dismissal of Emmanuel d'Astier as Minister of the Interior and his replacement by a career politician. D'Astier had not even been formally advised of the change: the news was given to him at a dinner held during his and Lucie's visit to Lyon, and he was incandescent with rage. A soupçon of revenge entered Lucie's arrangements.

As de Gaulle stood on a balcony in Marseille City Hall in the immense heat of September 1944, a motley parade of former *résistants* and *maquisards* poured past along with the uniformed FFI troops, a little drunk, shouting and singing, waving their guns, jubilant and confident. Riding on the bumpers of tanks recovered from the Germans, some still painted with swastikas, were hundreds of women, nurses and *résistantes*, wearing semi-transparent pink and white outfits cut from parachute silk. The general thought it all absolutely disgraceful. He enjoyed the dinner even less. His aides had planned for him to sit between the commanding officer of the FFI – a former officer in the French Army – and the President of the Committee of Liberation, but Lucie changed the seating plan without telling them. The general found himself between two local *résistants* and refused to utter a word to either throughout the dinner.

Serge Asher-Ravanel also met General de Gaulle on his victory tour of France, and had his first sad, concrete realization that the euphoria of a victorious resistance would not last long. He was left in no doubt of the general's wariness of armed civilians, particularly armed civilians whose political agenda he did not trust. Still only twenty-four years old, Serge had been promoted to colonel in the FFI and fought bravely in the liberation of the country. In Toulouse in August 1944, as shocked as Lucie by the news that Lib-Sud's leader, Emmanuel d'Astier, had just been dismissed as Minister of the Interior, Serge watched de Gaulle's cold, militaristic handling of the thousands who had come joyfully to see him, and felt the immense potential of the resistance begin to drain away as 'the symbol' made it clear they had no useful role to play in the reconstruction of the country they had fought for with ingenuity, passion and solidarity. 'I saw men of fifty years old crying … he wanted to emasculate the Resistance.'[32] That day, Germany's defeat became in Serge's eyes a 'bitter victory'.[33]

Lucie experienced moments of joy during her own tour of liberated France, but also moments of great sadness. In Lyon with d'Astier, she saw the damage caused by Allied bombs, dropped in May 1944 as part of the nationwide plan to destroy communications before the landings. The School of Military Medicine where Raymond had been tortured had been partly destroyed, and a thousand people had been killed. In the final weeks of fighting, fury and impotence had also driven certain German officers to wreak as much damage as they could before they were forced to leave. She attended the exhumation of Julien Chevalier, one of the *groupe franc* who had ambushed the prison van carrying Raymond to Montluc in October 1943, and who had been executed by firing squad in July 1944. He left four children, some of the thousands of young war victims for whom homes and futures had to be secured. In Marseille, Raymond told his wife, dozens of orphaned or abandoned children were living in bombed-out ruins. In November, Lucie embarked on a programme of creating homes for them. The first, specially chosen, was the kitschly decorated country house in Provence, formerly owned by Marshal Pétain, where the children of four men from the *groupe franc* that had rescued Raymond were taken.

In January 1945, Raymond was abruptly sacked from his post in Marseille. A man who had held high office before the war replaced him and the children's homes he and Lucie had set up, necessarily costly, were allowed to close, having served only about a hundred children. Like their old comrade Serge Asher-Ravanel, the Aubracs were realizing just how little place was allowed for *résistants* and the resistance in de Gaulle's France. Ejected from Marseille, they decided to head for Paris, barred to them in July 1940 but once again their own capital. After a long and difficult car journey, caught in the snowdrifts of another bleak and freezing winter, the couple moved into a requisitioned apartment at 39 Rue Marbeuf, a block backing onto the Champs-Élysées and formerly owned by Louis Renault, head of the car firm, who had been arrested as a collaborator and died in custody. Boubou and baby Catherine, whom Raymond had hardly seen, were retrieved from Ascot, and they found that their little boy had forgotten his French. 'Oh, the big green busy bus!' he exclaimed to his mother as he looked at the streets of Paris for the first time.[34]

As the Aubracs set about returning to normal life, the French around them struggled to do the same. In late 1944, the Red Army came across the first extermination camps in eastern Europe. In the spring of 1945, Allied armies liberated one death camp after another, and any remaining euphoria over liberation dissipated in the face of the film-reels which have not lost their power to shock and silence seventy years on. On 7 May 1945, the Allies accepted Germany's unconditional surrender. The millions who had been deported, held as prisoners of war, sent on compulsory work service, hidden in the mountains or fought as Free French servicemen were beginning to come home, and families to reunite and face the legacies of long, painful absence.

The Aubracs saw many of their friends come under strain after the initially celebrated return of spouses, parents, children, siblings and friends. Those returning from concentration camps, factories or active service had changed, but they came home to find the people they had left had changed just as much. Some men were bewildered to find that a submissive wife had become used to running her own life. Children who had been infants when their fathers disappeared had to adapt to a stranger demanding his place in their home and affections. Lucie noted:

> the case of one man, a prisoner of war who returned in good health, because he had been working on a farm, who could not tolerate seeing his wife, a *résistante* who had been deported and came back skeletal and ill. He did not understand, he asked 'what she had been thinking of, getting herself mixed up with the Resistance,' and demanded a divorce.[35]

Resistance comrades came to stay with the Aubracs in Paris as they had done in Lyon. Many were depressed, some destitute; Pascal Copeau came to them to convalesce after a suicide attempt. Even his remarkable resistance history had not been enough for some to overlook his homosexuality, and his post-war political career was stillborn. And those were the survivors, for many of their greatest friends were gone for good. Joseph Epstein, the old and dear friend of Lucie's whom she had last seen outside a Paris metro station in 1943, had been executed by firing squad at the prison of Mont-Valérian in April 1944. He had given nothing away under torture. He was thirty-three and left a widow and a two-year-old son whose identity the Nazis never discovered. The corpse of Jean Cavaillès, arrested in Paris in August 1943, tortured and executed in February 1944, was exhumed from the grave where it had been marked 'unknown number 5' by his killers, and transferred to the Crypt of the Sorbonne. They were two among tens of thousands.

In the first week of May 1945, the Aubracs had confirmation that Raymond's parents had been murdered in Auschwitz. Raymond would carry a feeling of guilt all his life that he had been the unwitting cause of his parents' death, and Lucie would carry her own guilt that she had let him down when he needed her. France celebrates a national holiday on 8 May, the day German forces were defeated in the First World War. In 1945, 8 May was the occasion of the most tremendous party in liberated Paris, and Lucie went out into the streets to join in, leaving Raymond at home with the children. Her action would create one of the very few lasting strains in their marriage. 'I was wrong to celebrate *that* 8 May,' she admitted when she was eighty-five, 'because, for Raymond, it signified the death of his parents,' adding, 'we have never spoken of it since.'[36]

\* \* \*

If normal rhythms and relationships were beginning to creep back into Lucie's personal and family life in 1945, she found herself struggling in her political and professional ones. Despite Raymond's brusque eviction from his post at Marseille, he was still considered a man of great potential. De Gaulle had offered him a senior position in the French Zone of Occupation in defeated Germany, but he had turned it down, as he had the offer of a job in the Rothschild bank. Instead he agreed, with some reluctance, to supervise the national demining programme which had to be carried out before reconstruction – in some places, the resumption of normal everyday life – could get underway. Unsure how best to present herself to the new world emerging around her, Lucie's professional progress was far less sure than her husband's.

On the face of it she was a success, being one of the tiny group of women in the provisional government. But it did not feel like success to her. On the contrary, it felt like a ringside seat at the death of a dream, for what Lucie had desperately wanted to emerge in post-war politics was a united resistance party: a renewal of public life through the movements of the resistance. Not only was that party stillborn, but Lucie herself was already being ostracized by former *résistants* for whom unity was a thing of the past, to be tossed away in the rebuilding of party political interests.

Political divisions which dated from before the war and had been briefly contained by Jean Moulin were already reappearing. Lucie's vision was always naive: Moulin had struggled mightily to bring about a temporary fusion even when distrust of Vichy and hatred of the Nazi Occupier formed the strongest of common bonds. Without that bond, the united resistance withered, under attack from both Left and Right, republicanism and communism. The far Left was rapidly withdrawing into isolation, and Lucie's combined naivety and generosity showed nowhere so clearly as in her relations with the post-war Communist Party. Communists had done more than any other group to resist fascism, but although the Party won the first post-war election, it could not maintain its momentum. Men and women whose resistance had been coloured red were suspect in post-war Europe, however heroic their wartime deeds. In occupied territories, Allied intelligence services were employing former Nazis as spies and consultants to contain the spread of Soviet Communism. The Aubracs did not know it, but Raymond's torturer, Klaus Barbie, was already on the American payroll in Berlin. And as relations between Moscow and Washington soured, a tragic tendency emerged within the French Communist Party, one now known to be a hallmark of all the former Communist regimes: the neurotic desire to control every aspect of its members' lives.

The impenetrability of Communist Party archives is such that neither Lucie's intentions when she re-contacted the Party in 1945, nor the Party's response, is completely clear. Laurent Douzou, Professor of History at the University of Lyon, attempted to access the archives a few years ago to write his biography of Lucie Aubrac, and the limited success of even his persistent and expert raids shows the impossibility of knowing the whole truth. Douzou believes that Lucie was not applying to join the Party, and indeed her character, her wartime experience and her previous refusal to be incorporated into the hierarchy suggest that card-carrying membership did not interest her. However, if it is clear that she wanted to return to working in some way for and within the Communist movement, it is equally clear that the Communist Party chose to hold her at a distance, beginning a series of investigations into her wartime conduct. Vercingetorix – Georges Marrane – was summoned and asked whether Lucie had always sought Party approval for her activities. Both Lucie and Raymond were required to send in detailed accounts of their wartime lives. Although she claimed that she had always kept contact with and asked advice from Vercingetorix, the obvious answer to their question as to whether she had waited on the Party's approval of her actions was that of course she had not: if she had done so, her husband would probably have been shot.

Raymond Aubrac was as perceptive about the post-war Communist Party in France as he had been about the Vichy administration in the summer of 1940. For him, there was a strange parallel between Communist and military hierarchies. Just as regular army officers were unprepared to allow resistance fighters to hold on to power and change the old ways of doing things, so were senior Communists, who distanced themselves from any movement towards the creation of a united left-wing government based on resistance ideals. But what really counted against Lucie in Communist circles was her outspoken wartime support for de Gaulle, and her public insistence, in London and since her return to France, that *résistants* and *résistantes* had come from all parties and all classes. She had failed to insist that the resistance belonged to the Communist Party, and that the Communist Party was the rightful political inheritor of its legacy. In October 1945, she even wrote a short book on the origin and nature of resistance within France, expanding on this heretical point of view.[37] 'What I really want this work to demonstrate,' ran the introduction:

> is the extraordinary vitality of underground activity during the Occupation, the secret life lived by the whole of France, as if she were a woman engaged in a secret love affair to which she dedicated the best of herself. A life which was fragmented, risky, and varied because it was lived by men and women of different classes, professions and traditions.[38]

The book was one of many nails Lucie banged into her own Communist coffin. It has since found its way into many resistance bibliographies, but it was little read at the time, and the Aubracs always believed that the Communist Party bought up enormous quantities and pulped them. 'They reproached me,' Lucie said, 'for talking about Cavaillès and other non-Communists, and saying almost nothing about the role of the Communist Resistance.'[39] Lucie Aubrac could not be controlled any more than Lucie Samuel, and for the Communist Party, control of its members was paramount.

Lucie was still trying to reach an accommodation with the Party when she embarked on an attempt to combine her cherished political vision with a new career: not teaching, despite the long pre-war struggle to be qualified, but journalism, the work she had carried out in Lyon and London. Her ambition now was to produce an intelligent, left-wing but not party-political women's magazine. Again, it was the dream that the cooperation and fraternity of wartime might inform the politics of peace which led her to failure. The first edition of *Privilèges des Femmes* appeared in October 1945, and the last in December of the same year. Despite support from many resistance 'names', it was strangled at birth by political opponents who were angered by her ecumenical vision. Snubbed by journalists and former comrades on the women's magazines already produced by the Socialist and Communist parties – she left one meeting in tears – Lucie always believed her magazine's failure was due to a 'boycott ... the socialists accused us of being communists, while the communists reproached us with not being communist enough!'[40] The failure of the business left the Aubracs with debts that would take ten years to pay off.

Despite the liberation of her country and the reunion of her family, 1945 was therefore a bewildering and painful year for Lucie. Her Communist comrades held her at a distance. She had run up serious debt. Raymond's work frequently took him away from home, and her parental duties were onerous, for she had taken the two children of a murdered *resistant* and old friend of Raymond[41] into her family. To cap it all, the neighbours in Rue Marbeuf were unfriendly. They looked at us, Lucie thought, 'as if we were out of place among them, as if we did not belong to the same society as them.'[42]

Raymond's journey into very senior governmental or para-governmental tasks was just beginning, but Lucie's seemed to be over. She stood for election to the National Assembly in summer 1946, her name placed third (and misspelt) on the local Communist list. When the Party received enough votes to send two deputies from her constituency to the Assembly, Lucie Aubrac was not one of them. Excluded by conviction and circumstance from party politics, she could not see where to act.

What saved her in this difficult time was family, and her own determination to turn unpromising circumstances into a positive narrative. Raymond's siblings, Yvon and Ginette Samuel, had survived the war. Having been held in a prisoner-of-war camp for several years, Yvon quietly returned to his medical practice when he was released. Ginette, who had narrowly escaped the patrol which came to arrest her parents in early 1943, had hidden in the countryside for over a year until the liberation allowed her to emerge. Lucie's sister, Jeanne, her brother-in-law, Pierre Norgeu, and their children had also survived, and Lucie's old estrangement from her parents had long since healed, perhaps made insignificant by the war. When Lucie's father died in November 1945, the mother who had done her best to set her daughters on the road to lives of fulfilment moved in with the Aubracs. The sadness of Louis Bernard's death was offset a little at the beginning of the next year when Lucie found to her joy that she was pregnant with her third child.

Perhaps spurred by the two events, she turned to the rehabilitation of her family with a will, incorporating Louise into her life and playing her new role with determination. In 1946, the Aubracs left the Rue Marbeuf apartment and bought a large house in Soisy, just outside Paris, where Louise spent much of her time. Here, Lucie would rest, gather the people she loved around her, have her old friends to stay and, after the bewildering, hectic speed of her life over the past five years, spend some time contemplating the future.

She saw this domesticity as a preference rather than an obligation. Her health was not always good and she 'preferred activities which were compatible with Raymond's career and bringing up the children. I needed to devote myself to family life, to peace and quiet, to my home … I needed a little time off.'[43] Her early married life had, after all, been spent in extraordinary circumstances and conditions. The Aubracs had spent seven years moving from rented flat to rented villa to safe houses in the Jura, hotel rooms in London, Algiers and Marseille and finally a requisitioned flat in a snooty part of Paris. The house in Soisy was the first they had ever chosen and furnished for themselves.

The Aubracs had been living in Soisy only a few months when an extraordinary guest came to stay, brought by an artful mixture of Communist Party investigation and the legacy of Raymond's wartime work. As Commissioner of the Republic in Marseille, Raymond had reacted vigorously to reports that a camp for Indochinese workers brought to work in French munitions factories was being dishonestly run, in particular that guards were selling off the workers' rations and forcing women into prostitution. He had acted immediately, arresting the guilty and sending in a new, cleaner crew to run the place, and thought no more about it until he was asked to a cocktail party in Paris and found himself face to face with Ho Chi Minh.

In September 1945, Ho declared the independence of the Democratic Republic of Vietnam in what had been the French colony of Indochina. Informed that a drinks party was to be thrown during their trip to Paris, the Vietnamese commission that had come to negotiate an independence timetable had requested that Commissioner Aubrac be invited. Shortly after the party, 'Uncle Ho' came knocking at the door in Soisy and invited himself to stay. Ho fitted in well with the family which Lucie had gathered around her, kith and kin, friends and comrades from the Latin Quarter, Strasbourg, Lyon, London and Marseille. He got on famously with Lucie's newly widowed mother, and insisted on becoming godfather to the third Aubrac child, Elisabeth, who was born during his stay, in August 1946. His arrival caused considerable difficulty, however, for it turned a family house full of small children into the de facto residence of a head of state. Policemen patrolled discreetly outside, and former resistance comrades efficiently ensured security within the garden fence. Journalists came and went. Every day half a dozen guests expected to be fed; Lucie became exhausted and eventually Raymond was forced to have a little chat with his guest. The result was that a nearby Vietnamese restaurant closed for the duration of Ho's visit; its proprietor-chef moved into the expanding Aubrac ménage and a stream of Vietnamese dishes issued from the kitchen to feed the family, Ho and his retinue.

The 'Uncle Ho' interlude was a colourful but brief one in the Aubracs' family life, but it did not bring Lucie any closer to the Communist Party or reopen the door to a political career. Still paying off the magazine debts and with five children to support, she had to start earning. In 1947, she took up a teaching position at a Soisy *lycée* and returned to the classroom for the first time since May 1943.

It was not always an easy transition from *résistante* and heroine to wife and schoolteacher. Lucie's rather febrile energy was not exhausted by running her household and teaching in Soisy any more than it had been in Strasbourg or Lyon. When a government commission – the first of many – was established to 'enquire into the totality of political, economic, diplomatic and military events which, between 1933 and 1945, preceded, accompanied and followed the armistice, in order to determine responsibilities and, if necessary, suggest political and judicial sanctions',[44] Lucie eagerly accepted the place she was offered. Correspondence over the next couple of years from the principal of her *lycée* would sound a familiar note of frustration. 'Mme Aubrac taught successfully last year,' ran an acerbic report from the principal in early 1948. 'This year, illness obliged her, in mid-November, to take two months off. And she has informed me that I cannot count on her between now and next July ...'[45] In April 1948, she asked for time off to visit Poland as representative of the French resistance at the inauguration of a monument dedicated to the French who died in Poland. It was refused: whatever Madame Aubrac had done in the past, it was time for her to get back to work, and stay there.

Even when brought to heel by her headmaster, Lucie did not allow her return to the classroom to remove her entirely from her country's public life. If the united resistance had been excluded, and had excluded itself, from government, the ideals it had fleetingly lived by might yet inform international and extra-governmental movements. The Aubrac name carried weight, and both she and Raymond were founder members of the 'Peace Movement' created in February 1947 by former *résistants* in response to the development of nuclear arms. In February 1948, the *Combattants de la Liberté* (forerunner of the *Mouvement de la Paix*, which is still France's largest peace movement) was founded with their support and the aim of supporting the republic and preventing the return of racism or dictatorship – any dictatorship. Three days later, Soviet tanks moved into Prague, ousting Czechoslovakia's fragile democracy and ushering in four decades of dictatorship. It was a brutal example of the challenges to Lucie's vision.

CHAPTER 5

# LUCIE AUBRAC

IN 1950, the Aubracs legally ceased to be called Samuel, instead adopting Raymond's wartime pseudonym as their name. Raymond's three years as head of the national demining programme had ended by then, and he had moved into international consultancy with a political tinge. The institution he and three colleagues founded in 1948, BERIM, was a civil engineering consultancy established to promote trade with Communist countries, in particular Czechoslovakia. It was both a return to his roots, and another step in the couple's continuing belief in inclusivity and solidarity, a belief to which they clung despite the sudden plunge in political temperature and the rolling-out of Stalinism across eastern Europe.

When Raymond founded BERIM he was, he said, 'un peu fellow traveller':[1] a sympathizer with, but not a member of, the Communist Party. It was a position which both he and Lucie had occupied on and off for nearly fifteen years. Although his directorship of BERIM would bring him, and occasionally Lucie, into increasingly frequent professional contact with Communist Party officials, the fifties saw the estrangement of the Aubracs from their allegiances to both French and international Communism.

The first half of the 1950s saw the Aubracs a happy, settled family. Raymond's career had taken off and Lucie had rediscovered her joy in teaching. Their debts had been reduced and they were able to employ a nanny, giving Lucie the freedom she craved. Participation in commissions investigating the Dark Years and support for peace movements were accompanied by a deep pleasure in family life, and in seeing France recover from its devastation. But in 1956, their belief in their own country and the way of life for which they had risked everything began to waver.

In the year 1956, the rotten centre of international Communism was exposed. In 1952, four years after the Soviet coup d'état in Czechoslovakia, Stalin ordered a purge of dissident and Jewish elements there. Fourteen Communist politicians – eleven of them Jewish – had been tried on trumped-up charges of high treason and espionage. Tortured into making false confessions, most were hanged and three were sentenced to life imprisonment. After Stalin's death in 1953, they were gradually released. When the best-known of the men, Artur London, left prison in 1956, Raymond Aubrac was among those who went to meet him in Prague. There Raymond discovered not only that Artur London's treatment by Communist police was the same as he had himself suffered at the hands of the Gestapo, but that French Communist Party officials had known the men were guilty of nothing all along, and had said nothing.

Both Aubracs watched the long perversion of Communism with great sorrow. Lucie always made a distinction between the Communism of Stalin and that of her wartime Communist comrades, 'so courageous, so devoted … I will always respect their conception of a Socialist ideal for which they gave their lives. That is why I do not accept the demonization of the word "Communist", which has nothing to do with the Stalinist regime.'[2] Asked whether she regretted the years of fellow-travelling, she replied honestly that she 'was not sufficiently discerning', but added that she did not want 'to slip into anti-communism. I thought another society was really possible.'[3] Raymond's condemnation was stronger. He felt wounded by those who had lied: by the leaders of international Communism who 'governed by terror under a mask of idealism' and by the French leaders who lied 'to cover up a terrible truth.'[4]

The same year that Artur London was released in Prague, the leaders of the French Communist Party demonstrated that they too had deviated from early principles and now put colour, race and creed above the universal fraternity of workers. The fifties saw the growth of vigorous independence movements in both the French and British empires. There were uprisings in the Algerian city of Constantine one week after Hitler's suicide and French repression was immediate and brutal. In 1945 France had to present herself as a strong and united country, and losing her empire would undermine her international status. A bloody decade ensued, for independence movements refused to be repressed. Indochina (now Vietnam, Laos and Cambodia) was the first colony to become independent, in April 1954. In November of the same year, freedom movements in France's most precious colony, Algeria, gained momentum when the *maquisards* of the Algerian National Liberation Front launched coordinated attacks throughout the colony with calls for 'the restoration of the Algerian state – sovereign, democratic and social – within the principles of Islam.'[5] The reaction of France's radical-socialist government was swift. The Minister of the Interior, a young François Mitterrand, announced that 'the only negotiation is war', and that 'Algeria is France, and France recognizes no authority except its own.'

The Aubracs were among those who disagreed with this assertion of French sovereignty over a foreign country. For them, there was a clear link between their own defiance of the Nazi Occupation in the 1940s, and Algerian defiance of France in the 1950s. For the Aubracs, 'resistance' was not something emblematically French, something to do with wine and cheese and *terroir* and the spirit of the Marseillaise; something to be wielded only by one European nation against another. It was *le refus*: the universal right to refuse oppression. They were appalled when the French Communist Party agreed to support the sending of troops to crush Algerian independence fighters. This was perhaps the greatest blow of all to Lucie's post-war vision. The Aubracs thought they had shared values with both a republican government and a Communist Party they did not wish to denounce but with which they could no longer travel in harmony. They took the betrayal of these values so seriously that in 1957 they emigrated. Their first destination was Morocco, a French protectorate which had become independent in 1956 and where their old friend Pascal Copeau was working. He suggested to the new Moroccan government that Raymond Aubrac would be a useful person to have on board in creating the infrastructure necessary to modernize the state, and the family moved to Rabat. It was a gesture of solidarity and, for Raymond, the start of a career in what is now called development.

If principle had driven the Aubracs to Morocco, the lovely life they found there certainly helped them stay. They lived in a comfortable villa with their children, able to afford domestic help and indulge their interests. Lucie discovered a new passion for archaeology. Friends came to stay. In 1960, nineteen-year-old Jean-Pierre – no longer Boubou – finished school and returned to France to study medicine: the first chick had flown the nest. In 1961, Lucie started teaching at the local French-government *lycée*, where she signed a petition calling for negotiations to begin to recognize Algerian independence. It would come a year later, declared to the French nation in July 1962 by President de Gaulle.

Seven years after they had arrived in Rabat, Raymond's work came to an end, and in 1963, the family moved to Rome, where Raymond had been offered employment at the UN's Food and Agriculture Organization. It was Lucie who urged him to accept the job, because of the opportunity it would give her to follow her new hobby. Raymond's initial contract was for six months, but they would end up spending twelve years in Italy, their daughters Catherine and Elisabeth successively leaving home. Raymond's work engaged him fully and frequently took him away. His previous contacts with Ho Chi Minh also brought him back to Vietnam for diplomatic visits, and then, after the end of the war with America in 1973, for reconstruction. Occasionally Lucie accompanied him, always interested in meeting new people and seeing new places, but more often she stayed in Rome with her work, her family, her friends and her archaeology. It was Lucie who oversaw the purchase of a family house in the Cévennes; who undertook the correspondence with the children; who ran the house and organized the social life. She relished it: these days as a well-to-do couple, alone together again after the children had gone, were very happy ones. 'He continues to delight me,' she wrote to her younger daughter Elisabeth in 1970, 'and I tell myself that I have been very lucky.'[6]

In 1975, the couple moved on to New York, where Raymond had work at the UN. Lucie explored the city, and beyond, and loved the country she had almost sailed for in 1939. Their happiness there was marred by the death of her mother, aged eighty-seven, who had remained in France. 'Nothing is the same,' she wrote to Elisabeth, 'I am now face to face with my own old age.'[7] She was sixty-three. Louise's death broke the last link with an impoverished childhood. Elegant wife of a senior

UN executive, owner of a country house and a Paris apartment, part of the 'development establishment', Lucie had come a long way. In 1976, Raymond retired and although Lucie would have liked to spend more time exploring the vast continent she had only just discovered, she gave in to his desire to return to France. They sailed aboard the *Queen Elizabeth II* for Cherbourg in July 1976. Taking up residence in their old Parisian apartment, Lucie realized how much her years in other cultures had changed her. A brief note slipped into the box of each of her neighbours in the block of flats announced simply that the Aubracs had returned, and sent their greetings. Outrage! Complaints to the management that these new neighbours had been 'soliciting for business',[8] which was strictly forbidden, shoulders haughtily turned in the foyer, dark looks in the lift ... only one man called, and told the couple he had looked them up in *Who's Who* to know who had been leaving him notes. A simple courtesy in America was an unacceptable intrusion in Paris.

The neighbour's recourse to *Who's Who* to know who his new neighbours were was a neat illustration not only of the culture to which the Aubracs had returned, but of their place within it. Outside their circle of friends, they were pretty much forgotten. That, however, was about to change. The personalities and movements of the Dark Years were about to become the subject of academic and popular scrutiny.

* * *

Among Lucie's memories of her return to a chaotic Brittany in July 1944 was a brutal encounter between a young woman suspected of having slept with a German soldier and a group of men who were shaving her head before an audience. She had intervened.

'This is unacceptable, we are re-establishing the rule of law here. Put this woman in prison if you think it necessary, but keep your hands off her!'

'Piss off,' shouted one of the men, very aggressive. 'Keep out of it or the same thing'll happen to you.'[9]

These *épurations sauvages* – violent purges – were the ugly side of liberation. It is estimated that about ten thousand French citizens were killed before special courts were set up – the *épuration legale*, or legal purge – to take vengeance out of the hands of the mob. Of the 120,000 individuals accused of collaboration, the special courts sentenced nearly seven thousand to death (over half of them in absentia), although only 791 were executed. Pierre Laval, Pétain's chief minister and regarded as the worst of the collaborators, was shot on 15 October 1945, shouting '*Vive la France!*' Henri Béraud, the newspaper editor and *bête noire* of Emmanuel d'Astier in the days of the Last Column, was sentenced to death, but the sentence was commuted to life imprisonment. So was that of Marshal Pétain, now very old and semi-senile, who was one of many pardoned by de Gaulle in the interests of national unity, and sent into life imprisonment on the tiny Breton island Ile d'Yeu. The special courts had largely completed their work by 1949, but suspicions and accusations would disturb French political life for decades.

The 1946 commission on which Lucie had sat, to the anger of her headmaster in Soisy, was only one of several set up by post-war governments in an attempt to investigate the Dark Years and establish some national modus vivendi which would allow France to move forward. In October 1944, there was a Commission on the History of the Occupation and Liberation of France; eight months later, the

Commission of the History of the War was set up; then came the
Commission of the History of the Second World War and a Commission
of the History of the Resistance. There were commissions seeking to
look after victims of the Occupation, to compensate *résistants* and
people who had been deported to concentration camps and ensure their
health needs were met, and to decide where honours should be granted
and where they should be withheld.

One of the very darkest chapters in the history of the Occupation
was the betrayal at Caluire of Max, now known by all to have been the
former parliamentarian and prefect of the Eure-et-Loir, Jean Moulin.
Moulin's bravery in June and November 1940, the derring-do of his
regular parachuting in and his undercover life, his complete refusal to
speak under horrendous torture in June 1943 and the final brutality of
his death had made him a national hero. That status was supported, in
part engineered, by the fact he had been the personal representative of
the man who became president of post-war France, General de Gaulle,
but Moulin had not only been manoeuvred into the forefront of national
memory by politics: he had left an indelible mark on those who knew
him. Many *résistants* might have disagreed with Moulin in 1943 about
politics or wartime strategy, but he had inspired devotion, respect and
affection. He was not only brave and intelligent, he was *sympathique*,
that most elusive and powerful quality. He had been betrayed, and his
betrayer must be found.

The man at whom the finger was most unwaveringly pointed was
still René Hardy, the only man to escape from the doctor's surgery
at Caluire, and again from Lucie's attempt to kill him with poisoned
jam. Another fissure in the united resistance had opened up in 1945
when, despite widespread distrust, Hardy was briefly given a place in
government, reporting to the former Combat *patron* Henri Frenay who

had been appointed Minister for Prisoners, Deportees and Refugees. Hardy's period in office was brief. In December 1945, a report turned up in the SS archives in Lyon. Known as the 'Flora report', 'Flora' being the German codename for the Caluire operation, it dated from July 1943 and stated baldly and without any possibility of misinterpretation that Hardy had enabled the arrest of Jean Moulin.

This apparent proof led to a bitterly contested trial which drove a wedge still further between former colleagues. Combat's Henri Frenay and Pierre de Bénouville were among Hardy's supporters, while Lucie and Raymond Aubrac, Serge Asher-Ravanel and others from Lib-Sud were among the most relentless of his accusers. Despite the 'Flora report', Hardy was acquitted in January 1947 because his lawyer persuaded the court that German documents were inherently untrustworthy and should not therefore be admitted as evidence. Hardy and his supporters left the court triumphant but, just two months later, a second document turned up which appeared to prove he had lied. Once again, Hardy was committed for trial.

This time, the incriminating paper came from the couchette department of the national railways archive, written by a French conductor on the Paris–Lyon express train. It stated that German officials arrested a passenger named René Hardy on 7 June at Chalon-sur-Saône and removed him from the train. This was the smoking gun, as it proved that first, Hardy had been arrested just before General Delestraint, head of the Secret Army, was seized in Paris and the Gestapo raided Caluire; and that second, against all the rules, he had not told his resistance comrades of the arrest, and broken off all contact with them. This time Hardy went before a military tribunal. The Aubracs were again called on for their evidence and they were trenchant and implacable in their accusations – but Hardy was given the benefit of the doubt and acquitted by a majority of one.

A few days later, Raymond was invited to a meeting in a house near the Trocadero where a pistol lay on the table. What transpired gave him such horrors that he would not talk about the meeting for over half a century. Hardy's 'friends' were there, he said. Despite the acquittal, they had been persuaded by the new evidence that their man was indeed guilty. Hardy was on holiday on Lake Constance, and their plan was to kidnap him, bring him in for interrogation and then induce him to shoot himself. Raymond was violently opposed to any such extrajudicial procedure: it was, he said, vital to follow the rule of law. Hardy remained alive and free.

The 'legal purge' tribunals set up to try collaborators finished their work in July 1949 and by then many people wished to leave the destructive divisions of the war behind. Responding to the national mood and the continuing dominance of Gaullist ideology, a comforting narrative was spun around the Dark Years with almost the same speed as the one that had been spun around Pétain's National Revolution. The French and anyone who read about them were soon presented with the thesis that Pétain's government had accepted power only because Pétain and his associates thought they could more easily protect French interests from within a German-dominated state than from without. It was what people like Henri Frenay and even Serge Asher-Ravanel had believed in 1940, and was now presented as fact. According to this version of events, Vichy had continually attempted to sabotage German policies by procrastination, inactivity and deliberate inefficiency. *Bref*, there had simply been a few bad apples in the French barrel.

There was a second element to this iron-fisted Gaullist rewriting. As the Gaullist government conjured up a collective memory of an entire nation of resisters, the true *résistants* and *résistantes* receded from view. In particular, the glorious heterogeneity of the real resistance was suppressed, and in its place emerged a republican, Christian or at least agnostic, rather conservative entity, of which the French republican civil servant Jean Moulin was the apogee. In 1964, Moulin's remains were removed to the Panthéon in Paris. As streets, places and boulevards all over France were named after *résistants*, and blue plaques went up at the places where men and women had 'died for France', the resistance was sanitized and Frenchified. No street was named after the Polish Communist Jew Joseph Epstein. The Spanish republicans who had fought fascism in their own country and then again in France went unrecorded.

When the Aubracs returned to France from New York in 1976, however, the discourse around the Dark Years was changing. The wartime generation might still be in power, but a new one was coming up behind them, and some thought it was time to look more closely at what, really, had happened in France. In 1972, an American historian, Robert Paxton, published a bombshell book. Dissatisfied with the prevailing opinions, he did what French historians had not done, and consulted German archives. The evidence he turned up of Vichy's eager, even proactive, collaboration with the Nazis resulted in *Vichy France: Old Guard and New Order 1940–44*. Paxton bluntly and convincingly showed that Vichy had not provided resistance from within, but had included senior members (Marshal Pétain himself was exonerated) who had even taken the initiative in persuading Hitler to let them collaborate. Paxton concluded that the Nazis would have been willing to let Vichy get on with running its part of France, if only to save on German administrative resources, and that it had been Vichy which had gone running to its German masters with ideas and results. *La vraie France, la France eternelle*, Paxton said, was not composed of people like the Aubracs and Jean Moulin but of people who had welcomed in the Germans as a force of law and order; a means to repress the left-leaning, socially avant-garde interwar society which they feared and mistrusted; a means to cleanse France of Jews and degenerates, bring back the proper balance between the sexes and the classes, and ensure the power of the Catholic church.

The first reaction to Paxton's book in France was of fury. Senior French academics denounced him as an amateur historian (a former Rhodes Scholar, he had received a doctorate from Harvard and taught history at Columbia University in New York); only eight when war broke out, they said he was too young to be able to pronounce on the war (a strange claim to make against any historian); as an American, he could not understand the subtleties and peculiarities of occupation; he was *not French* and therefore had no right to pronounce judgement. In one televised debate, the President of the Pétain Association told Paxton to his face that he was a liar. Paxton stood firm.

The 1970s saw not only the retrieval of new evidence by Paxton and others but a change in historical priorities. The Holocaust began to dominate Second World War studies, displacing the resistance as the central element in France's collective memories of the Occupation. Paxton's next book was specifically on Vichy's role in the deportation of Jews, a task which led him into severe depression. His conclusion was that Vichy had cooperated to a level 'virtually unparalleled' in Europe and that seventy-two thousand Jews, French and 'foreign', had been handed to the death camps virtually by French efforts alone.

When such painful facts were put in the public domain, it was inevitable that people began asking questions not just about what had really happened under Vichy, but about which members of the current political establishment had something to hide. As the belief in widespread resistance was challenged, politicians began to manipulate the questions being raised for their own purposes. The centrist Right which had governed France since the end of the Second World War was under increasing threat from a left-wing alliance under François Mitterrand, and people on both sides were wondering if stories from the past could be unearthed to destabilize or discredit their enemies. Just before the presidential elections of 1981, the satirical newspaper *Le Canard Enchaîné* published startling new evidence about the Budget Minister Maurice Papon. Papon had been a senior civil servant under Vichy, escaped condemnation by the post-war special tribunals and gone on to develop a very successful political and business career. Documents had just been found which proved he had also been responsible for deporting 1,690 Jews from Bordeaux during the war. Partly because of the Papon scandal, François Mitterrand won the election and among his first acts as President was the laying of a rose on the tomb of Jean Moulin in the Panthéon. Nonetheless, there were questions about Mitterrand's own youthful membership of the far-right *La Cagoule*, his relatively late entrance into the resistance, his association with André Bettencourt of the L'Oréal company, who had written anti-Semitic articles during the Occupation, and worst of all the infamous photograph which had recently surfaced showing him being awarded a medal by Pétain.

War records, war secrets, war shames: they were all a constant bubbling undercurrent to political life in France when the Aubracs returned. When it was announced in 1983 that Klaus Barbie, 'the Butcher of Lyon', would be returning to that city to stand trial for his actions during the Dark Years, joy was mingled with fear that some very uncomfortable stones were going to be turned over.

* * *

What had happened to Klaus Barbie? After fleeing Lyon in 1944, he lived briefly in Germany under a variety of aliases. The Americans identified him as early as 1945 and interrogated him about his activities in Lyon, when he told them that René Hardy had betrayed Jean Moulin. They employed him to infiltrate the Soviet zone of Berlin: a German-speaking expert on penetrating Communist networks was too valuable to be given up, whatever atrocities he had committed. When the French government requested Barbie's extradition after René Hardy's second trial in 1950, the CIA spirited him out of Europe down one of the Nazi ratlines to South America, where he lived an undisturbed and prosperous life for over twenty years, offering consultancy to dictatorships on how to suppress left-wing dissidence.

In 1972, the German Nazi-hunter Beate Klarsfeld had positive information that an elderly gentleman living in the Bolivian capital of La Paz and going by the name of Klaus Altmann was in fact Klaus Barbie. A French documentary team flew in and managed, at considerable personal risk, to track him down and briefly interview him. They were taken aback to find a small, quietly spoken man, nothing like the tall, booted and capped German officer of their imagination. Before they were told to stop filming, they asked him who betrayed Jean Moulin and his reply, reproduced in the newspaper *France Soir*, was clear. It was René Hardy. The team took its film immediately to the French Embassy in La Paz, from where it was flown to Paris. Raymond Aubrac was one of three of Barbie's former victims asked to identify him from a clip. In Raymond's careful recital of the traits he recognized in 'Klaus Altmann' there was a sickening intimacy, legacy of the relationship between abused and abuser; 'the mouth, the lips, certain facial expressions, the shape of his face, the way he had of lowering his eyes then suddenly looking up, the way he turned his head … when I looked at the picture of him, I felt fear."[10]

Despite the positive identification of Klaus Altmann as Klaus Barbie, he was still safe in his new life, for French efforts to extradite him were thwarted by the Bolivian government. Nor, privately, were French officials and politicians united in their approval of extradition even if the Bolivians agreed. A British Secret Service report of February 1972 was blunt, if mistaken, in its view of Jean Moulin's personal politics. The French government was dragging its feet over extradition, because it feared 'Altmann' would make embarrassing revelations. Jean Moulin, the British agent told his masters, had been a Communist. In 1943, he had been betrayed to Klaus Barbie not by a Gestapo informer, but by Gaullist *résistants* who believed he was working for Moscow and fatally undermining General de Gaulle's own influence over the resistance. Since some of those same Gaullists, the agent concluded, now held positions of power they were desperate to prevent Altmann from speaking.

It took ten years to extradite Barbie. In February 1982, intermediaries arranged another interview between French TV journalists and the man still calling himself 'Klaus Altmann'. 'I am not Barbie,' he replied in German to the journalist's question in French. 'My name is Klaus Altmann. I was born in 1915, in Berlin.' Asked in French if he had ever been to Lyon, he replied, in German, that he had not. He said he could not speak French. Given a photo of Jean Moulin, he said he had never met him. '*Who betrayed Jean Moulin?*' shouted the journalist as 'Altmann' left the room, but this time he did not answer. A year later, the Bolivian dictatorship fell, and Barbie lost his protectors. He was extradited and arrived on French soil in February 1983, and the French Minister of Justice decided that 'he must go to the place he committed

his crimes. He must, in his turn, spend the night in a cell there, awaiting
his fate.[11]

Forty years had gone by since Barbie had tortured Raymond in the
School of Military Medicine and sent his battered body back to Montluc
prison each night. He and Lucie watched the television footage on the
night of 5 February 1983: a van drawing up outside Montluc amid
immense crowds, a pale face glimpsed between the bars on the back
window; constant flashbulbs; police keeping back protestors. 'What
would you say to him?' an eager journalist rang to enquire. 'I would
say,' Raymond replied, in his inimitable style, 'welcome back, my dear
friend'.[12] But Barbie stayed in Montluc only a week, for photos in the
press gave the precise location of his cell, and assassination before he
came to trial was all too likely. Already one former victim had been
arrested making her way to Lyon with a gun in her bag, determined to
shoot her torturer.

With Barbie's extradition, the French media inevitably turned to a re-
examination of the events at Caluire and the controversy surrounding
Moulin's betrayal. In anticipation of renewed scrutiny of his role, René
Hardy had spent much of 1983 writing a book defending himself.[13]
A documentary by the film-maker Claude Bal showed him as a wild-
haired, wild-eyed man, seriously unwell, accusing Moulin of being a
Communist and denying he had ever had anyone arrested. Hardy
pointed the finger at two others. The first was Pierre de Bénouville,
formerly Captain Frenay's second-in-command at Combat and now a
close associate of President Mitterrand. Bénouville, Hardy claimed, had
known in June 1943 that he was under German surveillance following
his arrest on the Lyon–Paris train and subsequent interrogation by
Klaus Barbie, but had sent him to Caluire anyway, advising him to play
the dangerous game of double agent.

The other man onto whom Hardy attempted to deflect suspicion, initially to the bemusement of those who heard his claims, was Lib-Sud's Raymond Aubrac. How, Hardy asked, was it possible that a Jew and a Communist could have escaped immediate execution when arrested by the Gestapo? But the Germans had held Aubrac for over two months, in unknown conditions. Beneath the suggestion lay a subtext which could have come from the 1930s: who had sought to bring down France, to carry out a subterranean, poisonous, secret work? A Communist Jew. Who betrayed Jean Moulin? Raymond Aubrac, with the aid of his Communist wife.

The Claude Bal documentary, *Que la vérité est amère* (How bitter is the truth), also featured interviews with Maître Jacques Vergès, a fifty-eight-year-old mixed-race Franco-Vietnamese lawyer who had just taken on Klaus Barbie's defence. In certain ways, Vergès had much in common with the Aubracs. Like theirs, his personal and professional life had been conditioned by a hatred of racism and colonialism, although in Vergès' case this was largely because of the discrimination he had himself faced. However, this had led Vergès, unlike the Aubracs, to a hatred of France itself and he had dedicated his career to exposing *French* racism and imperialism. As a very young man in the French colony of Réunion, he had joined the wartime resistance, and later found his way to the Free French. Immediately after the Liberation, however, he discovered that French nationalism was inseparably linked to French imperialism – the same discovery the Aubracs had sadly made when the troops went into Algeria. Years before that, even as the Nuremberg trials were beginning, French forces had been crushing revolt in Madagascar and Vergès' mother's homeland of Vietnam. Vergès made his name during the Algerian War of Independence, defending 'terrorists', one of whom he married, converting to Islam when he did so and beginning the next great fight of his personal and professional life, against what he considered to be the illegitimacy of Israel.

Vergès was already famous in France, a favourite of the media to whom he gave lively conferences and juicy, outrageous quotes. His preferred method of running a trial was 'attacking the prosecution'. Muscling his way onto Barbie's defence team, he determined that the forthcoming trial would not be so much of his client, as of French hypocrisy. The question he would force the court, the witnesses and the country to answer would not be whether Barbie was guilty, but what right France had to prosecute him for offences during the Nazi Occupation which the French had themselves carried out in their colonies.

For Vergès, the resistance which he had once joined had proved itself as hypocritical as any other element of French life when it failed to give united support to colonized peoples seeking independence. Perhaps it was the René Hardy documentary which gave him the idea of how best to undermine its legacy, which would not only satisfy his personal grievance but further muddy the already dirty waters in which his Nazi client swam: any dividing tactic would have worked, any nasty insinuation would have been as good as any other – but Raymond Aubrac had been accused by Hardy of one of the greatest crimes of the Occupation. Vergès picked up the ball he was thrown and ran as fast as he could with it, stating on camera that Aubrac, like René Hardy, had been released by Klaus Barbie, and since Hardy had been obliged to give an explanation for that release, then so too should Raymond Aubrac. The Aubracs came out fighting. Their first riposte to the accusations was to sue for slander. Lucie's second was to give her own account of what had happened in 1943.

Forty years had passed since Lucie's resistance work. She had already written several accounts of it, and that of the larger resistance movements of which she was a part. Her first accounts were given to the British and Free French debriefers and journalists on her arrival in London in February 1944. In September 1945, newly in France, she gave a colourful interview to the Communist newspaper *La Marseillaise*, and in October 1945 she published the book which caused such displeasure to Communist headquarters. She also delivered a private report on her wartime actions to the Communist Party in February 1946. At René Hardy's two trials, she had again described her actions in statements which were transcribed in the court reports. Emphases were different among these versions – her contact with this rather than that person was stressed, occasionally she got dates and places wrong – but the broad narrative of her time in the resistance, particularly during the vital months of 1943, was the same: the early adherence to d'Astier and Lib-Sud; the newspaper, the attempts to rescue imprisoned comrades; the arrest of Raymond in March, the threats to the Attorney General and Raymond's release; his second arrest in May, the wedding plot and the rescue in October.

Nevertheless, while she had aimed for these accounts to be historical testimony, her lifelong passion for storytelling had increasingly played upon her memories of war just as they had upon her memories of childhood. Lucie's resistance friends, urging her to write a new book after Vergès' accusations, reminded her that she was, after all, a historian even if it was a long time since she had taught history. But 'the archives bored me,' she said bluntly. 'They put me off.'[14] Instead, she found a solution which served the immediate purpose while allowing her the freedom she had always demanded to create her own story. 'One night, I had the idea of writing it like a diary. That would allow me to evoke particular memories without having to describe the whole resistance.'[15] Her old pupil Simone Kaminker, now the film star Simone Signoret, put her in touch with helpful editors and a deal was done.

Entitled *Ils partiront dans l'ivresse*, after the message transmitted by the BBC in February 1944,[16] and translated into English as *Outwitting the Gestapo*, the book which Lucie published in 1984 was a memoir written in impressionistic style and largely in the present tense, as if being jotted in a diary at the time the events were lived.[17] It recorded Lucie's life in her triple capacities of wife, mother and *résistante* and was crafted around her pregnancy with Catherine. 'Like all mothers,' she wrote, 'I carried her for nine months … She was conceived on 14 May, 1943,'[18] the day that Raymond was released after his first arrest. A critical and popular success, the book catapulted Lucie, now aged seventy-three, back into the limelight in which she had found herself in 1944. 'A hugely valuable eye witness account from an exceptional woman,' ran a typical review.[19]

The publication of her book and the great publicity around Barbie's extradition introduced Lucie to a large new audience by way of television. A prime-time talk show called *Apostrophes* dedicated one broadcast to 'rebels', which saw Lucie in a lively exchange with the man who had defended Marshal Pétain in his post-war trial for treason. She put him energetically right on both his partisan assessment of de Gaulle as 'ignoble', and the fate of her old friend Jean Cavaillès, whom a collaborating novelist named Robert Brasillach had claimed to have saved, but who Lucie knew too well had been executed by firing squad. Her new celebrity, and her introduction to a generation which did not know the Aubrac name, was soon matched by state recognition. As interest in the now elderly band who had defended *la vraie France* during the Dark Years revived, President Mitterrand made Lucie Commander of the Légion d'Honneur in March 1985. It was a vote of public and governmental confidence. ('Disobeying the order of the officer in charge of protocol, she 'ostentatiously stepped forward on my left foot instead of my right.')[20] She was interviewed by newspapers and magazines, her opinion sought not only on the resistance but also on the issues of the day. She was always trenchant, robust, elegant and strong, despite her health having begun to fail. It seemed the Aubracs had quashed any suspicions raised by René Hardy and his lawyer.

The case against Barbie took four years to prepare. The judge in charge had to decide what, specifically, were the charges on which he was to be tried. Dozens of lawyers contacted him, representing families of *résistants* whom Barbie had tortured or killed; Jewish survivors, Jewish organizations, families of Jewish victims; the city of Lyon itself. The French Statute of Limitations did not allow most crimes committed more than twenty years ago to be prosecuted, but crimes against humanity were an exception. It was finally decided, therefore, that Barbie would be prosecuted not for his persecution of the resistance, but for his role in the Final Solution, and specifically his role in the deportation in April 1944 of forty-four Jewish children from a home in the small town of Izieu, east of Lyon, whom he sent to Poland just weeks before France was liberated.

* * *

The prosecution of Klaus Barbie began on 11 May 1987, in a special courtroom with seating for seven hundred people and, unusually, with cameras present. It was to be a traumatic and long-drawn-out affair. Although the charge related to the deportation of the Jewish children, victim after victim of other atrocities were invited *by the defence* to give evidence. Cathartic though it was for them to tell their terrible stories, it was also part of Vergès' own plan. Barbie refused to attend and as each witness was examined, Vergès twisted the questioning back to his main point: how could France try his client for acts it had itself carried out elsewhere? Under his adroit management, the trial, which should have been that of a blatantly guilty man faced with mountains of evidence, turned into 'a four-year war of legal attrition and, in the process ... acquired an entirely new nature. On the night of the verdict, it seemed as if the original issue, the justice of Klaus Barbie, had been lost in a sea of unwanted questions and discomforting moral dilemmas.'[21] But although Vergès' attacks succeeded in generating a great deal of painful coverage, soul-searching, reflection and fury, they were not in the end allowed to divert the court from deciding whether Barbie was guilty of the specific charges brought against him. For that, there could only be one verdict. On 4 July 1987, Barbie was sentenced to life imprisonment. His client had lost, but Vergès believed he had achieved what he sought: that he had forced the French to face up to their wartime collaboration, and their own role in repressing the legitimate resistance of other peoples.

One result of the spotlight shone by Barbie's trial on the role of wartime resistance was that the subject returned to prominence in schools and universities. The year after her return to France, in 1976, Lucie had been asked to address a group of high-school children by a Jewish woman who had survived deportation. She had not enjoyed or repeated the experience because 'excessive personalisation annoys me.'[22] Presumably she had been asked too much about 'how she felt' and too few hard questions about solidarity and oppression. Other *résistants* and deportees, she knew, had approached schools, asking to be allowed to talk to younger generations about the Dark Years, determined their sacrifice should continue to have meaning, but the schools had largely refused. 'All that changed with the Barbie trial in 1987'. Now invitations flooded in to *résistants* and deportees, so many 'we had trouble replying to them all.'[23] The famous author of *Ils partiront dans l'ivresse* was sought after. She was delighted to accept the invitations and equally delighted to find a new generation better able to engage with the questions she wanted them to consider.

Lucie Aubrac took on her new role with gusto. Everywhere she could, she presented the resistance as she had always fought for it to be: a movement of solidarity, whose values were still germane. She was heartened to find the questions from this new generation of listeners more thoughtful, 'less anecdotal than before ... more concerned with deeper motivations ... For the children of the first baby-boom, those born between 1940 and 1960, we belonged to the past.' For the next generation, they were the nation's conscience. And 'judging your father's behaviour is not easy. It's simpler with your grandfather.'[24] Her question and answer sessions were not just a matter of describing her own life during the Occupation, but also a call to vigilance. Nazism might be a thing of the past, but racism was not. The 1980s were years of riots in the large French cities. There were anti-immigrant demonstrations by French people who feared the influx of thousands, largely Muslim and African, into France, and anti-racist demonstrations such as *Touche pas à mon pote* (hands off my mate) which were backed by France's vocal left-wing celebrities. Racism, Lucie wanted her young listeners to know, had not disappeared along with the yellow star.

She enjoyed the work immensely, despite the onset in 1985 of a disease which gradually destroyed her sight. Soon, she found she could no longer read or write and within a couple of years her visual world was reduced to vague shapes. In one of the most touching elements of the Aubracs' long love-affair, Raymond devoted hours of his time to recording entire books for her to listen to. Outside the privacy of their house, Lucie did not let her increasing blindness slow her down. She had always shunned and detested pity; she had never allowed what others might perceive as disadvantage to stand in her way. Criss-crossing the country, she continued to perform in hundreds of classrooms, putting on and taking off her glasses as if they made any difference; spreading notes on a table in front of her as if she could see them. It was a denial of, and a challenge to, what was happening to her: a final disobedience in the face of the laws of nature.

In 1990, there was a postscript to the Klaus Barbie trial. France's laws had not allowed criminal charges to be brought against him for his torture of *résistants*, but the failure to make him answer for so much suffering had angered many. As his trial for crimes against humanity began, a civil action was also brought against him, by the families of Bruno Larat and André Lassagne, two *résistants* arrested at Caluire alongside Raymond Aubrac. Both men had been transferred from Lyon to Paris, and then deported to concentration camps where Larat had died and Lassagne, an old friend of the David brothers, had been liberated in 1945. As Barbie began his life sentence in 1987, therefore, he and Jacques Vergès had begun to prepare the defence against this new charge. The disgust which Vergès had aroused for his manner of defending Barbie had not swayed his convictions. He was determined to run the new trial as he had the last: defending his client by launching an attack on the prosecution. This time, Vergès' counter-accusation was aimed specifically at two people whom he had tried but failed to bring down during the trial just ended, but who had instead found themselves elevated to the status of resistance icons: Lucie and Raymond Aubrac.

Klaus Barbie, now very sick with the cancer which would soon kill him, did not attend his second trial. Questions were put to him in his prison cell about the transfers from Lyon to Paris of Bruno Larat and

André Lassagne and Vergès read his answer in open court. Why did Barbie not transfer Raymond Aubrac to Paris with most of the other men arrested with Jean Moulin? According to a statement read to the court by Jacques Vergès, the reason was that Raymond Aubrac, threatened with the death penalty, had agreed to work for Klaus Barbie.

The tiny hook on which this momentous accusation of treachery hung was this: a frail scrap of evidence had turned up suggesting that Raymond's first arrest had not been on 15 March 1943, as he and Lucie had always claimed, but on 13 March. During those two 'lost' days, Vergès now alleged, he had been 'turned' by the Gestapo, and persuaded to betray the comrades arrested on 15 March at 7 Rue de l'Hôtel de Ville (Serge Asher-Ravanel and Maurice Kriegel-Valrimont) and, a little later, Jean Moulin and the others at Caluire. The 'evidence' for this claim was a document found in German archives which had not previously been considered. A report on the arrests written at the time by Officer Kaltenbrunner of the Gestapo, to whom Barbie had delegated the matter, it stated that Raymond Aubrac had been arrested on 13 March. And if that were thought to be inadmissible, or judged to be a simple typing error, Maître Vergès had another 'proof' up his sleeve. At René Hardy's second trial, Raymond Aubrac himself had referred to his arrest as occurring on 13 March. For Vergès, this was no mere confusion of dates or slip in the memory of chaotic events which took place decades ago: it was a fatal mistake in which Aubrac revealed the truth he had attempted to keep hidden for over forty years: he and his wife had become Gestapo agents and betrayed Jean Moulin.

Lucie appeared on television to denounce this extraordinary accusation, and the press, again, pronounced its disgust at the lawyer's tired and disgraceful tactics. It was pointed out that Barbie had never previously mentioned Raymond Aubrac's name in connection with

Caluire, and that when interviewed by his own superior officers in Paris just after the arrests, he had named René Hardy, as he had when interviewed by the Americans in 1948, and again when he was discovered in Bolivia in 1972. The Americans had specifically asked him why Raymond Aubrac was kept in Montluc prison in Lyon when the others were transferred to Paris, and his reply had been 'I do not know why Aubrac stayed in Lyon.'[25] So why did he suddenly produce this apparent recollection of Raymond Aubrac's treachery now?[26] Was Barbie a simple mouthpiece for Vergès, or, knowing he did not have long to live, was this a last desperate attempt to prolong his trial and spend some of his remaining years in relative freedom?

The civil case brought by Larat's and Lassagne's families went on for months. In July 1991, the judge was given a sixty-three-page document apparently penned by the dying defendant, which Vergès claimed was an exhaustive account of events leading to the arrests at Caluire, and in particular of Raymond Aubrac's alleged treachery. What Vergès announced pompously as his client's 'Testament' was almost certainly not produced by Klaus Barbie, despite being written in the first person, but by Vergès himself with the help of researchers. In fact, it came too late for the renewed sensation which Vergès wished: when German police files proved that Barbie had been ordered by his superiors to send Bruno Larat and André Lassagne to Paris, the civil case against him had to be dropped, to the families' great distress. The 'Testament' was never produced in court. A few weeks later, Barbie died of cancer and it seemed that Vergès' painful pseudo-revelations and attempt to rake muck had to cease. But Vergès had not finished. Despite the convictions for slander against Vergès and René Hardy following the documentary in which Hardy had first made his accusations against Raymond Aubrac, Vergès began leaking revelations in the 'Testament' which repeated them, and these appeared to inculpate Lucie, too:

> The German police's trusted man at the head of the Secret Army
> was Raymond Aubrac.
> Aubrac was the first to know the time and place of the meeting, he
> had known it since the Saturday evening.
> Mme Aubrac telephoned me on the Sunday to tell me about it.
> Mme Aubrac's visits to the offices of the Gestapo in Lyon [when
> attempting to arrange the fake marriage] show that she had been
> known there since May when, her husband having been freed, she
> agreed to work as a liaison agent between him and us.[27]

Perhaps the strangest claim of all those made in the 'Testament' was that
the attack on the Gestapo van in the Boulevard des Hirondelles was in
fact mounted by an entirely different resistance group and that, having
got wind of it, Barbie allowed it to go ahead as an opportunity to release
Raymond Aubrac. Contradicted by a mass of evidence, including the
testimonies of the surviving members of Serge Asher-Ravanel's *groupe
franc*, Vergès' would-be sensational accusations and the story pieced
together to support them were denounced by the vast majority of media
and did nothing to dislodge Lucie and Raymond Aubrac from the status
of revered senior citizens. The invitations kept coming. Lucie was asked
to participate in conferences at American universities; a film named
*Boulevard des Hirondelles* appeared, based on the rescue in October
1943, and she continued to travel across France to talk to schoolchildren.
In 1995, President Jacques Chirac made her a Grand Officer of the
Légion d'Honneur. 'From the first hours of the occupation,' he said,
'she rose up against defeatism and surrender. She was an emblematic
figure of the central role of women in the Resistance.'[28] The same year,

the film director Claude Berri, fresh from the success of *Jean de Florette*, came to see the couple about adapting Lucie's 1984 book as a film. Neither Aubrac was particularly taken by Berri, his angle on the story or the resulting media circus, but Lucie saw it as an extension of her work keeping alive memories of resistance, and gave her permission, with all profits going to the Resistance Foundation, a recently founded charity dedicated to the same aim. For the vast majority, the Aubracs had become an iconic part of French history: the *couple mythique de la résistance française*, representing all that was good about the nation. Vergès' smears had failed.

* * *

In early 1997, both Aubracs participated in advance publicity for Claude Berri's much-trailed film *Lucie Aubrac*, alongside its stars Daniel Auteuil and Carole Bouquet. Expectations were varied. The Aubracs knew there would be tension between what they knew to have really happened and the commercial requirements of a film production company which knew its audiences might have little idea of the background. Berri was not giving a history lesson; he was telling a love story against a historical backdrop and ramping up the drama.

*Lucie Aubrac* came out in February 1997. Its respectable if not enormous commercial success was matched by a patchy reception from critics, whose consensus was that the film portrayed an appealing romance, and featured some good performances and nice period detail, but was essentially empty. The historians invited into the arts pages for the occasion took that criticism further, lamenting the fact that Berri's film gave no time to the political context and complexity of the resistance, and in particular the bitter rivalries within it. It was, they said, a politically correct, sanitized version of the resistance, in which all the goodies were on one clearly defined and united side and all the baddies were on the other.

But not everyone found the film anodyne. Many of the protagonists were dead, including René Hardy, whom Berri's script made no bones of fingering as the man responsible for betraying Jean Moulin. After years of illness and reclusion, Hardy had died a few days before Klaus Barbie's trial began, near the town of Niort in Deux-Sèvres. 'You will see,' he told a journalist in one of his last interviews. 'People will be fighting [about the accusations] even over my dead body.'[29] In March 1997, Raymond Aubrac attended a première of the film in Niort, followed by a debate. In the audience were Marie-Claire Boutet, Hardy's companion at the time of his death, and his daughter Sophie. Both publicly attacked Raymond: Boutet with the reminder that her lover had been acquitted twice, and Sophie with a cry from the heart. 'You,' she accused Raymond, 'have cast a shadow over my whole life by saying that René Hardy was guilty.'[30] Raymond did not back down. He had, he replied, an 'intimate conviction' of Hardy's responsibility for Moulin's betrayal. It was about to be challenged, yet again, and by a tougher combatant than Sophie Hardy. The same month, Raymond and Lucie heard that a book was about to be published which promised to burst the bombshell which Maître Vergès had tried unsuccessfully to explode in 1987.

The book was entitled *Aubrac, Lyon 1943*, and its author, the Lyon historian and journalist Gérard Chauvy, intended it to be iconoclastic. It was first trailed in a history magazine the same day *Lucie Aubrac* reached the screen, under the title *The Three Aubrac Mysteries*, and was marketed as an attempt to subject 'Legend' to the more rigorous requirements of 'History'. The book consisted of 267 pages of dense text, centred around Chauvy's contention that, although Barbie's 'Testament' could not be regarded as impartial, it was impossible to act as if it did not exist. Chauvy did not explicitly defend the accusations thrown out by Hardy and Vergès – they had, after all, been condemned as slander – but instead exposed the mass of inconsistencies in all the evidence which had come to light about the arrests in Caluire, and particularly in the many accounts the Aubracs themselves had given. Reproducing Barbie's entire 'Testament' as one of his twenty-one appendices, he left it to readers to draw their own conclusions.

Chauvy's book was front page news in the French newspapers and made the main television news broadcasts for several days. Most of the press condemned the renewed attacks on the Aubracs. Chauvy was derided, as Robert Paxton had been in 1973, as an 'amateur historian', but he fought back. The Aubracs had put their story into the public realm, he said, and had thus made it a legitimate area of examination. The fact that they were revered resistance figures did not mean their accounts of historical events were sacrosanct, or could not be compared with others, as all historical evidence should be used to illuminate the truth. Moreover, the 'Testament' was a document with legal standing, submitted as evidence during a court case even if not in the end called upon: it could not simply be dismissed. Chauvy's editor came to his defence, suggesting that it was time to put patriotic fervour aside and subject the legend of the resistance to the same historical examination as any other episode.

Chauvy's questions were supported by his painstaking assembly of documents and testimonies taken from German, French and British sources. First of all, there were the three documents dating from 1943. The first of these was the 'Kaltenbrunner report' of 27 May 1943, drawn up by a Gestapo officer, which appeared to incriminate Raymond by recording his arrest as having happened on 13, not 15, March 1943. The other two, on the other hand, pointed to Hardy's guilt. The 'Flora report' of July 1943 was written after the arrests at Caluire and stated that Hardy had been responsible for giving the information leading to those arrests. Lastly the report from the couchette assistant proved Hardy had been arrested by the Gestapo on the train to Paris, a few days before the betrayal of first General Delestraint and then Jean Moulin.

As well as these, Chauvy reproduced or quoted from the testimonies given at René Hardy's two trials by many witnesses for defence and prosecution, including Raymond and Lucie Aubrac; interviews given by the Aubracs and other former *résistants* since the war; debriefings of hundreds of *résistants* in London, Algiers and France; and dozens of memoirs and contributions made to commissions and committees. And even Chauvy's harshest critics could not deny that comparison of these did indeed show that while Raymond Aubrac could not be definitively proven guilty, there were what he called many 'evident improbabilities', even in the Aubracs' own accounts.[31] A pardonable lapse given either pressure of events (in the earliest testimonies, for example their debriefings in London in February 1944); or passage of time (in the later ones, such as Lucie's book *Outwitting the Gestapo*)? Or a deliberate attempt to spin a web of obfuscation around a terrible truth?

Raising Vergès' old question as to whether Raymond Aubrac had been arrested on 13 or 15 March 1943, Chauvy went on to ponder which of his identities had in fact been known to the Germans at the time of that first arrest. If they really believed he was François Vallet, small-time black marketeer, he would have been no use to them as a double agent. But if they had realized he was in fact 'Balmont' or 'Aubrac', senior officer of the Secret Army, he was worth a great deal. Now, sometimes Raymond had said since then that the Gestapo had not realized that François Vallet was the same person as Raymond

Aubrac, but on other occasions he had said either he did not know, or that possibly they had. So which was it? When Chauvy moved on to explore Lucie's role in releasing her husband, he reached the tentative conclusion that despite all claims to the contrary, she had had no role at all in rescuing him either in May or October 1943, and that another agency – by implication, the Gestapo – had been behind both releases. 'I don't claim to explain everything,' Chauvy told *Le Journal du Dimanche*. 'I simply state that the hagiographical accounts that have been produced up to now are unacceptable.'[32] The Aubracs, he pointed out, had been 'happy to present themselves to the world as the emblematic Resistance couple, in their interviews, in their many publications' and in Berri's recent film.[33]

The Aubracs sued Chauvy for slander as they had successfully sued Claude Bal after his documentary was broadcast in 1984, and it seemed that Chauvy's attack would be dismissed as those of René Hardy and Jacques Vergès had been. In the newspaper *L'Évènement du Jeudi* an angry letter appeared, signed by nineteen surviving *résistants*. It was an absolute rebuttal of Chauvy's insinuations. 'We will not accept this strategy of [sowing] suspicion, insinuation and rumour; it is morally contemptible and historically (as real historians know) unfounded.'[34] Within months, resistance historian François Delpla published *Aubrac: the Facts and the Slander*, which answered Chauvy point by point, and yet another archival document exonerating Raymond was produced. This last was a police report dating the arrest of the inexperienced liaison agent whose list of addresses, found by the Germans in his sock in March 1943, had caused the arrest of Raymond, Serge Asher-Ravanel and Maurice Kriegel-Valrimont in the Rue de l'Hôtel de Ville. That police report dated the agent's arrest as having taken place on the night of 13–14 March: as Raymond's own arrest had been subsequent to the liaison agent's, it was impossible that he had been arrested on 13 March and then 'turned', as Vergès and Barbie claimed. The date in the Kaltenbrunner report must have been wrong. With that discovery, Chauvy's allegations seemed to have no more substance to them than the previous ones. But then a surprising – and, to the Aubracs, deeply hurtful – voice was raised, apparently in Chauvy's defence. It was that of Daniel Cordier, who in 1943 had been Jean Moulin's secretary and who was now his devoted biographer and the keeper of his flame. Using an article in the left-wing newspaper *Libération*, Cordier stated that the Aubracs had, it was true, been among those who had risked their lives in the struggle to liberate France, but added that 'if they had stayed anonymous, they would not have to defend themselves to anyone, except their comrades and their peers but as soon as they started putting themselves and their versions into the media, they had to defend them to all French people.'[35] It was an astonishingly ungracious challenge to former comrades.

Had the Aubracs, in allowing themselves to become a celebrity couple, been hoist by their own petard? Had they been brought down by hubris, and exposed themselves to rivalry and jealousy? Despite the swirl of insinuation and innuendo Chauvy's book had stirred up in the press and on the fledgling internet, and despite the doubts expressed even by men such as Daniel Cordier, very few people really believed that the Aubracs had worked for the Gestapo in 1943. The sole fact that Raymond had identified Barbie in 1972, knowing his trial might follow, would have been sufficient to quash any such accusation. What the drip of suggestion ever since 1983 had finally done was provoke doubts not about the Aubracs' loyalty to France, but about their loyalty to one resistance faction over another. The Aubracs had been skewered not so much by Chauvy's insinuation that Raymond had become a Gestapo informer to save his own and his wife's skin, as by two other implied accusations, both rooted in the rivalries of the 1940s and the Aubracs' rumoured close association with the Communist Party. These implied accusations were equally vitriolic and mutually exclusive: firstly, that the Aubracs had been secretly working for Moscow and had eliminated Moulin in order to prevent de Gaulle from taking over the resistance; and secondly, that *Moulin* had been secretly working for Moscow, and the Aubracs found out and eliminated him on de Gaulle's behalf.

The military preoccupations of the twenty-first century have swung violently away from Communism, the Cold War, the hunt for Nazi criminals and the murky archives of the Second World War. But in 1997, in France, the events of the Dark Years were not affairs of the past, squabbles among a generation which no longer mattered: even forty years on they still had a direct bearing on the present. What Chauvy's book had done was to re-highlight, very publicly, the differences which Jean Moulin and others had worked so hard to overcome. The political and personal differences between the various *résistants* and their movements, which had been grudgingly put aside to fight a common enemy, had yet again emerged, and two elderly people found themselves on very public trial. 'I do not think,' Daniel Cordier wrote, 'that the Aubracs have told the entire truth about 1943, and I hope that they will explain themselves, of course not before a court, but before a commission of historians.'[36] The Aubracs, hurt and furious, accepted the gauntlet thrown down. When journalists from the newspaper *Libération* asked Raymond for his reaction to Cordier's words, he suggested they organize exactly what Cordier had asked for.

* * *

On 17 May 1997, the heavily trailed commission took place at the offices of *Libération*. The panel assembled to question the Aubracs contained three former *résistants*, Daniel Cordier among them, and five historians of the resistance, and all parties had agreed that the transcripts would be published in the newspaper. If the Aubracs had agreed to the questioning in the expectation they would be swiftly and formally cleared of the accusations raised successively – mendaciously, maliciously or mistakenly – by Hardy, Barbie, Vergès and Chauvy, they were disappointed. 'They were a little Machiavellian,' Raymond said with his habitual gentle understatement. After a morning of comradely agreement, the members of the panel suddenly went on the attack, and a strange sort of chest-beating competition began to emerge as comradeship vanished.

Each panellist first announced that he or she believed there was absolutely no foundation to the accusations of treachery. Daniel Cordier assured the Aubracs that he had defended their reputation since the suggestions of wrongdoing first surfaced in 1983. But having dismissed the accusations, the panel did not rise. Instead, their questions became something different, more inquisitorial and harder. Why, they suddenly pressed Raymond, had he been allowed to remain at Montluc prison in Lyon after the arrests at Caluire, when most of the other *résistants* arrested had been transferred to Paris? Taken aback, he could only repeat what he had said many times since that date: that he did not know. They turned to Lucie. Why did documents suggest she paid twelve separate visits to the Gestapo during Raymond's second imprisonment? She had not made twelve visits, she protested. She saw Klaus Barbie twice, and the other two officers seven times in all, for the purpose of arranging the marriage.

They continued. Why, when documents showed Raymond had been

released on 10 May 1943 (as 'François Vallet'), had Lucie sometimes claimed he was released on 12 May and, in *Outwitting the Gestapo*, that it had been on 14 May? The 12 she could not explain. As for her stating it was on 14 May, she confessed it was because her publishers had wanted her to make the date of Raymond's release coincide with the date of their anniversary to give the story added pathos. A forgivable licence, or a looseness with one truth from which one might infer a looseness with others? The questioning hardened further.

'What are you hiding?' Cordier asked Raymond abruptly.

'Aubrac, we've seen through you,' added historian Jean-Pierre Azéma, for no apparent reason.[37]

Why were the German officers who had helped Lucie arrange the marriage not punished after Raymond's escape? She did not know.

Why did Lucie tell the judge in Hardy's 1947 trial that she had seen her husband in Montluc prison on 29 June when in *Outwitting the Gestapo* she said she had not been allowed to see him at all?

That story about confronting the Attorney General with a message to be broadcast on Radio Londres – was that credible? Had Lucie really done that, or was it another of her stories? Why would she identify her husband as a secret Gaullist agent? Would it not have put him in even more danger?

The exchange was reprinted verbatim in *Libération*:

> Lucie Aubrac: It is true that I made a mistake. He [Raymond] would perhaps have been provisionally released anyway. It was extremely rash, it's true, to go and threaten the attorney. But that's my character, I sometimes go off the rails, I go too far sometimes, and that day, I went too far, I'd had enough. Do the messages from the BBC announcing parachute arrivals still exist? If you can

consult them, you'll find my message.

Daniel Cordier: That message was never broadcast.

Lucie Aubrac: *Continuez de gravir les pentes*, I'm sure that was the message I gave the attorney to prove I came from the Resistance.

Daniel Cordier: *Chère Lucie*, that message was never broadcast by the BBC. I have searched the National Archives, where all the messages are kept, and that one is not there.[38]

Despite the cold fury she displayed to the ruthlessly probing historians before her, Lucie could not prevent a truth coming out. If the commission did not unearth any evidence of Communist resistance fighting Gaullist resistance behind the meeting at Caluire, what they did expose was Lucie Aubrac's endemic inability to tell the truth. Not that she had betrayed Jean Moulin, never that; but that she had embroidered her own past, and that of the resistance, to the point of fictionalization. *Outwitting the Gestapo*, it emerged, had not been the work of history it had been taken as when it was published in 1984. It was, Lucie was now forced to admit, an account of a different truth; not a historical one, but an emotional one; one which was true to the spirit of the resistance. Again, it did not matter much in itself: it was no proof of treachery or conspiracy or anything else, but it was another indication that Lucie Aubrac's testimony was unreliable. The conclusion of one of the historians, François Bédarida, was humiliating. 'Your strategy, designed to perpetuate the image of the Resistance, has been a disaster … Why? Because, by seeking to render the past more immediate, you have embroidered, tidied up – in fact, you have invented stories, instead of sticking strictly to fact, and have thus left yourself shockingly exposed.'[39]

The panel then strayed onto even more sensitive territory. Had Lucie, mused Daniel Cordier and Jean-Pierre Azéma aloud, been the cause of the Gestapo's finding Raymond's parents? Was it not possible that after one of her visits to arrange the marriage, Gestapo officers had secretly followed her home and learnt her real identity? If such were the case, she might have indirectly brought about the identification and arrest of Raymond's parents in late 1943. The accusation was breathtakingly insensitive,[40] and had nothing to do with the subject under discussion. Raymond immediately defended his wife, but Daniel Cordier told him he could not disprove her guilt, even if it was unintentional. And was not Raymond equally guilty? The deaths of his family were not Raymond's fault, Cordier said, but he had nonetheless caused them. Raymond could have pointed out these things were pure speculation, and anyway outside the remit of the commission. Instead, he told the panel the painful story of how his parents had been detected following the arrest and torture of a cousin. 'Prove it,' said Cordier, unforgivably.[41] Hurt and furious, the Aubracs walked out.

Whatever Lucie's failings, the commission stank of a horrible, sordid jealousy; of the tall poppy syndrome applied to two venerable, remarkable and elderly people. One of the younger historians on the panel, Laurent Douzou, said as much later. He had been invited to participate because of the ground-breaking work he had done in a 1995 book on the development of Lib-Sud, which should alone have quashed any suggestions that the Aubracs had been Communist submariners. 'I think,' Douzou said, 'we were, collectively, wrong, very wrong, to have done it.' Much of the press agreed, distancing itself from the verbal lynching the commission had meted out. Not all coverage was supportive, however: the Aubracs' long association with the French Communist Party, Raymond's radical management of Marseille in 1944, BERIM's work with Communist regimes after the war, the couple's well-known support of left-wing and anti-colonial causes – all these were mentioned by writers who would not let the subject drop, whatever the evidence, or lack of it. When *Libération* published the commission's transcripts, its own editor's conclusion was that 'areas of doubt' remained in what was now known as *l'affaire Aubrac*. It was a difficult conclusion to defend, and another group of historians reacted furiously to the distasteful spectacle their colleagues had put on. The commission was 'the complete opposite of a history lesson,' they wrote in an open letter. 'There is no "*affaire Aubrac*", merely the question of how history is conceived of and used by the media.'[42] Inundated by post, Raymond had to rise at five o'clock each morning to keep up with the correspondence. He was at his desk when he suffered a heart attack: he was eighty-three and 'for a moment,' Lucie 'was terribly afraid of being left a widow'.[43] She consoled herself fearfully that 'Raymond is two years younger than me, and I don't think that will happen,'[44] and was proved right. Raymond recovered his good health, and it was Lucie's which began to decline.

In April 1998, the slander case against Chauvy and his publisher reached a kinder conclusion for the Aubracs. The judgement of the *tribunal de grande instance* in Paris found a more perceptive as well as a more generous way of dealing with the intersection of legend and history than had the members of the commission.

> The judge cannot, in the name of any superior imperative of historical truth, give up the protection of the right to honour and consideration of those who, thrown into the torment of war, were forced but courageous actors. These men and women may have been put on a pedestal by their contemporaries, but that does not mean they have become simple objects of study, deprived of personality or sensibility, or that their own destiny can be taken

from them in the cause of scientific utility.[45]

Chauvy's publisher was ordered to pay a large fine. Appeals as far as the European Court of Human Rights confirmed the judgement, but the verdict in her favour was not enough for Lucie. Despite her age, she did as she had always done, and went on the attack. Last time it had been *Outwitting the Gestapo*; this time it was a series of interviews with a sympathetic journalist, Corinne Bouchoux, which appeared later that same year in a book under the title *Cette exigeante liberté* (This Demanding Liberty). It was another salvo fired against the doubters, in defence of her aim of keeping alive her own conception of the spirit of resistance and keeping control of how her own story was told. 'I will be eighty-five this year,' she wrote in the introduction. 'My life is nearly over. Since my youth, the same principles have inspired my actions … The defence of liberty and the dignity of all.'[46]

*Cette exigeante liberté* covered far more of Lucie's life than the contested nine months on which *Outwitting the Gestapo* had concentrated. Under the very gentle probing of Mme Bouchoux, stories tumbled from her of her childhood, her adolescence, her recollections of peasant grandparents and the ancient rhythms of a land on the soil; her years in Paris between the wars, her wartime activities and her life with Raymond. Again, she spoke of a united resistance: in Lib-Sud, she said, 'some were church-goers, there were Jews, freemasons, old chaps fed up with people requisitioning their lettuces, grocers who'd had enough of cutting coupons into tiny pieces, and Communists! We were all different, but we shared the same hope: for the liberation of our country.'[47] *Cette exigeante liberté* was sympathetically received. Along with the verdict in their favour against Chauvy's editor, and the natural sympathy felt towards two old people who had fought with rare courage for their convictions and their country, the 1997 commission did not, in the end, succeed in dislodging the Aubracs from their place as symbols of national virtue.

Despite the affronts, the repeated, if minor, attacks on their reputation, their advanced age and Lucie's almost complete blindness, both Aubracs continued speaking to schoolchildren about the resistance. Lucie's visits even increased: history teachers across France and Belgium received the upright old lady who became affectionately known as 'the white wolf', and perhaps twenty thousand school children listened to Madame Aubrac tell her tales in their schools between 1997 and 2004, the year that accelerating ill health forced her to slow down. Neither she nor the teachers who continued to invite her, nor the children who listened open-mouthed to this vigorous old lady who had braved machine guns, ever thought her speeches dated. Her slogan was *resister se conjugue au present*, which flows less neatly in English than in its original language: 'to resist is always in the present tense'. Demonstrating the truth of this, she added another element to her talks on resistance and racism: fundamentalism in all its varieties. 'Every time an idea is polarized, even a secular idea, it leads to madness. Fundamentalism is intolerance. The practice of intolerance leads to social regression and the logic of war. Those who claim to be God's chosen ones, or that they alone own the truth eliminate all others!'[48]

All this time, she and Raymond lived in greater intimacy than had perhaps ever been the case. Their family had flowered around them. Jean-Pierre, Catherine and Elisabeth had begun the next generation, some of whom had already started on a third. The couple played host not only to children and grandchildren but to their enormous number of friends and acquaintances and, continually, to journalists, writers, documentary makers and others interested in the testimony they never refused to give on their years of resistance. It was Lucie who interested the interviewers the most: she was more talkative and more fiery, and more engaged in the whole process. And she was a woman, and history had turned to unearthing the participation of women in all events, Resistance included. Lucie's greater celebrity never bothered her husband. He would sit near his wife, watching to make sure she did not become tired or distressed by questions, occasionally intervening discreetly to tone down some overly vigorous assertion which might get her into hot water but uninterested in claiming any share of her limelight.

Summers and Christmases were spent at their house in the Cevennes, and the rest of the year in Paris. Here they lived contented lives, devoted to each other. Interviewed at the age of eighty-five, Lucie said they never missed an opportunity to show their love for each other. 'He never,' she told her interviewer, 'serves himself at table before he serves me.'[49] A small courtesy, but one on which marriages have foundered. Lucie's last public appearance came in October 2006, when she attended the inauguration of a memorial to twenty-four Jewish children deported to Auschwitz in 1942. The following month, she was taken into hospital and in March 2007, she died. She was ninety-four.

Obituaries appeared across the world. 'One of the most beautiful pages in the history of the Resistance is turned,' Nicolas Sarkozy declared. 'In the name of freedom, she rejected submission, hatred and anti-Semitism.'[50] Her funeral took place on a cold and drizzly day. A salute was fired over her coffin in the Cour des Invalides and President Chirac spoke. 'Certain exceptional beings,' he said, 'carry the highest values of humanity. The spirit of resistance, courage, patriotism, love of family: Lucie Aubrac, without a doubt, was one of these great figures ... Lucie Aubrac, we will not forget your message.'[51] There was a minute's silence, and then Raymond, surrounded by his ten grandchildren, leaning on a cane, trod carefully over the wet and slippery cobblestones behind his wife's coffin as it was carried away to the sound of the *Chant des Partisans*, a Resistance anthem written by Emmanuel d'Astier in 1943.

Raymond continued passing on the message which he and his more famous wife had been transmitting all their lives: resistance to oppression; liberty in solidarity. Aged ninety-three, he stepped up his school visits. As soon as he was invited, he explained with the courteous wit which never left him, he went. 'It means I am not alone and, you know, the classrooms are heated, and the school dinners are good ...'[52] A clip of film shows him, a very old man surrounded by primary school children, one of whom asks brightly, 'What was Lucie for you?' 'Ah,' he replies, as teachers cast agonized looks at each other in the background, 'we were together for sixty-seven years – you know, it is not easy to live without her.'[53]

\* \* \*

In 2009, Laurent Douzou wrote the most complete biography of Lucie Aubrac so far (and one to which my own is hugely indebted). Douzou had been a member of the commission which questioned the Aubracs in 1997, and had expressed his remorse for the way in which it dealt with the couple. He clearly admired Lucie, not just for her resistance work but for the uncompromising manner in which she attacked life, but when his investigations unearthed even more inconsistencies in her various autobiographical works than the 1997 commission had found he was obliged, as a historian, to grapple with them. The surprising thing about the string of fantasies he discovered was that they were of no apparent importance: not even the most neurotic anti-Communist could claim there was anything political behind them. And the *extraordinary* thing about them is that she had told them to the journalist interviewing her just after the commission, when her reputation was being mauled because of the fabrications and 'reconstructions' she had given in her first book! The very moment one might have expected her to be scrupulous in not giving her enemies any more ammunition, she was telling what can only be called lies.

Out came the story that her own birth in Paris had been by chance, the same story spun to Corinne Bouchoux that she had told many years ago to young Lieutenant Samuel: her parents were vine-growers, peasants from Burgundy who just happened to be in Paris to attend a wedding when her mother went into labour. Why? There was nothing to hide here – even after all her celebrity and renown, her status as national heroine, had she wanted to claim a more 'authentic' Frenchness for herself?

She spoke of how her father suffered trauma-based amnesia after the First World War and that her mother did not find him again until 1921. 'When he finally came home,' she said, 'he was almost a stranger.'[54] Again, why? No obvious purpose was served by prolonging his absence from the home for a further four years and making him an amnesiac except a ramping-up of drama.

Turning to the entrance examination for teacher training college, she told Corinne Bouchoux, as she had told countless others, that she accompanied her mother to Paris to take the examinations one day in 1929, passed the written examination and came a national second in the entrance. Her parents had been so furious about her decision not to take up the offered place that they had refused to see her for four years! In the Latin Quarter, she had made her living not as a classroom assistant but as a washer-up in workers' restaurants. Recalling the autumn after the defeat in 1940, when she was newly settled in Lyon with Raymond, she spoke of the post she had taken up at the *lycée des jeunes filles*, even describing the febrile atmosphere into which she walked: 'Madame Brunschwig, our headmistress, a physicist who had previously worked as laboratory assistant with the Curies, was sent away in October under the new Jewish law. This means of sending her into early retirement revolted me. In the staffroom, we dared to say loud and clear that it was unjust ...'[55] But Lucie had not started teaching until October 1941, so why was she recounting, not just in passing, but in some detail, events which had not happened?

Laurent Douzou's book is an academic one: scrupulous, meticulous, issue of a huge amount of original research, comparison of many conflicting sources, and careful analysis. He clearly admired her: 'this lady,' he exclaims fondly, 'really liked playing games!'[56] It was one explanation, but another is that Lucie herself no longer really knew which of her own stories were true and which were fantasy.

Raymond made no public reaction to Douzou's respectful 'outing' of Lucie as a serial fibber, although the revelations that her childhood and adolescence were not as she had described them seemed as much news to him as they had been to everyone else. Despite his wartime reproof that she must stop fantasizing, it seems she had never admitted that she had told him a few fairy tales when they were very young. How many of us do not have similar skeletons in the cupboard? When their bones came tumbling out a couple of years after his wife's death, Raymond may have been shocked, but I suspect he simply chuckled. As he himself observed, looking back to his own young days, 'the manner in which you conduct yourself ... ends by becoming part of your character,' for him as much as for the wife he loved so much.[57]

The year after Douzou's biography was published, 2010, Raymond, too, was awarded the Grand Croix de la Légion d'Honneur. His speech both reflected the values he and Lucie had cherished, and echoed back to the struggle in the 1940s in his insistence that the anonymous thousands who had made up the resistance should not be forgotten, or hidden by the more resplendent uniforms and military titles which had come in at the last moment and attempted to eclipse them. 'I will wear this insignia … while thinking of these men and women who deserved it for the services they rendered to France and to Humanity, and whose life was cut short by a cruel destiny.'[58] The same year he undertook his last long voyage, going back to Vietnam by invitation of the government for celebrations of the thirty-fifth anniversary of independence.

The man who conducted Raymond's last interviews was a French artist and documentary maker named Pascal Convert, who spent many months visiting the ninth-floor apartment where he lived alone. Convert passed over the matter of Lucie's lies diplomatically. For him, the recent revelations that she had not only fictionalised episodes of her early life, but had kept the truth secret even from her own husband, should be seen as the mark of a person determined to make herself and not be made by others. It was a gentle way to regard the matter, and perhaps one suggested privately by Raymond. Instead, Convert asked the man he clearly admired and cared for kinder questions about the origin of their relationship and the reason for its longevity – the famous secret which all long-married couples are asked for eventually. 'We were not a mythical couple,' Raymond replied, 'we were a real couple. We lived sixty-seven years together. We were a couple who had the fortune of being happy in all our various and sometimes difficult adventures, with all the many children whom a happy couple acquires, three children, ten grandchildren, twelve great grandchildren at present tally. One goes ahead,' he added, 'and the other is punished, and has to accept his punishment. Maybe he deserved it, I don't know.'[59]

Raymond Aubrac died in April 2012, at the age of ninety-seven. His coffin was taken to the same Cour d'Honneur des Invalides where Lucie's had rested five years earlier. President Nicolas Sarkozy was among hundreds who came to pay their respects, in mid-election campaign, but the Aubracs' daughter Elisabeth publicly insisted there be no politicking around her father's funeral, and that the only speeches should be made by other *résistants*. Two very elderly gentlemen spoke, an army choir sang the *Chant des Partisans*, and there was a salute from the Republican Guard.

In the many obituaries in French and international newspapers, Raymond Aubrac was spoken of as the last of the surviving *grands résistants* and, in death as in life, Lucie's name invariably appeared alongside her husband's. *Les Aubracs*, as the elderly Nazi-hunter Serge Klarsfeld wrote in *Le Figaro*, had become 'a legendary couple who will survive … because of what they achieved, and because they achieved it with a gun in their fist' ('*qui militait revolver au poing*').[60]

A few days later, Raymond Aubrac's ashes were placed in the family tomb in the Burgundy town of Salornay-sur-Guye, alongside those of Lucie.

# NOTES

**Introduction**

1. Jean-Louis Crémieux-Brilhac, quoted in Douzou, *Lucie Aubrac*, p. 144.

**Chapter 1**

1. L. Aubrac, *Cette exigeante liberté*, p. 21.
2. Ibid., p. 23.
3. Ibid., p. 20.
4. Ibid., p. 18.
5. Ibid., p. 9.
6. Ibid., p. 25.
7. Lebesque, *Chroniques du Canard*.
8. André Ternet, quoted in Convert, *Raymond Aubrac, résister, reconstruire, transmettre*, p. 38.
9. Quoted in Douzou, *Lucie Aubrac*, p. 66.
10. Laurent Douzou, 'Lucie Aubrac n'avait pas froid aux yeux', *Libération*, 16 March 2007.
11. Amat, *L'histoire au present*.
12. L. Aubrac, *Cette exigeante liberté*, p. 28.
13. Ibid., p. 29.
14. Quoted in Douzou, *Lucie Aubrac*, p. 55.
15. Amat, *L'histoire*.
16. Quoted in Douzou, *Lucie Aubrac*, p. 75.
17. Ibid., p. 76.
18. L. Aubrac, *Cette exigeante liberté*, p. 44.
19. Douzou, *Lucie Aubrac*, p. 83.
20. L. Aubrac, *Cette exigeante liberté*, p. 8.
21. 'Corps of Bridges and Roads', now the École des Ponts ParisTech.
22. Convert, *Raymond Aubrac, résister, reconstruire, transmettre*, p. 54.
23. Ibid., p. 57.
24. L. Aubrac, *Outwitting the Gestapo*, p. 19.
25. L. Aubrac, *Cette exigeante liberté*, p. 203.
26. Ibid., p. 51.

27. Ibid., p. 52.

28. Ibid., p. 68.

29. Ibid., p. 68.

**Chapter 2**

1. Signoret, *Nostalgia Isn't What It Used to Be*, pp. 37–8.

2. 'Paris falls to the Germans', *The Guardian*, 15 June 1940, http://www. theguardian.com/century/1940-1949/Story/0,6051,128218,00.html.

3. '1939–1945 dans les souvenirs d'un general', *Le Télégramme*, 18 September 2013, http://www.letelegramme.fr/local/morbihan/vannes-auray/vannes/1939-45-dans-les-souvenirs-d-un-general-18-09-2013-2238238.php.

4. Quoted in Douzou, *Lucie Aubrac*, p. 296.

5. L. Aubrac, *Cette exigeante liberté*, p. 55.

6. Amat, *L'histoire au present*.

7. L. Aubrac, *Cette exigeante liberté*, p. 203.

8. Ibid., p. 67.

9. Ibid., p. 7.

10. Béatrice Vallaeys, 'Très peu de Français ont été courageux. Les Aubrac le furent', *Libération*, 11 April 2012, http://www.liberation.fr/societe/2012/04/11/tres-peu-de-francais-ont-ete-courageux-les-aubrac-le-furent_811132.

11. A graduate of the elite *polytechniques*, further education institutes specializing in science and engineering.

12. Quoted in Jackson, *France*, p. 111.

13. L. Aubrac, *Cette exigeante liberté*, p. 68.

14. Convert, *Raymond Aubrac, résister, reconstruire, transmettre*, p. 75.

15. L. Aubrac, *Cette exigeante liberté*, p. 57.

16. Convert, *Raymond Aubrac, résister, reconstruire, transmettre*, p. 74.

17. L. Aubrac, *Outwitting the Gestapo*, p. 30.

18. Ibid., p. 180.

19. Convert, *Raymond Aubrac, résister, reconstruire, transmettre*, p. 69.

20. L. Aubrac, *Outwitting the Gestapo*, p. 56.

21. Convert, *Raymond Aubrac, résister, reconstruire, transmettre*, p. 74.

22. L. Aubrac, *Outwitting the Gestapo*, p. 121.

23. d'Astier de la Vigerie, *Emmanuel d'Astier de la Vigerie*, p. 25.

24. Orwell, *Collected Works: I Belong to the Left*, p. 22.

25. R. Aubrac, *Où la mémoire s'attarde*, p. 60.

26. Amat, *L'histoire au present*.

27. d'Astier de la Vigerie, *Emmanuel d'Astier de la Vigerie*, p. 49.

28. L. Aubrac, *Cette exigeante liberté*, p. 61.

29. Convert, *Raymond Aubrac, résister, reconstruire, transmettre*, p. 83.

30. Jackson, *France*, p. 255.

31. Ravanel, *L'esprit de Résistance*, p. 52.

32. Jackson, *France*, p. 281.

33. d'Astier de la Vigerie, *Emmanuel d'Astier de la Vigerie*, p. 58.

34. L. Aubrac, *Cette exigeante liberté*, p. 78.

35. Convert, *Raymond Aubrac, résister, reconstruire, transmettre*, p. 103.

36. L. Aubrac, *Cette exigeante liberté*, p. 62.

37. d'Astier de la Vigerie, *Emmanuel d'Astier de la Vigerie*, p. 67.

38. L. Aubrac, *Outwitting the Gestapo*, p. 32.

39. Quoted in Douzou, *Lucie Aubrac*, p. 100.

40. L. Aubrac, *Cette exigeante liberté*, p. 61.

41. Quoted in Weisberg, *Vichy Law*, p. 379.

42. Quoted in Douzou, *Lucie Aubrac*, p. 92.

43. L. Aubrac, *Outwitting the Gestapo*, p. 27.

44. Ibid., p. 27.

45. Ibid., p. 67.

46. Ibid., p. 28.

47. Ibid., p. 23.

48. Ibid., p. 70.

49. Ibid., p. 25.

50. Ibid., p. 25.

51. L. Aubrac, *Cette exigeante liberté*, p. 73.

52. L. Aubrac, *Outwitting the Gestapo*, p. 131.

53. Quoted in Douzou, *Lucie Aubrac*, p. 107, endnote.

54. L. Aubrac, *Cette exigeante liberté*, p. 69.

55. Ibid., p. 206.

56. Ibid., p. 206.

57. Douzou, *Lucie Aubrac*, p. 112.

58. Jacques Brunschwig-Bordier, quoted in Douzou, *Lucie Aubrac*, pp. 109–10.

59. L. Aubrac, *Cette exigeante liberté*, p. 68.

60. L. Aubrac, *Outwitting the Gestapo*, p. 160.

61. Ibid., p. 160.

62. Ibid., p. 33.

63. Convert, *Raymond Aubrac, les années de guerre*.

64. Ravanel, *L'esprit de Résistance*, p. 59.

65. Quoted in Morton, *War in the Pacific*, p. 158.

66. L. Aubrac, *Cette exigeante liberté*, p. 80.

67. Quoted from an exhibit at the exhibition 'Jean Moulin: une vie d'engagements', July 2013, Panthéon, Paris.

68. d'Astier de la Vigerie, *Emmanuel d'Astier de la Vigerie*, p. 105.

69. Ibid.

70. L. Aubrac, *Outwitting the Gestapo*, p. 86.

71. Ibid., p. 36.

72. L. Aubrac, *Cette exigeante liberté*, p. 128.

73. L. Aubrac, *Outwitting the Gestapo*, p. 67.

74. Douzou, *Lucie Aubrac*, p. 112.

75. L. Aubrac, *Cette exigeante liberté*, p. 85.

76. Ravanel, *L'esprit de Résistance*, p. 77.

77. He did so under the additional codename of 'Fouquet', although I continue to refer to him as Kriegel-Valrimont for simplicity.

78. Convert, *Raymond Aubrac, résister, reconstruire, transmettre*, p. 103.

79. Ravanel, *L'esprit de Résistance*, p. 71.

80. L. Aubrac, *Outwitting the Gestapo*, p. 131.

81. Quoted in Douzou, *Lucie Aubrac*, p. 113.

82. Eisenhower, *Crusade in Europe*, p. 107.

83. Ravanel, *L'esprit de Résistance*, p. 84.

84. Quoted in Moorehead, *A Train in Winter*, p. 53.

85. L. Aubrac, *Outwitting the Gestapo*, p. 124.

86. Quoted in d'Astier de la Vigerie, *Emmanuel d'Astier de la Vigerie*, p. 211.

87. 'Interview: La première arrestation de Raymond Aubrac (première partie)', *Libération*, 9 July 1997, http://www.liberation.fr/societe/1997/07/09/special-aubrac-chapitre-deux-mars-mai-1943_211253.

88. Ravanel, *L'esprit de Résistance*, p. 126.

89. Ibid., p. 98.

90. Ibid., p. 101.

91. Convert, *Raymond Aubrac, résister, reconstruire, transmettre*, p. 152.

92. Ravanel, *L'esprit de Résistance*, p. 110.

93. Ibid., p. 103.

94. Quoted in Douzou, *Lucie Aubrac*, p. 118.

95. Ibid.

96. Ravanel, *L'esprit de la Résistance*, p. 107.

97. Convert, *Raymond Aubrac, résister, reconstruire, transmettre*, p. 160.

98. Ravanel, *L'esprit de Résistance*, p. 159.

99. Douzou, *Lucie Aubrac*, p. 19.

100. Ibid.

101. L. Aubrac, *Outwitting the Gestapo*, p. 39.

102. Convert, *Raymond Aubrac, résister, reconstruire, transmettre*, p. 158.

103. Ravanel, *L'esprit de Resistance*, p. 106.

104. Convert, *Raymond Aubrac, résister, reconstruire, transmettre*, p. 161.

105. L. Aubrac, *Outwitting the Gestapo*, p. 24.

106. Ibid., p. 42.

107. Ibid., p. 20.

108. Douzou, *Lucie Aubrac*, p. 119.

109. L. Aubrac, *Cette exigeante liberté*, p. 89.

110. Ibid.

111. L. Aubrac, *Outwitting the Gestapo*, p. 15.

112. Ibid., p. 23.

113. Ravanel, *L'esprit de Résistance*, p. 113.

114. L. Aubrac, *Outwitting the Gestapo*, p. 30.

115. Ravanel, *L'esprit de Résistance*, p. 113.

116. Ibid., p. 114.

117. L. Aubrac, *Outwitting the Gestapo*, p. 31.

118. Ibid., p. 45.

119. Ibid., p. 34.

120. Ibid., p. 41.

121. Ibid., p. 38.

122. Ibid., p. 41.

123. Ibid., p. 44.

### Chapter 3

1. L. Aubrac, *Outwitting the Gestapo*, pp. 48–9.

2. L. Aubrac, *Cette exigeante liberté*, p. 85.

3. Ibid.

4. Ibid., p. 86.

5. L. Aubrac, *Outwitting the Gestapo*, p. 64.

6. Amat, *L'histoire au present*.

7. L. Aubrac, *Outwitting the Gestapo*, p. 69.

8. L. Aubrac, *Cette exigeante liberté*, p. 87.

9. L. Aubrac, *Outwitting the Gestapo*, p. 73.

10. Ibid., p. 77.

11. Ravanel, *L'esprit de Résistance*, p. 160.

12. Ibid.

13. Ibid.

14. Ibid., p. 161.

15. L. Aubrac, *Outwitting the Gestapo*, p. 89.

16. Ibid., p. 91.

17. 'Old maid'. Lucie Aubrac later said she had used false papers in the name of 'Ghislaine de Barbentane', after an aristocratic family for whom her mother had once milked cows. However, when she was examined by British intelligence officers in February 1944, she told them she had used the name 'Lucie Montet'. As we know from another source that she did indeed carry identity papers in that name, and also that she sometimes changed details to present a more appealing story, I think it most likely she actually used the Montet identity. Whichever name she used, the story she told the Gestapo was the same.

18. L. Aubrac, *Outwitting the Gestapo*, p. 79.

19. Ibid., p. 80.

20. Ibid.

21. Ibid.

22. Ibid., p. 87.

23. Ibid., p. 123.

24. Ibid., p. 100.

25. Ibid.

26. Ravanel, *L'esprit de Résistance*, p. 151.

27. Ibid., p. 163.

28. Ibid., p. 134.

29. L. Aubrac, *Outwitting the Gestapo*, p. 101.

30. Ibid.

31. Ibid.

32. Ibid, p. 103.

33. Ibid., p. 105.

34. Ravanel, *L'esprit de Résistance*, p. 161.

35. L. Aubrac, *Outwitting the Gestapo*, p. 108.

36. Ibid., p. 47.

37. Ibid., p. 104.

38. Ibid., p. 125.

39. Ibid., p. 129.

40. Ibid., p. 132.

41. Convert, *Raymond Aubrac: les années de guerre.*

42. L. Aubrac, *Outwitting the Gestapo*, p. 135.

43. Ibid., p. 137.

44. Ibid., p. 162.

45. Ibid.

46. Ibid., p. 163.

47. Ibid.

48. Ibid., p. 164.

49. Ibid.

50. Ibid., p. 165.

51. Ibid., p. 167.

52. Ibid.

53. Quoted in Douzou, *La désobéissance*, p. 221.

## Chapter 4

1. L. Aubrac, *Cette exigeante liberté*, p. 118.

2. Ibid.

3. L. Aubrac, *Outwitting the Gestapo*, p. 177.

4. L. Aubrac, *Cette exigeante liberté*, p. 119.

5. Ibid., p. 120.

6. Ibid., p. 121.

7. Ibid.

8. Ibid.

9. Ibid., p. 123.

10. Ibid., p. 126.

11. Ibid.

12. Ibid.

13. Ibid., p. 127.

14. Ibid., p. 129.

15. Ibid., p. 130.

16. Ibid., p. 131.

17. Ibid., p. 227.

18. Ibid.

19. Ibid., p. 135.

20. Ibid.

21. Ibid.

22. Ibid., p. 142.

23. *The Times*, 24 March 1944 (issue 49813), p. 3.

24. Ibid.

25. L. Aubrac, *Outwitting the Gestapo*, p. 187.

26. L. Aubrac, *Cette exigeante liberté*, p. 138.

27. Quoted in Douzou, *Lucie Aubrac*, p. 151.

28. L. Aubrac, *Cette exigeante liberté*, p. 145.

29. For many years, the German commander Von Choltitz maintained he had disobeyed Hitler's orders to destroy the city. Maurice Kriegel-Valrimont was one of the first to reject this claim as a 'shameless falsification of history' (in the 1978 documentary, *Libération: Porte-Parole des Gauchistes*) and archival research carried out by German historians supports his rebuttal.

30. L. Aubrac, *Cette exigeante liberté*, p. 152.

31. Ibid., p. 152.

32. Ravanel, *L'esprit de Résistance*, p. 16.

33. Ibid., p. 17.

34. Convert, *Raymond Aubrac, résister, reconstruire, transmettre*, p. 230.

35. L. Aubrac, *Cette exigeante liberté*, p. 167.

36. Ibid., p. 158.

37. *La résistance: (naissance et organisation)*, Paris: Lang, 1945.

38. Quoted in Douzou, *Lucie Aubrac*, p. 161.

39. Amat, *L'histoire au present*.

40. L. Aubrac, *Cette exigeante liberté*, p. 159.

41. Max Barel, a Communist *résistant* tortured with particular barbarity by Barbie just before the liberation.

42. L. Aubrac, *Cette exigeante liberté*, p. 160.

43. Ibid., p. 197.

44. Quoted in Douzou, *Lucie Aubrac*, p. 189.

45. Ibid., p. 188.

## Chapter 5

1. Bartosek, *Les Aveux des archives*, p. 121.

2. L. Aubrac, *Cette exigeante liberté*, p. 159.

3. Ibid.

4. Convert, *Raymond Aubrac: résister, reconstruire, transmettre*, p. 633.

5. Proclamation of the Algerian National Liberation Front, 1 November 1954.

6. Douzou, *Lucie Aubrac*, p. 317.

7. Ibid., p. 237.

8. L. Aubrac, *Cette exigeante liberté*, p. 189.

9. Ibid., p. 146.

10. Français Docu, *Klaus Barbie*.

11. Ibid.

12. Ibid.

13. René Hardy, *Derniers Mots-Mémoires* (Last Words), Paris: Fayard, 1984.

14. L. Aubrac, *Cette exigeante liberté*, p. 195.

15. Ibid.

16. The English-language version is entitled *Outwitting the Gestapo*.

17. As discussed later in this book, although *Outwitting the Gestapo* is a wonderfully vivid primary source, it is flawed. I have therefore used it cautiously, principally for what it reveals about Lucie's emotions, personality and relationships, and have substantiated her memories of events from other sources.

18. L. Aubrac, *Outwitting the Gestapo*, p. 13.

19. Quoted in Douzou, *Lucie Aubrac*, p. 251.

20. L. Aubrac, *Cette exigeante liberté*, p. 8.

21. 'Nazi war crimes trial: Klaus Barbie', *Jewish Virtual Library*, https://www.jewishvirtuallibrary.org/jsource/Holocaust/barbietrial.html.

22. L. Aubrac, *Cette exigeante liberté*, p. 193.

23. Ibid., p. 194.

24. Ibid., p. 194.

25. Quoted in Convert, *Raymond Aubrac: résister, reconstruire, transmettre*, p. 636.

26. Jacques Gelin, who has spent over twenty years researching what happened at Caluire, has suggested Maître Vergès had a personal grievance against Raymond Aubrac, suspecting him of having been an undercover American agent in France's negotiations with Ho Chi Minh ('Entretien avec Jacques Gelin', *La Cliothèque*, 19 July 2013, http://clio-cr.clionautes.org/ENTRETIEN-AVEC-JACQUES-GELIN.html#.VCvEQcJ0zrc).

27. '"Aubrac Lyon 1943", la stratégie du soupçon', *l'Humanité*, 16 April 1997, http://www.humanite.fr/node/155662#sthash.GnXrb4OI.dpuf.

28. 'Lucie Aubrac, a French WWII Resistance hero', *European Jewish Press*, 19 March 2007, http://ejpress.org/index.php?option=com_content&view=article&id=7269&catid=10:western-europe&Itemid=6.

29. 'Controversial Resistance figure dead', *Associated Press*, 14 April 1987, http://

www.apnewsarchive.com/1987/Controversial-Resistance-Figure-Dead/id-0da3
88ed06e3f7cfe975906d02f34874.

30 'Incident entre Raymond Aubrac et la veuve de René Hardy', *Libération*, 4
March 1997, http://www.liberation.fr/culture/1997/03/04/incident-entre-
raymond-aubrac-et-la-veuve-de-rene-hardy_200925.

31. Chauvy, *Aubrac Lyon 1943*, p. 10.

32. Ben MacIntyre, 'Resistance heroes reject Nazi "double agent" slur', *The Times*,
31 March 1997, p. 13.

33. Ibid.

34. 'Nous n'acceptons pas …', *L'Evènement du Jeudi*, 3–9 April 1997.

35. 'En tant que camarade des Aubrac, je souhaiterais qu'ils s'expliquent',
*Libération*, 15 March 2007, http://www.liberation.fr/societe/2007/03/15/en-
tant-que-camarade-des-aubrac-je-souhaiterais-qu-ils-s-expliquent_13897.

36. Ibid.

37. Quoted in Convert, *Raymond Aubrac: résister, reconstruire, transmettre*, p. 652.

38. 'Le couple Aubrac et l'énigme de la mort de Jean Moulin', *Nouvelles de France*,
17 April 2012, http://www.ndf.fr/nos-breves/17-04-2012/le-couple-aubrac-et-
lenigme-de-la-mort-de-jean-moulin?print=pdf.

39. Ibid.

40. And inaccurate: the arrest and deportation of the elder Samuels was
unconnected to their son's activities.

41. Quoted in Convert, *Raymond Aubrac: résister, reconstruire, transmettre*, p. 653.

42. 'Une déplorable leçon d'histoire', *Libération*, 25 July 1997, http://www.
liberation.fr/tribune/1997/07/25/la-reaction-d-un-collectif-d-historiens-au-
supplement-publie-le-9-juillet-dans-liberation-les-aubrac_210095.

43. L. Aubrac, *Cette exigeante liberté*, p. 207.

44. Ibid.

45. Quoted in Douzou, *Lucie Aubrac*, p. 273.

46. L. Aubrac, *Cette exigeante liberté*, p. 9.

47. Ibid., p. 173.

48. L. Aubrac, *Cette exigeante liberté*, p. 198.

49. Ibid., p. 205.

50. 'Décès de Lucie Aubrac: les réactions politiques', *La Dépêche*, 15 March 2007,
http://www.ladepeche.fr/article/2007/03/15/392745-deces-de-lucie-aubrac-les-
reactions-politiques.html.

51. 'La France rend hommage à Lucie Aubrac', *l'Express*, 21 March 2007, http://
www.lexpress.fr/actualite/politique/la-france-rend-hommage-a-lucie-

aubrac_463571.html.

52. Convert, *Raymond Aubrac: résister, reconstruire, transmettre*, p. 672.

53. 'Raymond Aubrac à l'école des Renards à Fontenay-aux-Roses, le 20 mai 2011', *YouTube*, 17 April 2012, https://www.youtube.com/watch?v=YICa38ZyeZA.

54. L. Aubrac, *Cette exigeante liberté*, p. 13.

55. Ibid., p. 65.

56. Douzou, *Lucie Aubrac*, p. 275.

57. Convert, *Raymond Aubrac: résister, reconstruire, transmettre*, p. 54.

58. Ibid., p. 256.

59. Ibid., p. 60.

60. 'Hommage à Aubrac, "figure héroïque de la résistance"', *Le Figaro*, 11 April 2012.

# SELECT BIBLIOGRAPHY

Amat, Jorge, *L'histoire au present* (broadcast), 2002

Aubrac, Lucie, *Cette exigeante liberté, entretiens avec Corinne Bouchoux*, Paris: L'Archipel, 1997

Aubrac, Lucie, *Ils partiront dans l'ivresse*, Paris: France Loisirs, 1984, trans. Bieber, Konrad, *Outwitting the Gestapo*, University of Nebraska Press, 1993

Aubrac, Raymond, *Où la mémoire s'attarde*, Paris: Odile Jacob, 1996

d'Astier de la Vigerie, Geoffroy, *Emmanuel d'Astier de la Vigerie, combattant de la Résistance et de la Liberté, 1940–44*, Chaintreaux: Éditions France-Empire Monde, 2010

Bartosek, Karel, *Les Aveux des archives – Prague-Paris-Prague, 1948–1968*, Paris: Éditions du Seuil, 1996

Chauvy, Gérard, *Aubrac Lyon 1943*, Paris: Albin Michel, 1997

Convert, Pascal, *Raymond Aubrac, résister, reconstruire, transmettre*, Paris: Éditions du Seuil, 2011

Convert, Pascal, *Raymond Aubrac, les années de guerre* (documentary film), 2010

Cordier, Daniel, *Jean Moulin, La République des catacombes*, Paris: Éditions Gallimard, 2014

Douzou, Laurent, *Lucie Aubrac*, Paris: Éditions Perrin, 2009

Douzou, Laurent, *La désobéissance: histoire d'un mouvement et d'un journal clandestins*, Clermont-Ferrand: Éditions Odile Jacob, 1995

Eisenhower, Dwight, *Crusade in Europe*, New York: Doubleday, 1948

Français Docu, *Klaus Barbie Agent de la CIA Criminel Nazi* (film), 2012

Jackson, Julian, *France: the Dark Years 1940–1944*, Oxford: Oxford University Press, 2003

Karel, William, *Jean Moulin (Résistance Occupation)* (film), 2013

Kedward, H. Roderick, and Roger Austin, eds., *Vichy France and the Resistance: Culture and Ideology*, New York: Barnes and Noble, 1985

Lebesque, Morvan, *Chroniques du Canard*, Paris: Jean-Jacques Pauvert, 1960

Moorehead, Caroline, *A Train in Winter: an Extraordinary Story of Women, Friendship, and Resistance in Occupied France*, London: Harper, 2011

Morton, Louis, *War in the Pacific: Strategy and Command*, Washington DC: Dept.

of the Army, 2000

Orwell, George, *Collected Works: I Belong to the Left*, Singapore: Utopia Press, 1945

Paxton, Robert O., *France: Old Guard and New Order, 1940–44*, New York: Columbia University Press, 1972

Ravanel, Serge, *L'esprit de Résistance*, Paris: Éditions du Seuil, 1995

Reporter, Remy, *Les detectives de l'histoire: qui a trahi Jean Moulin?* (television documentary, *France 5*), 2007

Signoret, Simone, *Nostalgia Isn't What It Used to Be*, London: Penguin, 1979

Weisberg, Richard H., *Vichy Law and the Holocaust in France*, Amsterdam: Harwood Academic Publishers, 2013

# PICTURE CREDITS

Map of occupied France © Eric Gaba for original blank map, Rama for zones, distributed under licence CC BY-SA 4.0

Lucie and Raymond as a young married couple © Sipa Press/REX Shutterstock

Jean Cavaillès © Laboratoire d'Histoire des Sciences et de Philosophie – Archives Henri-Poincaré (Nancy, France). With grateful thanks to the Société des Amis de Jean Cavaillès.

Parisians watching German troops enter the city © US National Archives

Handshake between Pétain and Hitler © Heinrich Hoffmann/Bundesarchiv

Emmanuel d'Astier de la Vigerie © Hulton Archive/Getty Images

Révolution Nationale poster, © Victoria and Albert Museum, London, gift of the American Friends of the V & A; gift to the American Friends by Leslie, Judith and Gabri Schreyer and Alice Shreyer Batko

Lucie Aubrac aged thirty © Sipa Press/ REX Shutterstock

German propaganda poster © Mary Evans Picture Library/Onslow Auctions Limited

Jean Moulin © Keystone/Getty Images

*Lucie to the Rescue* comic strip story published by *True Comics*, Inc. / Parents' Magazine Institute, True Comics issue 049. Image by kind courtesy of Michigan State University Libraries Special Collections

Klaus Barbie © Gabriel Hackett/Hulton Archive/Getty Images

Lucie and Raymond, 1991 © Nahassia/Sipa/REX Shutterstock

# INDEX